MAR 0 8 2005

DATE DUE

JUN 01 2006	

ANNOTATION FOR THE SEMANTIC WEB

Frontiers in Artificial Intelligence and Applications

Series Editors: J. Breuker, R. López de Mántaras, M. Mohammadian, S. Ohsuga and W. Swartout

Volume 96

Recently published in this series

Vol. 95. B. Omelayenko and M. Klein (Eds.), Knowledge Transformation for the Semantic Web
Vol. 94. H. Jaakkola et al. (Eds.), Information Modelling and Knowledge Bases XIV
Vol. 93. K. Wang, Intelligent Condition Monitoring and Diagnosis Systems – A Computational Intelligence Approach
Vol. 92. V. Kashyap and L. Shklar (Eds.), Real World Semantic Web Applications
Vol. 91. F. Azevedo, Constraint Solving over Multi-valued Logics – Application to Digital Circuits
Vol. 90. In preparation
Vol. 89. T. Bench-Capon et al. (Eds.), Legal Knowledge and Information Systems – JURIX 2002: The Fifteenth Annual Conference
Vol. 88. In preparation
Vol. 87. A. Abraham et al. (Eds.), Soft Computing Systems – Design, Management and Applications
Vol. 86. R.S.T. Lee and J.H.K. Liu, Invariant Object Recognition based on Elastic Graph Matching – Theory and Applications
Vol. 85. J.M. Abe and J.I. da Silva Filho (Eds), Advances in Logic, Artificial Intelligence and Robotics – LAPTEC 2002
Vol. 84. H. Fujita and P. Johannesson (Eds.), New Trends in Software Methodologies, Tools and Techniques – Proceedings of Lyee_W02
Vol. 83. V. Loia (Ed.), Soft Computing Agents – A New Perspective for Dynamic Information Systems
Vol. 82. E. Damiani et al. (Eds.), Knowledge-Based Intelligent Information Engineering Systems and Allied Technologies – KES 2002
Vol. 81. J.A. Leite, Evolving Knowledge Bases – Specification and Semantics
Vol. 80. T. Welzer et al. (Eds.), Knowledge-based Software Engineering – Proceedings of the Fifth Joint Conference on Knowledge-based Software Engineering
Vol. 79. H. Motoda (Ed.), Active Mining – New Directions of Data Mining
Vol. 78. T. Vidal and P. Liberatore (Eds.), STAIRS 2002 – STarting Artificial Intelligence Researchers Symposium
Vol. 77. F. van Harmelen (Ed.), ECAI 2002 – 15th European Conference on Artificial Intelligence
Vol. 76. P. Sinčák et al. (Eds.), Intelligent Technologies – Theory and Applications
Vol. 75. I.F. Cruz et al. (Eds.), The Emerging Semantic Web – Selected Papers from the first Semantic Web Working Symposium
Vol. 74. M. Blay-Fornarino et al. (Eds.), Cooperative Systems Design – A Challenge of the Mobility Age
Vol. 73. H. Kangassalo et al. (Eds.), Information Modelling and Knowledge Bases XIII
Vol. 72. A. Namatame et al. (Eds.), Agent-Based Approaches in Economic and Social Complex Systems
Vol. 71. J.M. Abe and J.I. da Silva Filho (Eds.), Logic, Artificial Intelligence and Robotics – LAPTEC 2001
Vol. 70. B. Verheij et al. (Eds.), Legal Knowledge and Information Systems – JURIX 2001: The Fourteenth Annual Conference
Vol. 69. N. Baba et al. (Eds.), Knowledge-Based Intelligent Information Engineering Systems and Allied Technologies – KES'2001

ISSN 0922-6389

Annotation for the Semantic Web

Edited by

Siegfried Handschuh

University of Karlsruhe, Institute AIFB, Karlsruhe, Germany

and

Steffen Staab

University of Karlsruhe, Institute AIFB, Karlsruhe, Germany

IOS Press

Ohmsha

Amsterdam • Berlin • Oxford • Tokyo • Washington, DC

ISBN 1 58603 345 X (IOS Press)
ISBN 4 274 90599 3 C3055 (Ohmsha)
Library of Congress Control Number: 2003106105

Publisher
IOS Press
Nieuwe Hemweg 6B
1013 BG Amsterdam
The Netherlands
fax: +31 20 620 3419
e-mail: order@iospress.nl

Distributor in the UK and Ireland
IOS Press/Lavis Marketing
73 Lime Walk
Headington
Oxford OX3 7AD
England
fax: +44 1865 75 0079

Distributor in the USA and Canada
IOS Press, Inc.
5795-G Burke Centre Parkway
Burke, VA 22015
USA
fax: +1 703 323 3668
e-mail: iosbooks@iospress.com

Distributor in Germany, Austria and Switzerland
IOS Press/LSL.de
Gerichtsweg 28
D-04103 Leipzig
Germany
fax: +49 341 995 4255

Distributor in Japan
Ohmsha, Ltd.
3-1 Kanda Nishiki-cho
Chiyoda-ku, Tokyo 101-8460
Japan
fax: +81 3 3233 2426

PRINTED IN THE NETHERLANDS

Foreword

Like all truly great ideas, Tim Berners-Lee's principal idea of the *Semantic Web* may be easily summarized: When computers not only retrieve but also understand what data is available on the Web, we will have a new kind of Web and new types of intelligent applications in the Web. In the foreseeable future, however, machines will be too dumb to understand what people have put on the Web. Therefore, let us put *computer-understandable data* next to human-understandable data. Then, the computers will be smarter.

To make this dream come true, we need a number of building blocks, some of them elaborated on in recent writings [4,6,3,1,2,8,7]. For instance, we need standardized languages to describe semantic data, i.e. data that is computer-understandable as it is semantically self-describing, and we need programmes and protocols to actually exchange and understand semantic data. As a *primus inter pares*, however, we need semantic data.

This book is about providing semantic data, a process often referred to as "semantic annotation" because it frequently involves the decoration of existing data, e.g. plain text, that is only understandable for the human with semantic metadata that describes, e.g., the text.

Understandably, semantic annotation is now one of the core challenges for building the Semantic Web. In this challenge, one must deal with all the different data that now exists on the Web, i.e. text, tables, pictures, sound, movies and dynamic services. In this challenge, one must consider the user from whom the additional effort of constructing semantic data is required and how he deals with it. And, in this challenge, one must close the loop and, eventually, motivate the user explaining the benefits that he derives from it.

In this book we attempt to cover these issues ranging from the annotation of text to the annotation of multimedia, ranging from manual to more efficient semiautomatic and automatic means (where possible) and ranging from the few, early geek adopters to applications that already show benefits to the more common type of user.

A Guide to the Content

The book commences with pioneering work contributed by people outside of what is now considered the Semantic Web community proper. It started with a team of people who aimed to solve the problem of fast and convenient communication in the mathematics community by publishing their writings and describing these writings in a semantically concise form. Dalitz et al. will acquaint us with their work in the department we titled '**The Digital Library Approach**'.

The Digital Library Approach

- Wolfgang Dalitz, Winfried Neun and Wolfram Sperber: Semantic Annotation in Mathematics and Math-Net

The department on **Manual Annotations** presents two approaches which aim at the creation of semantic data that can be used alike by human and machine. The history of the two contributions dates back to the 90s and, thus, to the very early beginning of the Semantic Web. Nevertheless, they show here ongoing, recent developments. In particular,

CREAM has evolved through several life-cycles springing off from its earliest incarnation, the OntoPad, in the OntoBroker project [5]. It has now become a multiple means for the annotation of static as well as dynamic web pages. Koivunen and Swick were among the first to actively promote and exploit RDF for semantic annotation in general and for supporting collaboration in particular.

Manual Annotations

- Siegfried Handschuh and Steffen Staab: Annotating the Shallow and the Deep Web
- Marja-Riitta Koivunen and Ralph R. Swick: Collaboration through Annotations in the Semantic Web

A lot of metadata can be harvested quite easily as there are many data sources that come with explicit data descriptions – though often not in a format digestible for the standard Semantic Web agent. Baumgartner et al. show how to flexibly build and configure so-called wrappers for extracting semantic data from regular HTML code, such as tables generated from databases. Klein directly exploits structures that are explicit, as he ties RDF Schema to XML documents, marking up XML content with a concise semantics.

Wrapping

- Robert Baumgartner, Sebastian Eichholz, Sergio Flesca, Georg Gottlob and Marcus Herzog: Semantic Markup of News Items with Lixto
- Michel Klein: Using RDF Schema to Interpret XML Documents Meaningfully

Linguistic annotations of sentences referring to grammar (e.g. in the famous Penn treebank), but also to word senses, already have a tradition now in the computational linguistics community. The objectives there were that natural language systems should not only be built in a normative way by insight into one's own introspection of language understanding, but also by following the distributional hypothesis that syntactic analysis and language understanding performed by humans arises from the observation of linguistic constructs within the language. Thus, in the department on **Linguistics and Information Extraction**, Buitelaar and Decklerck share some of the corresponding insights. Subsequently, Ciravegna and Wilks adopt the distributional hypothesis building on syntax and other sign posts in order to learn rules for performing (semi-)automatic semantic annotations on structurally and/or linguistically similar web pages. DeKlerck et al. then show that the information extraction systems that result from such training (or from normative definitions) are not restricted to plain text only. Rather, they can be extended to serve the needs for semantic annotation of multimedia documents also.

Information Extraction & Linguistics

- Paul Buitelaar and Thierry Declerck: Linguistic Annotation for the Semantic Web
- Fabio Ciravegna and Yorick Wilks: Designing Adaptive Information Extraction for the Semantic Web in Amilcare
- Thierry Declerck, Jan Kuper, Horacio Saggion, Anna Samiotou and Peter Wittenburg: Content-based Indexing and Searching of Multimedia Documents

The subject of **Graphics** is further approached in the subsequent section. In particular, Wielemaker et al. describe their approach of dealing with annotations and use of metadata explicitly for images. Rather than by considering the object to detect information adequate for annotation, Santini and Champin & Prié observe what the user does with the object at hand, such as digital pictures, in order to derive meaningful annotations.

Graphics

- Jan Wielemaker, August Th. Schreiber and Bob J. Wielinga: Supporting Semantic Image Annotation and Search
- Simone Santini: Image Semantics without Annotations
- Pierre-Antoine Champin and Yannick Prié: MUSETTE: Uses-based Annotation for the Semantic Web

Eventually, we examine two papers that directly link annotation to uses. Bechhofer & Goble describe a widely applicable usage scenario, viz. conceptual open hypermedia, which allows for further spinning of the semantic as well as the syntactic Web. Finally, Brase & Nejdl describe their concrete experiences engineering ontologies and describing metadata for an open learning repository – one of the hot application areas of current metadata development and provisioning.

Usage of Annotations

- Sean Bechhofer and Carole Goble: COHSE: Conceptual Open Hypermedia Service
- Jan Brase and Wolfgang Nejdl: Annotation for an Open Learning Repository for Software Engineering, Case Study

We hope you enjoy reading the book as much as we did putting it together – and think differently about semantic annotation having read the book.

Acknowledgements

We gratefully acknowledge the intellectual stimulus contributed by many fruitful discussions and inspiration from the research and development environment in Karlsruhe. In particular, this was the research group on knowledge management of Rudi Studer at the Institute for applied informatics and formal description methods (AIFB) at the University of Karlsruhe, our colleagues of WIM (knowledge management research group) at the research center for information technologies (FZI), and our colleagues at the Ontoprise office. Furthermore, we have benefited from the EU IST Thematic Network OntoWeb SIG5 on 'Language Technology in Ontology Development and Use' as a forum. Special thanks go to Carry Koolbergen and Anne Marie de Rover of IOS Press, who have been very supportive of the publication of this book.

Work for this book had to be financed! We thank the DARPA DAML programme for funding our work on semantic annotation in the project OntoAgents, and Stefan Decker for taking us on board of his OntoAgents project. Furthermore, we gratefully acknowledge current funds from the EU IST project DOT.KOM (Designing adaptive InfOrmation extraction from text for KnOwledge Management) for our work on the integration of semantic annotation with information extraction.

We gratefully thank our families for their devotion and for putting up with us, which is in fact an enormous undertaking in itself!

Karlsruhe, January 27, 2003

Siegfried Handschuh & Steffen Staab

Bibliography

[1] Yih-Farn Robin Chen, László Kovács, and Steve Lawrence, editors.
WWW-2002 – Proceedings of the Twelfth International Conference on the World Wide Web. ACM Press, 2003.
Budapest, Hungary, May, 2003.

[2] Panos Constantopoulos, Vassilis Christophides, and Dimitris Plexousakis, editors.
SemWeb 2000 – Proceedings of the First International Workshop on the Semantic Web, 2000.
Workshop at ECDL-2000, Lisbon, Portugal, September, 2000.

[3] Dave DeRoure and Arun Iyengar, editors.
WWW-2002 – Proceedings of the Eleventh International Conference on the World Wide Web. ACM Press, 2002.
Honululu, Hawaii, May, 2002.

[4] D. Fensel, H. Lieberman, J. Hendler, and W. Wahlster, editors.
Spinning the Semantic Web, Cambridge, MA, USA, 2002. MIT Press.

[5] Dieter Fensel, Stefan Decker, Michael Erdmann, and Rudi Studer.
Ontobroker: The very high idea.
In *FLAIRS Conference*, pages 131-135. AAAI Press, 1998.

[6] J. Hendler and I. Horrocks, editors.
ISWC-2002 – Proceedings of the First International Semantic Web Conference, LNCS 2342. Springer, 2002.

[7] S. Staab, M. Frank, N. Fridman-Noy, editors.
Proceedings of the International Workshop on the Semantic Web, CEUR Workshop Proceedings Vol. 55. http://sunsite.informatik.rwth-aachen.de/Publications/CEUR-WS/Vol-55/, 2002.
Workshop at WWW-2002, Honululu, Hawaii, USA, May, 2002.

[8] S. Staab, S. Decker, D. Fensel, and A. Sheth, editors.
SemWeb 2001 – Proceedings of the Second International Workshop on the Semantic Web, CEUR Workshop Proceedings Vol. 40. http://sunsite.informatik.rwth-aachen.de/Publications/CEUR-WS/Vol-40/, 2001.
Workshop at WWW-2001, Hong Kong, China, May 1, 2001.

Contents

The Digital Library Approach

Annotation for the Semantic Web
S. Handschuh and S. Staab (Eds.)
IOS Press, 2003

Semantic Annotation in Mathematics and Math-Net

Wolfgang Dalitz   Winfried Neun   Wolfram Sperber
ZIB Berlin
Takustr. 7
D-14195 Berlin

Abstract. The Web of the future will provide a huge amount of information. We need better ways for dealing with and managing the information. A qualified semantic annotation of the information plays a key role for the Web of the future. This article gives an overview about the efforts of the mathematical community to build up a distributed and open information and communication system for mathematics: the Math-Net. The Math-Net Initiative has developed metadata schemas for some classes of Web resources which are relevant in mathematics. Math-Net Services process this information and enable the user to efficiently search and access the information.

1 Introduction

1.1 Web Resources in Mathematics

The Web is a huge data and information pool also for mathematics. The well-known search engine Google lists more than 10,000 mathematical Web sites. Each of these Web sites provides hundreds of documents as

- mathematical publications (the important mathematical journals, digitized literature, preprints, etc.),
- software (numerical software, computer algebra systems, etc.),
- teaching materials (textbooks, exercises, examples, etc.),
- personal homepages of mathematicians,
- information about mathematical institutions,
- etc..

The information is located at different servers of mathematicians, mathematical departments, libraries, publishing houses, software companies, etc.
The information is given in different formats (e.g. TEX, ps, pdf, HTML, also Word, special formats for software, etc.), and is described by different methods and data sets (metadata).

This is a typical situation in the Web: the information is heterogeneous and located at various servers. And the user is confronted with such problems as

- How can I find and use the relevant information I need?
- What about links to other resources that are important and relevant in this field?
- How can I integrate results from other resources in my work?

1.2 Semantic annotation

The Web as it is at present cannot solve problems of this kind in a suitable way.
The content of the Web documents has to be better structured and marked up ("semantically annotated") to allow a semantic processing of the information. In recent years, the W3C has started various initiatives and activities to develop concepts and methods for the so-called Semantic Web, the Web of the next generation.

One of the basics of the Semantic Web is the term "metadata". From a naive point of view metadata are simple "data about data".
The Dublin Core Metadata set (DC metadata), see [1], is a prominent example for metadata elements which allow a semantic annotation. The DC metadata define a set of 15 elements plus qualifiers for a standardized bibliographic description of electronic documents. The metadata elements cover attributes as the title, the creator, or the subject of a resource. In many cases, these metadata are helpful for the content analysis of an Internet resource and for an efficient search.

2 The Math-Net Project

2.1 The aim

The story of Math-Net began with the Math-Net project in Germany (1997-1999). At that time, many mathematical institutions, e.g. departments and institutes, started to build up their own Web sites. The most important aims of the Math-Net project were to

- establish high quality Web sites of mathematical institutions,
- make the information searchable and accessible in a user-friendly and effective way.

Especially, the Math-Net project has developed

- methods for the standardization of the semantic annotation for the main types of information offered by a mathematical institution,
- services allowing an efficient retrieval and access to the information.

Building up Math-Net is not only a technical problem, but an organizational, too. A network of persons is necessary to realize such a project. The mathematical departments and institutes in Germany have appointed information coordinators who are responsible for the information provided on the local Web sites.

2.2 Web Sites of Mathematical Institutions and Math-Net Pages

The Math-Net project started with the information provided by the departments and institutes on the local servers of the institutions.
In a first step, the existing Web sites of mathematical institutions were analyzed. The result was not surprising: the Web sites of mathematical institutions have a common core.[1] The evaluation has led to a hierarchical schema for the core information of mathematical departments and institutes. The updated schema of the information objects is the following

- General
  - About us
  - Organization of the Department/Institute
  - Information for Prospective Students
  - Community Outreach
  - Information for Visitors
- People
  - Faculty/Staff
  - Students
  - Long-term Visitors/Associates
- News
  - Schedule of Events
  - Information for Dep. Members/Members of the Institute
  - Positions Available
- Research
  - Research Groups
  - Preprints/Publications
  - Projects
  - Software Development
- Teaching
  - Academic Programs/Curricula
  - Class Schedules
  - Course Information and Materials
- Information Services
  - Computing Services

[1] But it was a hard and long-term job to reach an agreement on the standard.

- Libraries
- Journals
- Bibliographic Search

Core information of mathematical departments and institutes

The groups and subgroups of this list define a classification schema for the information of mathematical departments and institutes. The objects in the classes given by the groups and subgroups have a well-defined subject.
This classification schema was used for the definition of the Math-Net Page.
The Math-Net Page is designed for the role of a secondary homepage for the Web site of a mathematical department. The mathematical departments should install a Math-Net Page as a portal to the information offered by them.

2.3 Preprints and Metadata

The medium "preprint" has been a vehicle for the presentation of new results in mathematics for a long time. With the advent of the WWW, preprints became more and more popular in the mathematical community. Publishing preprints in the Web has some advantages:

- Research results can directly be published by the authors in the Web, without time delay and without additional costs.
- Preprints provided on Web servers are accessible from all over the world.

Preprints were the first resource class which was investigated in the Math-Net project.[2] Preprints are offered on the Web sites of mathematical departments, specialized preprints servers organized by the mathematical community, and other institutions. The semantic annotation of the preprints (in form of metadata) differs between various providers.
Within the Math-Net project, a metadata set for preprints was defined basing on the Dublin Core metadata set. The encoding of the metadata was realized in HTML.
The metadata cover

- the author(s) (with the subelements last name, first name, e-mail address),
- the title of the paper,
- the URLs of the paper (different formats are allowed),
- the language,
- the title of the series, if the paper is published in a series,
- the size of the paper,
- important dates of the publication (upload, updates),

[2]This is based on investigations made by J. Plümer and R. Schwänzl, see [26].

- classification codes: primary Mathematical Subject Classification (MSC), a secondary MSC, the classification codes used by the Zentralblatt f'ür Didaktik der Mathematik (ZDM) and Computing Reviews (CR), Physics and Astronomy Classification Scheme (PACS),
- keywords,
- abstract.

2.4 *Web Sites of Individuals and Professional Homepages*

More and more persons and especially scientists provide information about themselves in the Web. Professional homepages of mathematicians are also an important Web resource. A first model for the description of persons was developed.
Professional homepages of mathematicians are often not only simple Web pages, they are Web sites covering the curriculum vitae, the affiliation, research interests, preprints and publications, teaching activities, etc.
Similarly as for the Math-Net Pages of institutions, it makes sense to define standardized professional homepages containing metadata information for persons.
Especially, a professional homepage should contain

- name, affiliation, address, phone, fax, email

and the following groups

- General
- Collaborations and Cooperations
- News and Miscellaneous
- Research
- Teaching
- Professional Societies and Activities

2.5 *Tools*

Authors need tools to create a Math-Net Page or metadata for preprints and professional homepages in an easy and standardized way. Therefore some software, the Page Maker and the Mathematics Meta Maker (MMM), was developed by the University of Osnabrück and ZIB Berlin.

2.6 *Math-Net Services*

The institutions taking part in Math-Net make their information resources electronically available in a standardized fashion. They have full responsibility for the quality, accuracy, timeliness, and appropriateness of the data they contribute. Math-Net Service Providers combine these data into services. The Math-Net Services aim at providing fast and well-structured access to the mathematical resources within Math-Net.

Technically, the local information stored on the servers of the Math-Net Members worldwide can be harvested automatically. Machines collect the information from the local Web sites and process it.
A high quality semantic annotation of the objects is the basis for high quality services.
The first Math-Net Service was a preprint index, called **MPRESS** [3] today, the Mathematical PREprint Search System [2].
MPRESS started harvesting of the information about the preprints offered on the Web servers of german math departments. The authors were asked to give a semantic annotation of their preprints described above. Moreover, MPRESS uses some technics for an automatic extraction of metadata.
Here is a list of the current Math-Net Services:

- **SIGMA**[4] is a further Math-Net Service, which is generated by gathering the whole information of Math-Net members, for the URL see [3].
- **PERSONA MATHEMATICA**[5] gathers the information about mathematicians given on the Web sites of mathematical institutions, for the URL see [4].
- **MathJournals**[6] provides an efficient access to the available information of mathematical journals, for the URL see [5].
- The **Math-Net Navigator**[7] collects and processes the information of the Math-Net Pages, for the URL see [6].
- The **Math-Net Links**[8] are a general portal to mathematically relevant Web sites, for the URL see [7].

2.7 The Harvest Software – a technical base for Math-Net Services

The Harvest software, for the URL see [8], is a tool to collect and process data from the Web. After gathering the information will be indexed. In more detail,

- First Harvest collects the data from the servers and works out how to read the data. This depends on the format of data. Harvest supports a lot of different data formats. Summarizers analyze the content, e.g. for HTML, ps, pdf, TEX, plain text, etc. Especially, Harvest can be used to collect the metadata information from the local servers.
- Then the data are converted into a special format: SOIF, the Summary Object Interchange Format. The generated data are the so-called "resource descriptions".
- Eventually, these resource descriptions are stored in a database. This can be done by the Glimpse software (default) or, alternatively, by any other database.

[3]But MPRESS is no fulltext archive. MPRESS delivers the information about preprints.
[4]is provided by ZIB Berlin
[5]is provided by the University of Cologne
[6]is provided by the University of Osnabrück
[7]is provided ZIB Berlin
[8]is provided ZIB Berlin

The user interface of Harvest makes the data and especially the metadata of the information searchable. The results provide links to the full-texts.
MPRESS, SIGMA, PERSONA MATHEMATICA and MathJournals use the Harvest software to gather the information of the departments.

3 The Internationalization of Math-Net

Efficient access to the information in mathematics is one of the important issues for the International Mathematical Union (IMU). In 1998, the IMU founded the Committee on Electronic Information and Communication (CEIC) to improve information and communication in mathematics.[9]
CEIC has declared the further development and internationalization of the Math-Net activities a major aim of its work. This affects as well the organizational as the conceptual and technical development of Math-Net.
A worldwide mathematical information and communication system must be distributed and open. So that all mathematicians, mathematical institutions and other information providers have the possibility to supply mathematically relevant information.
The Math-Net Initiative defines the concepts and develops tools for such a system putting on the general developments and trends in the Web. The aims, the principles, and the organization of Math-Net are formulated in the Math-Net Charter, see [9].
Standardized metadata sets are the basis for a distributed information and communication system enabling a cross-linking of resources, powerful services, and guaranteeing an efficient search.

4 RDF and its use in Math-Net

4.1 RDF

In the Math-Net project the metadata were encoded in HTML.
To encode the metadata within HTML the META-tag in the header of an HTML object can be used. Primarily, metadata are intended to allow a processing of the information by machines. The metadata are positioned in the header and are not visualized by Web browsers.
Semantic metadata sets, e.g., the DC elements, can be expressed in HTML as attribute-value pairs. The DC elements define the attribute. Within an HTML document all values are related to exactly one object, e.g. a preprint.
But the use of HTML as syntax is a strong limitation and only a first step towards a high quality semantic annotation of Web objects.
One example:
A lot of publications have more than one author. Important information about each author is, e.g., her/his name, surname(s), and her/his e-mail address as contact information. HTML has no possibility to group this information. If a publication has more than one author, it can be a problem to find a correspondence between the name, the surname, and the e-mail address.
The Resource Description Framework (RDF), [10], is a general model and syntax for the encoding of metadata, which was developed for a comprehensive and flexible content analysis of Web objects, see [11].

Triples are a convenient method to express semantics. The term "statement" is used in the RDF specification to describe such a triple. Triples are a native extension of the attribute-value pairs which were used in HTML. The subject defines the resource to which the statement is related. The predicate of the statement is the attribute and the object of the statement is the value. It is possible to combine statements.
RDF statements have different representations. A first is the triple representation. A second form is the graph representation which can be visualized if the schema is small. RDF statements can also be expressed in the Extensible Markup Language (XML). The use of XML to express RDF statements combines the advantages of XML for a precise description of the structure of resources with the capabilities of RDF to describe semantics.
The RDF schema, see [12], provides additional possibilities to describe semantic interrelations.

4.2 Use of RDF on the Math-Net Page

Math-Net has used RDF to improve the semantic annotation of mathematical resources. This will now be described in more detail for the Math-Net Page.
The original Math-Net Page developed in the Math-Net project was an HTML document with sparse metadata. These metadata were restricted to

- the title: Local Math-Net Guide,
- a subject,
- keywords, e.g., Math-Net, Math-Net Guide, etc.,
- and a link to the used Math-Net schema.

Especially, these metadata don't describe the main function of the Math-Net Page: to be a portal to the local resources which are characterized by the corresponding subjects.
In more detail, the DC element relation can be used to describe the linking to the local resources. But it is not possible to add more information to the references, e.g.

- to characterize the subject of the groups and subgroups of the Math-Net Page,
- to assign other labels to groups and subgroups.

Summarizing, the DC/HTML description was not sufficient for the semantic annotation of the Math-Net Page.
For the semantic annotation of the Math-Net Page a customized metadata set was defined. The metadata schema makes statements about

- the groups and subgroups of the Math-Net Page,
- the institution and the information coordinator.

Established metadata sets such as the Dublin Core metadata set or the vCard metadata set for the description of persons and affiliations were used as far as possible.
The semantic annotation of the Math-Net Page was developed in RDF. Therefore a subject

and a type schema were introduced:
Each of the groups and subgroups on the Math-Net Page has a well-defined content: this is expressed by the subject schema, see [13].
On the other hand, a group or a subgroup defines a resource class. The resources of each class are characterized by the same subject. The classification is represented in the type schema of the Math-Net Page, see [14]. The subject and the type scheme express different aspects of the groups and subgroups of the Math-Net Page described above.
The so-called descriptors [15] define the groups and subgroups of the Math-Net Page using the RDF Schema Language. The descriptors refer to the subject and type schema described above.
The vocabulary defined by this schema is accessible via a namespace.
The metadata on the Math-Net Pages are expressed in RDF/XML. The consequence: The new Math-Net Page is an XML object. The visible part of the Math-Net Page is encoded in XHTML, the metadata part in RDF/XML.

4.3 Use of RDF on the Math-Net Page - an Example

The use of metadata on the Math-Net Page is illustrated by an example:
The topic "Preprints/Publications" is a subgroup of the group "Research" of the Math-Net Page.
The subgroup "Preprints/Publications" is linked to a resource which covers information about the research papers of an institution, e.g. preprints or articles published in journals.
In a first step, the vocabulary of the Math-Net Page is defined. Therefore so-called "descriptors" for the groups and subgroups of the Math-Net Page were introduced allowing a smart formal definition.
Especially, the descriptor refer to the subject and type schema which define the subject of the class, e.g., the class "Preprints/Publications".

The descriptor for Preprints/Publications can be represented in a RDF/XML schema in the following form:

```
<mnst:Descriptor rdf:about="&mnstns;PreprintsPublications">
<rdfs:label>Preprints and Publications</rdfs:label>
<rdf:value>information about research paper</rdf:value>
<rdfs:comment>A class of resources, which contain information
about (a) given research paper(s).</rdfs:comment>
<rdfs:seeAlso rdf:resource="&iwi;scheme/Subject/"/>
<rdfs:seeAlso rdf:resource="&iwi;scheme/Type/"/>
<rdf:type rdf:resource="&rdfsns;Class"/>
<rdfs:subClassOf rdf:resource="&mnstns;Research"/>
<rdfs:isDefinedBy rdf:resource = "&mnstns;"/>
</mnst:Descriptor>
```

The entries in the type and subject schema are the following

- in the **subject schema**:

Descriptor: Preprints and Publications
URI: http://www.iwi-iuk.org/material/RDF/1.1/descriptor/#PreprintsPublications
value: information about research papers
use with subject: The current resource describes, lists or references resources which contain information about (a) given research paper(s).

- in the **type schema**:
Descriptor: Preprints and Publications
URI: http://www.iwi-iuk.org/material/RDF/1.1/descriptor/#PreprintsPublications
value: information about research papers
use with type: The current resource contains information about (a) given research paper(s).

The statement on the Math-Net Page that the resource http://X provides information about the preprints and publications can be expressed in RDF in various representations

a) Graph form [9]

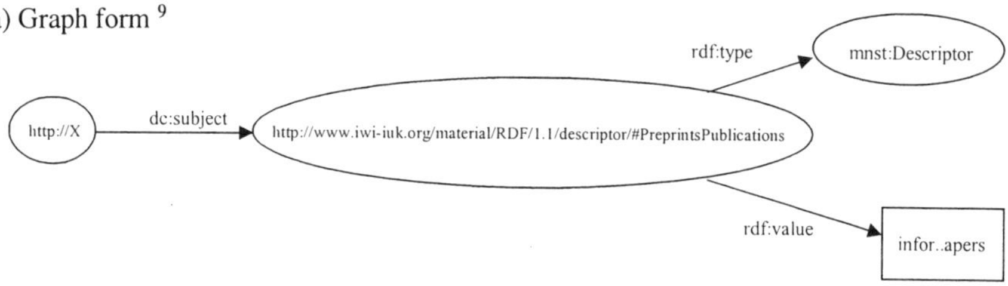

Figure 1: Metadata for the subgroup 'Preprints/Publications" on the Math-Net Page: graph form

The graph covers statements about resources. Resources have an identifier. They are represented by ovals in the graph.

This graph means (from left to right):
The resource given by the URL http://X has a subject which is given by the resource http://www.iwi-iuk.org/material/RDF/1.1/descriptor/#PreprintsPublications.
The type of this resource is given by the resource mnst:Descriptor.
The resource has the value " information about research paper".
The graph uses different vocabularies: mnst:Descriptor is the resource where the Math-Net Descriptors are defined.
The property "subject" is derived from the DC vocabulary (dc:subject).
Type and value are explained in the RDF vocabulary (rdf:type and rdf:value).
The object "information about research paper" is a string (represented by a rectangle in the graph).

b) Triple form [10]

[9]The graph was created automatically from the XML representation with the RDF API CARA, see [16]. CARA was developed within the CARMEN project, [23], by the University of Osnabrück.

[10]The representation as triples was created automatically with the RDF API CARA.

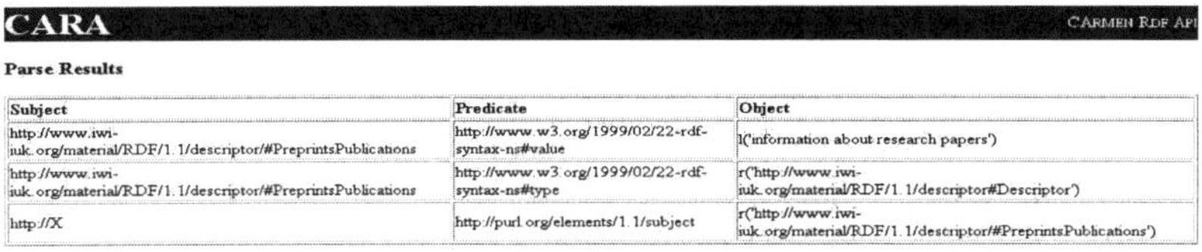

CARA CARMEN RDF API

Parse Results

Subject	Predicate	Object
http://www.iwi-iuk.org/material/RDF/1.1/descriptor/#PreprintsPublications	http://www.w3.org/1999/02/22-rdf-syntax-ns#value	l('information about research papers')
http://www.iwi-iuk.org/material/RDF/1.1/descriptor/#PreprintsPublications	http://www.w3.org/1999/02/22-rdf-syntax-ns#type	r('http://www.iwi-iuk.org/material/RDF/1.1/descriptor#Descriptor')
http://X	http://purl.org/elements/1.1/subject	r('http://www.iwi-iuk.org/material/RDF/1.1/descriptor/#PreprintsPublications')

Figure 2: Metadata for the subgroup 'Preprints/Publications" on the Math-Net Page: tiple form

The triple form of the schema lists the three statements given in the graph representation above.
The subject of a statement must be a resource. The object of a statement can be a resource or a string (literal).
The information if a object is a resource respectively a literal is marked up by the "r" respectively "l".

c) XML representation[11]

```
<rdf:Description rdf:"about=http://X">
     <dc:subject>
         <mnst:Descriptor rdf:value="information about research"
          papers"
          rdf:about="http://www.iwi-iuk.org/material/RDF/1.1/
          descriptor/#Preprints Publications"/>
    </dc:subject>
</rdf:Description>
```

The XML representation begins with the resource which is described.
The second line defines the property.
The next lines contain the object of the first statement, the resource http://www.iwi-iuk.org/material/RDF/1.1/descriptor/#Preprints/Publications which has a type (defined in mnst:Descriptor) and a value ("information about research").

Combining Statements

The semantic annotation of the resource in the example can be extended by the fact that the Math-Net Page provides a link to "Preprints/Publications". Then the corresponding RDF model is described as

[11]The XML representation was created by R. Schwänzl, University of Osnabrück.

a) Graph form

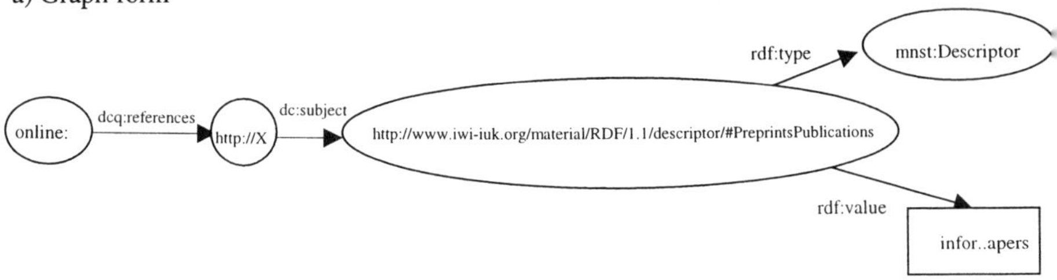

Figure 3: More metadata for the subgroup 'Preprints/Publications" on the Math-Net Page: graph form

The statement that the Math-Net Page (the resource which is generated is described by "online") references to the resource which is given by http://X is added to the graph. The predicate "references" is defined in the DC vocabulary.

b) Triple form

CARA CARMEN RDF API

Parse Results

Subject	Predicate	Object
http://www.iwi-iuk.org/material/RDF/1.1/descriptor/#PreprintsPublications	http://www.w3.org/1999/02/22-rdf-syntax-ns#value	l('information about research papers')
http://www.iwi-iuk.org/material/RDF/1.1/descriptor/#PreprintsPublications	http://www.w3.org/1999/02/22-rdf-syntax-ns#type	r('http://www.iwi-iuk.org/material/RDF/1.1/descriptor#Descriptor')
http://X	http://purl.org/elements/1.1/subject	r('http://www.iwi-iuk.org/material/RDF/1.1/descriptor/#PreprintsPublications')
online:	http://purl.org/dc/terms/references	r('http://X')

Figure 4: More metadata for the subgroup 'Preprints/Publications" on the Math-Net Page: triple form

c) XML representation

```
<rdf:Description rdf:about="http://X">
     <dc:subject>
        <mnst:Descriptor rdf:value="information about
          research papers"
          rdf:about="http://www.iwi-iuk.org/material/RDF/1.1/
         descriptor/#PreprintsPublications"/>
     </dc:subject>
</rdf:Description>
<rdf:Description rdf:about=" ">
     <dcq:references rdf:resource="http://X"/>
</rdf:Description>
```

The examples should illustrate the use of the RDF within the Math-Net Page only. The complete RDF part for the Math-Net Pages is more comprehensive, e.g.,

- It should be possible to assign other labels to the groups and subgroups. This can be modeled by the RDFS element label.

- Besides the metadata of the groups and subgroups the Math-Net Page covers metadata about the institution and the information coordinator, the person responsible for the Math-Net activities of the institution. For this purpose the vCard vocabulary is used.

Of course, within the RDF part the corresponding vocabularies have to be defined. Especially, the Math-Net Page uses metadata elements defined in different metadata sets. The used vocabularies are

- RDF,
- RDFS (RDF Schema),
- DC,
- DCQ (DC Qualified),
- MN (Math-Net Classes),
- MNST (Math-Net descriptors), and
- vCard.

XML uses namespacesto refer to vocabularies. The URIs of the namespaces are termed at the beginning of the RDF part of the Math-Net Page:

```
<rdf:RDF xmlns:rdf="http://www.w3.org/1999/02/22-rdf-syntax-ns#"
xmlns:rdfs="http://www.w3.org/2000/01/rdf-schema#"
xmlns:dc="http://purl.org/elements/1.1/"
xmlns:dcq="http://purl.org/dc/terms/"
xmlns:mn="http://www.iwi-iuk.org/material/RDF/1.1/Schema/Class/mn#"
xmlns:mnst="http://www.iwi-iuk.org/material/RDF/1.1/descriptor#"
xmlns:vCard="http://www.imc.org/2001/vcard-rdf/3.0#">
```

4.4 More about the Math-Net Page

The following image shows the (Standard) Math-Net Page of the TU München. The left column on the Math-Net Page provides links to the current Math-Net Services, the main part of the Math-Net Page (on the right hand side) covers links to the local information resources of the institution. The attribute "Standard" means that there is used a controlled English vocabulary. Besides "Standard" Math-Net Pages there are "Alternative" Math-Net Pages with customized labels, possibly in English or another language.
It is expensive to create a Math-Net Page manually. Misspellings in the XHTML part can produce trouble in the layout of the Math-Net Page, errors in the RDF part produce trouble in the automatic processing of the Math-Net Pages.
For that reasons a tool is needed to generate a Math-Net Page in an easy way. The Math-Net Page Maker, see [17], is a form-based tool for this task. The user has to insert several data in a cgi-script via a form.
The script generates the complete Math-Net Page.
On April 12,2002, CEIC and IMU endorsed a recommendation to all mathematical departments and institutes to create and install Math-Net Pages, see [27]. In the mean time more

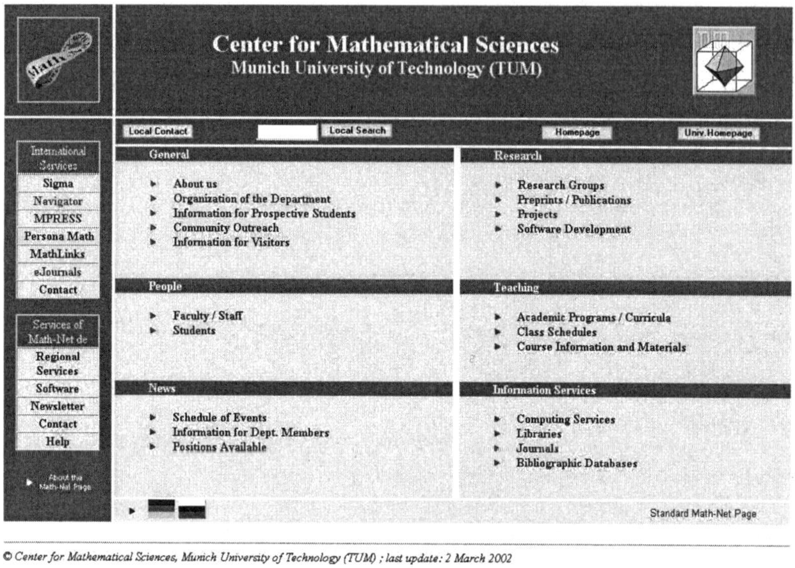

Figure 5: The Math-Net Page of the Technical University Munich

than 180 departments and institutes have generated and installed Math-Net Pages.
Of course, the concept of the Math-Net Page is not restricted to describe a portal to the information of mathematical departments. It can be used to model portals for different purposes. Especially, the idea can be used to develop a proposal for a standardized professional homepage.

4.5 *The Math-Net Navigator: Processing of Math-Net Pages*

Generally, the RDF metadata in the Math-Net Page allow the processing of the information by arbitrary search engines. Therefore, the search engines must be able to process RDF/XML resources.
The Math-Net Navigator is the Math-Net Service processing the Math-Net Pages. The backbone of the Math-Net Navigator is a database (for that purpose the public domain database MySQL is used).
At first the URL of each new Math-Net Page has to be inserted in the database [12]. The complete Math-Net Pages are daily gathered and processed by an automatic procedure.
The Math-Net Navigator combines seaching and navigation at different levels. In more detail, the Math-Net Navigator provides on the top level

- a search function (over the servers of all Math-Net Members worldwide);

[12]Standardized paths for the Math-Net Pages support the gathering of Math-Net Pages. Hence, Math-Net has a URL convention to localize the Math-Net Pages on the server of mathematical departments.

- geographical-oriented views of the Math-Net Members (a clickable map and a list of countries);
- subject-oriented views of the information provided by the Math-Net Members (e.g. lists of all Math-Net Members offering preprints).

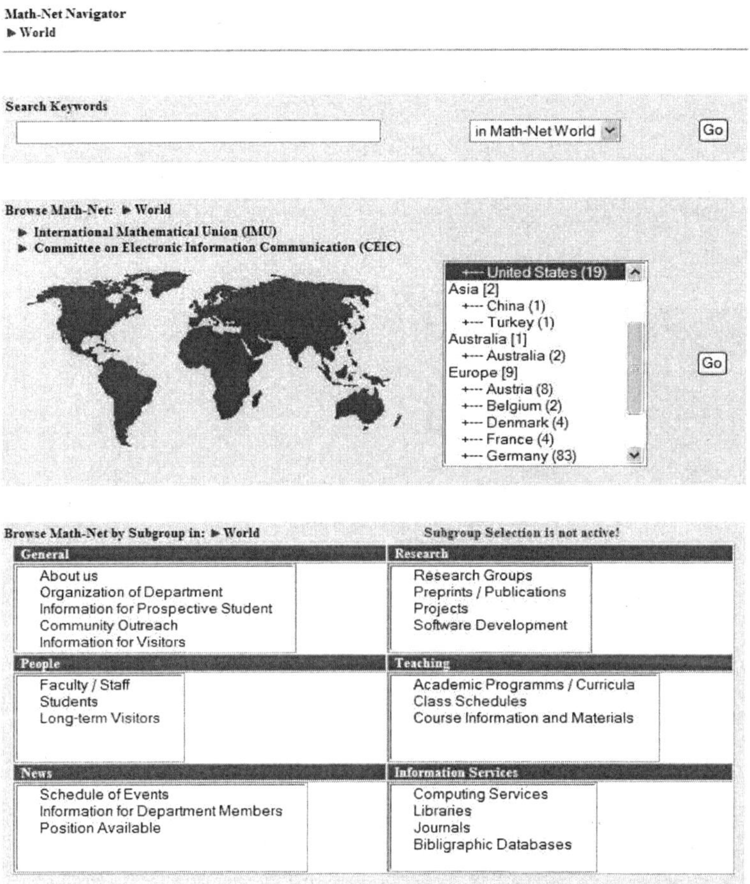

Figure 6: The Math-Net Navigator (top level)

If you choose a country (e.g., Canada) you get, essentially, the same functionality restricted to the Math-Net Members in Canada, namely

- a search function (over all Canadian Math-Net Members);
- a list of Math-Net Members in Canada;
- subject-oriented views of the information provided by the Math-Net Members (e.g., lists of all Math-Net Members offering preprints). [13]

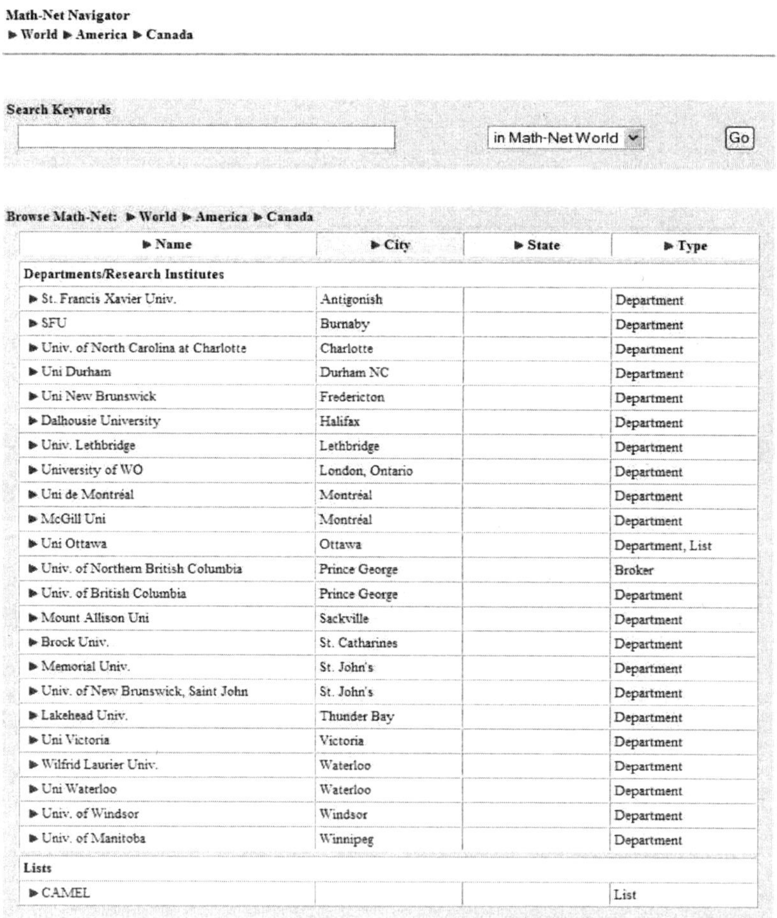

Math-Net Navigator
▶ World ▶ America ▶ Canada

Search Keywords

in Math-Net World | Go

Browse Math-Net: ▶ World ▶ America ▶ Canada

▶ Name	▶ City	▶ State	▶ Type
Departments/Research Institutes			
▶ St. Francis Xavier Univ.	Antigonish		Department
▶ SFU	Burnaby		Department
▶ Univ. of North Carolina at Charlotte	Charlotte		Department
▶ Uni Durham	Durham NC		Department
▶ Uni New Brunswick	Fredericton		Department
▶ Dalhousie University	Halifax		Department
▶ Univ. Lethbridge	Lethbridge		Department
▶ University of WO	London, Ontario		Department
▶ Uni de Montréal	Montréal		Department
▶ McGill Uni	Montréal		Department
▶ Uni Ottawa	Ottawa		Department, List
▶ Univ. of Northern British Columbia	Prince George		Broker
▶ Univ. of British Columbia	Prince George		Department
▶ Mount Allison Uni	Sackville		Department
▶ Brock Univ.	St. Catharines		Department
▶ Memorial Univ.	St. John's		Department
▶ Univ. of New Brunswick, Saint John	St. John's		Department
▶ Lakehead Univ.	Thunder Bay		Department
▶ Uni Victoria	Victoria		Department
▶ Wilfrid Laurier Univ.	Waterloo		Department
▶ Uni Waterloo	Waterloo		Department
▶ Univ. of Windsor	Windsor		Department
▶ Univ. of Manitoba	Winnipeg		Department
Lists			
▶ CAMEL			List

Figure 7: The Math-Net Navigator (Canada)

[13]not in the cutout

Resume:

- The Math-Net Pages and the Math-Net Navigator provide multiple views about the Web sites of the Math-Net Members, especially
  - an effective and user-friendly navigation along the subject and type scheme we defined as "core information" of mathematical departments and institutions, see above;
  - a search about the Web sites of Math-Net Members at different levels;
  - a geographical based access to the Web sites of the Math-Net Members.

  Universal search engines such as Google, AltaVista, etc., are not able to perform particularly the first view.
- The Math-Net Page is a uniform portal to the local information of mathematical institutions,
- The Math-Net Navigator is a central portal to the Web sites of mathematical institutions.

4.6 RDF Metadata for preprints - MPRESS

The original metadata set for preprints was substituted by an RDF schema in the mean time, see [18].
The RDF schema allows, e.g., a precise description grouping of the authors, particularly of names, surnames, and email adresses as well as of URIs and various formats.
The visualization of the graph metadata presentation is given in [19].
Again, the user needs a simple tool to generate a standardized metadata description of her/his preprint. Version 3.1 of the Mathematics Meta Maker (MMM), see [20], generates this description. The MMM tool produces an XML document containing the metadata which are encoded in RDF/XML.
The MMM tool can be downloaded and installed locally.
MPRESS, [2] , mainly gathers the metadata information for preprints. Today, more than 50,000 mathematical preprints located on more than 150 servers worldwide are indexed in MPRESS. MPRESS provides browsing and search functionalities.
The Mathematical Subject Classification (MSC), see [21], is the structure used for browsing. Searching combines a fulltext and a metadata search.

4.7 Metadata for persons - PERSONA MATHEMATICA

The concept for the Web presentations of persons is currently discussed by the Math-Net Initiative. The aim is to develop a standardized professional homepage as a portal to the information.
For details of the discussion see [22].
The structure of the professional homepage defines the classes and fixes the metadata. The procedure can be the same as for the Math-Net Page.
The Math-Net Service PERSONA MATHEMATICA, see [4], processes the metadata to realize efficient search facilities for mathematicians.

4.8 Relations between Math-Net Services

Initially the Math-Net Services were stand-alone services. Of course, the various kinds of documents provided in Math-Net are linked:

- Math-Net Pages refer to preprints and information about persons;
- Professional homepages have links to preprints and the institutions;
- etc..

As a consequence, all Math-Net Services should cooperate to allow the user a comprehensive access to the information available in Math-Net. Of course, the various kinds of documents provided in Math-Net are linked together. It starts with simple links:

- Math-Net Navigator and SIGMA
  As said before, the Math-Net Navigator provides also a search about the information of the Math-Net Members. Therefore must be added the URLs of new Math-Net Members to SIGMA to make harvesting these Web sites possible.
- Math-Net Navigator, MPRESS, and PERSONA MATHEMATICA
  If a new Math-Net Page is registered providing links to preprints and to information about the staff respectively this information must be integrated also into the services MPRESS and PERSONA MATHEMATICA respectively.
- Update of the Math-Net Links
  The Math-Net Links should be updated by using the information provided by the other Math-Net Services, particularly Navigator, MPRESS, MathJournals.

Moreover, the retrieval of the information contained in Math-Net should allow a refinement in searching, e.g., by types. This can be done, e.g., by a standardized navigation bar on the portal pages. Such a navigation bar can provide links to and/or a searching about the other Math-Net Services.

4.9 The technical base of Math-Net Services: Upgrade of Harvesting/Glimpse-Software

As said before, the resource descriptions in Harvest have a special format: SOIF. SOIF is a flat format. Metadata are presented in the form of attribute-value pairs.
The summarizing, indexing and retrieval components in the Harvest/Glimpse software are not sufficient to process the XML/RDF information and to make the information searchable in an enhanced way. Under the CARMEN project, [23], a prototype for the processing and retrieval of RDF/XML documents was developed by the University Osnabrück and the University Dortmund. This prototype, the X-Harvest/HYREX software, allows processing deeply structured documents, e.g. RDF/XML formatted documents, and combines this with enhanced functionalities of the information retrieval (e.g., stemming, soundex, etc.). For more information see [24].

5 Expressing mathematics on the Web

So far, this article dealt with the Web sites of mathematical institutions and a better semantic annotation for some typical and important resource classes. This is a first and important step towards improving the visibility of mathematical information in the Web and developing the basics for a Semantic Web in mathematics.

More in detail, the developed methods and tools addressed the semantic annotation of Web objects on a macro level. But what about the semantic annotation of a mathematical formula in a preprint or a publication?
Therefore it is necessary to analyze the mathematical content of the documents on a micro level. Fortunately, XML can be used for a uniform logical markup of mathematical objects on the micro level too. The advantages: a uniform and extensible platform to express mathematics and mathematically relevant information, to add semantic annotation, and to develop standardized retrieval methods and tools, etc.

Up to now, TeX is the most important format to express mathematical terms and statements in digital objects. TeX was the first Markup language. TeX allows an adequate presentation of the mathematical terms and statements. It has well-defined tags for a lot of mathematical functions, but it is not convenient to add further semantic annotation.
Some years ago, the mathematical community under the aegis of the W3C has started to develop the Mathematics Markup Language MathML. The advantage of MathML is that it uses XML as platform. MathML was the first XML specification that was recommended by the W3C. The current version MathML 2.0 is available at [25].
MathML seems to be a concept that facilitates an improved expression of mathematics on the Web. Especially, MathML Content Markup can be used for the automatic annotation and processing of mathematical terms, e.g., by computer algebra systems. Semantic annotation in MathML, however, is not standardized yet.

6 Concluding remarks

Knowledge management in mathematics is at its beginning. The examples described above show that the mathematical community launches a lot of activities to improve the quantity and quality of mathematics information on the Web.
But they also show that it is no trivial task to build up a better information and communication system in mathematics:

- The mathematical community is required to define its specific requirements and to contribute to the mathematical information structure in the future. MathML is an example for the influence of the mathematical community on the future development of the Web.

- The main goal is to improve the access to mathematical information for all interested in mathematical science and results.

- The mathematical community must take an active part in the development of concepts and foundations for better information and communication systems.

- New techniques must be designed in accordance with the general developments of the Internet and the Web.
- A qualified semantic annotation of the Web objects will play a key role for the presentation of scientific information in the Web.

References

[1] http://dublincore.org/documents/dces/

[2] http://mathnet.preprints.org/

[3] http://www.math-net.org/search/germany/

[4] http://www.mi.uni-koeln.de/Math-Net/persona_mathematica/

[5] http://elib.uni-osnabrueck.de/Math-Net/

[6] http://www.math-net.org/navigator/

[7] http://www.math-net.org/links/show?collection=math

[8] http://webharvest.sourceforge.net/ng/

[9] The International Mathematical Union, Committee on Electronic Information and Communication: Recommendations on Information and Communication, General Assembly, Shanghai,August 2002, also electronically available at http://www.math-net.org/charter

[10] http://www.w3.org/RDF/

[11] http://www.w3c.org/TR/1999/REC-rdf-syntax-19990222/

[12] http://www.w3c.org/TR/rdf-schema/

[13] http://www.iwi-iuk.org/material/RDF/1.1/scheme/Subject/

[14] http://www.iwi-iuk.org/material/RDF/1.1/scheme/Type/

[15] http://www.iwi-iuk.org/material/RDF/1.1/descriptor/

[16] http://zoe.mathematik.uni-osnabrueck.de/cgi-bin/RDF/parser.cgi

[17] http://www.math-net.org/pagemaker

[18] http://www.iwi-iuk.org/material/RDF/1.1/profile/MNPreprint/

[19] http://www.iwi-iuk.org/material/RDF/1.1/profile/MNPreprint/mnpreprinttest.rdf.png

[20] http://www.mathematik.uni-osnabrueck.de/cgi-bin/MMM3.1.cgi

[21] http://mathnet.preprints.org/msc/

[22] http://triton.mathematik.tu-muenchen.de/~kaplan/talks/Halle_DMV_IuK_2002/ Personendaten in einem verteilten Informationssystem-Dateien/frame.htm

[23] http://www.mathematik.uni-osnabrueck.de/projects/carmen/

[24] http://ls6-www.cs.uni-dortmund.de/ir/projects/carmen/wp7.html

[25] http://www.w3.org/TR/MathML2/

[26] J. Plümer and R. Schwänzl: Harvesting Mathematics, Euromath Bulletin Volume 2, No.1, 1996, also electronically available at http://www.emis.de/epub/harvest.ps.gz/

[27] The International Mathematical Union, Committee on Electronic Information and Communication: Recommendations on Information and Communication, General Assembly, Shanghai,August 2002, also electronically available at http://www.math-net.org/Math-Net-Recommendation.html

Manual Annotations

Annotation of the Shallow and the Deep Web

Siegfried Handschuh[1] and Steffen Staab[1,2]
[1]*Institute AIFB, University of Karlsruhe, 76128 Karlsruhe, Germany*
{sha, sst}@aifb.uni-karlsruhe.de
http://www.aifb.uni-karlsruhe.de/WBS
[2]*Ontoprise GmbH, 76131 Karlsruhe, Germany*
http://www.ontoprise.com/

Abstract. The success of the Semantic Web crucially depends on the easy creation of ontology-based metadata by semantic annotation. We provide a framework, CREAM, that allows for the creation of semantic metadata about static and dynamic Web pages, i.e. for semantic annotation of the Shallow and the Deep Web. CREAM supports the manual and the semi-automatic annotation of static Web pages, the authoring of new web pages with the simultaneous creation of metadata, and the deep annotation of Web pages defined dynamically by database queries.

1 Introduction

The Semantic Web supports its users to find accurate information, to combine easily related pieces of information into an overarching picture and to compose new applications without programming knowledge.

To achieve these objectives not only human readers have to understand what is offered on a web page, software agents also must be able to interpret existing information. This is only possible when the relevant information is represented in a declarative and semantically precise way and when it is thus understandable for the computer. This need creates the necessity to generate semantically accurate, ontology-based metadata. We describe how the problem is tackled by means of our annotation framework, CREAM — CREAting Metadata for the Semantic Web. CREAM comprises methods for:

- Manual annotation: The transformation of existing syntactic resources (*viz.* textual documents) into interlinked knowledge structures that represent relevant underlying information [18].
- Authoring of documents: In addition to the annotation of existing documents the authoring mode lets authors create metadata — almost for free — while putting together the content of a document [16].
- Semi-automatic annotation: Efficient semi-automatic annotation based on information extraction that is trained to handle structurally and/or linguistically similar documents [17].

- Deep annotation: Annotation of dynamic Web documents that results in a semantic mapping to the underlying database if the database owner cooperates in the Semantic Web and allows for direct access to the database [19].

In the following we wrap up several previous contributions ([18, 16, 17, 19]). We start to describe core requirements for semantic annotation. For a more concise description, we first define our terminology and give an example of the kind of metadata the generation of which we support by CREAM (Section 2). In Section 3 we derive the design of CREAM from the requirements elaborated before. In Section 4, we explain the major modes of interaction supported by CREAM. We briefly sketch the integration of CREAM with a learnable information extraction component in Section 5, before we outline the basic building blocks for deep annotation in Section 6. Finally, we discuss related works and offer conclusions.

2 Creating Metadata for the Semantic Web

CREAM is an annotation and authoring framework suited for the easy and comfortable creation of relational metadata. OntoMat-Annotizer (OntoMat for short) is its concrete implementation.

2.1 Requirements for CREAM

Given the problems with syntax, semantics and pragmatics in earlier experiences (e.g. KA2 [3]), we list here a set of requirements. Thereby, the principal requirements apply for *a-posteriori annotation* as well as for the *integration of web page authoring with metadata creation* as follows:

- **Consistency**: Semantic structures should adhere to a given ontology in order to allow for better sharing of knowledge. For example, it should be avoided that people use an attribute, where the ontology requires a concept instance.

- **Proper Reference**: Identifiers of instances, *e.g.* of persons, institutes or companies, should be unique. For instance, the metadata generated in the KA2 case study contained three different identifiers for our colleague Dieter Fensel. Thus, knowledge about him could not be grasped with a straightforward query.[1]

- **Avoid Redundancy**: Decentralized knowledge provisioning should be possible. However, when annotators collaborate, it should be possible for them to identify (parts of) sources that have already been annotated and to reuse previously captured knowledge in order to avoid laborious redundant annotations.

- **Relational Metadata**: Like HTML information, which is spread on the Web, but related by HTML links, knowledge markup may be distributed, but it should be semantically related. Current annotation tools tend to generate template-like metadata, which is hardly connected, if at all. For example, annotation environments often support Dublin Core [9, 10, 22], providing means to state, e.g., the name of authors of a document, but not

[1]The reader may see similar effects in bibliography databases. E.g., query for James (Jim) Hendler at the —otherwise excellent —DBLP: `http://www.informatik.uni-trier.de/~ley/db/`.

their IDs[2]. Thus, the only possibility to query for all publications of a certain person requires the querying for some attribute like fullname — which is very unsatisfying for frequent names like "John Smith".

- **Dynamic Documents**: A large percentage of the Web pages are not static documents. For dynamic web pages (e.g. ones that are generated from a database) it does not seem to be usefull to annotate every single page. Rather one wants to "annotate the database" in order to reuse it for its own Semantic Web purpose.

- **Maintenance**: Knowledge markup needs to be maintained. An annotation tool should support the maintenance task. In the remainder of the paper we will provide some infrastructure support for the task.

- **Ease of Use**: It is obvious that an annotation environment should be easy to use in order to be really useful. However, this objective is not easily achieved, because metadata creation involves intricate navigation of semantic structures, e.g. taxonomies, properties and concepts.

- **Efficiency**: The effort for the production of metadata is a large restraining threshold. The more efficiently a tool supports metadata creation, the more metadata users tend to produce. This requirement is related to the ease of use. It also depends on the automation of the metadata creation process, e.g. on the preprocessing of the document.

- **Multiple Ontologies**: HTML documents in the semantic web may contain information that is related to different ontologies. Therefore the annotation framework should cater for concurrent annotation with multiple ontologies.

Our framework, CREAM that is presented here, targets a comprehensive solution for metadata creation during web page authoring and a-posteriori annotation. The objective is pursued by combining advanced mechanisms for inferencing, fact crawling, document management, meta ontology definitions, metadata re-recognition, content generation, and (as explained in Section 5) information extraction. These components are explained in the subsequent sections.

2.2 Relational Metadata

We elaborate the terminology here because many of the terms that are used with regard to metadata creation tools carry several, ambiguous connotations that imply conceptually important differences:

- **Ontology**: An ontology is a formal, explicit specification of a shared conceptualization of a domain of interest [15]. In our case it is constituted by statements expressing definitions of DAML+OIL classes and properties [13].

- **Annotations**: An annotation in our context is a set of instantiations attached to an HTML document. We distinguish *(i)* instantiations of DAML+OIL classes, *(ii)* instantiated properties from one class instance to a datatype instance — henceforth called attribute instance

[2]In the web context one typically uses the term 'URI' (uniform resource identifier) to speak of 'unique identifier'.

(of the class instance), and *(iii)* instantiated properties from one class instance to another class instance — henceforth called relationship instance.

Class instances have unique URIs, e.g. like 'http://www.aifb.uni-karlsruhe.de/WBS/sst/#Steffen'. They frequently come with attribute instances, such as a human-readable label like 'Steffen'.

- **Metadata**: Metadata are data about data. In our context the annotations are metadata about the HTML documents.

- **Relational Metadata**: We use the term relational metadata to denote the annotations that contain relationship instances.

  Often, the term "annotation" is used to mean something like "private or shared note", "comment" or "Dublin Core metadata". This alternative meaning of annotation may be emulated in our approach by modelling these notes with attribute instances. For instance, a comment note "I like this paper" would bc related to the URL of the paper via an attribute instance 'hasComment'.

  In contrast, relational metadata also contain statements like 'Siegfried cooperates with Steffen', *i.e.* relational metadata contain relationships between class instances rather than only textual notes.

- **Generic Annotations**: In a *generic annotation*, a piece of text that corresponds to a database field and that is annotated is only considered to be a place holder. I.e. a variable must be generated for such an annotation. For example, a concept Institute in the client ontology may correspond to one generic annotation for the Organization identifier in the database.

  In consequence to the above terminology, we will refer to generic annotation in detail as *generic class instances*, *generic attribute instances*, and *generic relationship instances*.

Figure 1 illustrates our use of the terms "ontology", "annotation" and "relational metadata". It depicts some part of the SWRC[3] (semantic web research community) ontology. Furthermore it shows two homepages, viz. pages about Siegfried and Steffen (http://www.aifb.uni-karlsruhe.de/WBS/sha and http://www.aifb.uni-karlsruhe.de/WBS/sst, respectively) with annotations given in an XML serialization of RDF facts. For the two persons there are instances denoted by corresponding URIs (http://www.aifb.uni-karlsruhe.de/WBS/sst/#Steffen and http://www.aifb.uni-karlsruhe.de/WBS/sha/#Siegfried). The swrc:name of http://www.aifb.uni-karlsruhe.de/WBS/sha/#Siegfried is "Siegfried Handschuh".

In addition, there is a relationship instance between the two persons, *viz.* they cooperate. This cooperation information 'spans' the two pages.

The objective of CREAM is to allow for the easy generation of such a target representation irrespective of whether the major mode of interaction is a-posteriori annotation or web page authoring.

[3]http://ontobroker.semanticweb.org/ontos/swrc.html

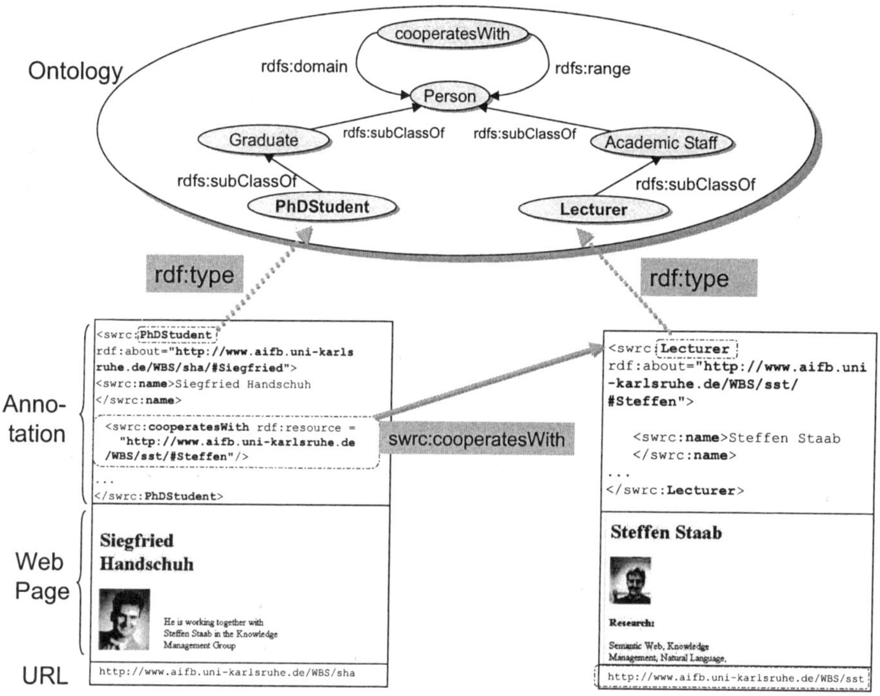

Figure 1: Annotation example

3 Design of CREAM

3.1 CREAM Modules

The difficulties sketched before directly feed into the design rationale of CREAM. The design rationale links the requirements with the CREAM modules. This results in a N:M mapping (neither functional nor injective). A tabular overview of the matrix can be found in [18, 16].

- **Document Editor**: The document editor may be conceptually — though not practically — distinguished into a viewing component and the component for generating content:
  - **Document Viewer**: The document viewer visualizes the document contents. The metadata creator may easily provide new metadata by selecting pieces of text and aligning it with parts of the ontology. The document viewer should support various formats (HTML, PDF, XML, etc.). For some formats the following component for content generation may not be available.

    The document viewer highlights the existing semantic annotation and server-side markup the of web page. It distinguishes visually between semantic annotation and markup that describes the information structure of a underlaying database.

  - **Content Generation:** The editor also allows the conventional authoring of documents. In addition, instances already available may be dragged from a visualization of the content of the annotation inference server and dropped into the document. Thereby, some piece of text and/or a link is produced taking into account the information from the meta ontology (cf. module meta ontology).

    The newly generated content is already annotated and the meta ontology guides the construction of further information, e.g. further XPointers (cf. [7], [14]) are attached to instances.

- **Ontology Guidance and Fact Browser**: The framework needs guidance from the ontology. In order to allow for sharing of knowledge, newly created annotations must be consistent with a community's ontology. If metadata creators instantiate arbitrary classes and properties the semantics of these properties remains void. Of course the framework must be able to adapt to multiple ontologies in order to reflect different foci of the metadata creators. In the case of concurrent annotation with multiple ontologies there is an ontology guidance/fact browser for each ontology.

- **Crawler:** The creation of relational metadata must take place *within* the Semantic Web. During metadata creation, subjects must be aware of which entities exist already in their part of the Semantic Web. This is only possible if a crawler makes relevant entities immediately available. So, metadata creators may look for proper reference, i.e. decide whether an entity already has a URI (e.g. whether the entity named "Dieter Fensel" or "D. Fensel" has already been identified by some other metadata creators) and only by this way metadata creators may recognize whether properties have already been instantiated (e.g. whether "Dieter Fensel" has already been linked to his publications). As a consequence of metadata creators' awareness, relational metadata may be created, because class instances become related rather than only flat templates are filled.

  A crawler partially fulfills the requirements of proper reference and the avoidance of redundancy. For example, one might crawl the homepages of his community before he starts to annotate his homepage in order to reuse and reference existing metadata. However, a crawler reduces and doesn't solve the problems since it is obviously not possible to crawl the whole web.

- **Annotation Inference Server**: Relational metadata, proper reference and avoidance of redundant annotation require querying for instances, i.e. querying whether and which instances exist. For this purpose as well as for checking of consistency, we provide an annotation inference server in our framework. The annotation inference server reasons on crawled and newly created instances and on the ontology. It also serves the ontological guidance and fact browser, because it allows to query for existing classes, instances and properties.

- **Meta Ontology**: The purpose of the meta ontology is the separation of ontology design and use. It is needed to describe how classes, attributes and relationships from the domain ontology should be used by the CREAM environment. Thus, the ontology describes how the semantic data should look like and the meta ontology connected to the ontology describes how the ontology is used by the annotation environment to actually create semantic data. It is specifically explained in [16].

- **Deep Annotation Module**: This module enables the deep annotation scenario. It manages the generation of mapping rules between the database and the client ontology. For this purpose, it combines the generic annotation stored in the annotation inference server and the server-side markup provided with the content (cf. Section 6. On demand it publishes the mapping rules derived from the generic annotations.

- **Document Management**: In order to avoid redundancy of annotation efforts, it is not sufficient to ask whether instances exist at the annotation inference server. When an annotator decides to capture knowledge from a web page, he does not want to query for all single instances that he considers relevant on this page, but he wants information whether and how this web page has been annotated before. Considering the dynamics of HTML pages on the web, it is desirable to store foreign web pages one has annotated together with their annotations. Foreign documents for which modification is not possible may be remotely annotated by using XPointer (cf. [7], [14]) as a addressing meachanism. When the foreign web page changes, the old annotations may still be valid or they may become invalid. The annotator must decide based on the old annotations and based on the changes of the web page.

  A future goal of the document management in our framework will be the semi-automatic maintenance of annotations on foreign web pages. When only few parts of a document change, pattern matching may propose revisions of old annotations.

- **Metadata Re-recognition & Information Extraction**: Even with sophisticated tools it is laborious to provide semantic annotations. A major goal thus is semi-automatic metadata creation taking advantage of information extraction techniques to propose annotations to metadata creators and, thus, to facilitate the metadata creation task. Concerning our environment we envisage three major techniques:

  1. First, metadata re-recognition compares existing metadata literals with newly typed or existing text. Thus, the mentioning of the name "Siegfried Handschuh" in the document triggers the proposal that URI, `http://www.aifb.uni-karlsruhe.de/WBS/sha/#Siegfried` is co-referenced at this point.
  2. "Wrappers" may be learned from given markup in order to automatically annotate similarly structured pages (cf., e.g., [24]).
  3. Message extraction like systems may be used to recognize named entities, propose co-reference, and extract some relationship from texts (cf., e.g., [28, 33]).

This component has been realized by using the Amilcare information extraction system (Section 5)[4], but it is not yet available in the download version of OntoMat.

Besides the requirements that constitute single modules, one may identify functions that cross module boundaries:

- **Storage**: CREAM supports two different ways of storage. The annotations will be stored inside the document that is in the document management component. Alternatively or simultaneously it is also possible to store them in the annotation inference server.

[4]`http://www.dcs.shef.ac.uk/~fabio/Amilcare.html`

- **Replication**: We provide a simple replication mechanism by crawling annotations into our annotation inference server. Then inferencing can be used to rule out formal inconsistencies.

3.2 Architecture of CREAM

The architecture of CREAM is depicted in Figure 2. The Design of the CREAM framework pursues the idea to be flexible and open. Therefore, OntoMat, the implementation of the framework, comprises a plug-in structure, which is flexible with regard to adding or replacing modules.

The core OntoMat, which is downloadable, consists of an Ontology Guidance and Fact browser, a document viewer/editor, and a internal memory data-structure for the ontology and metadata. However, one only gets the full-fledged semantic capabilities (e.g. datalog reasoning or subsumption reasoning) when one uses a plug-in connection to a corresponding annotation inference server.

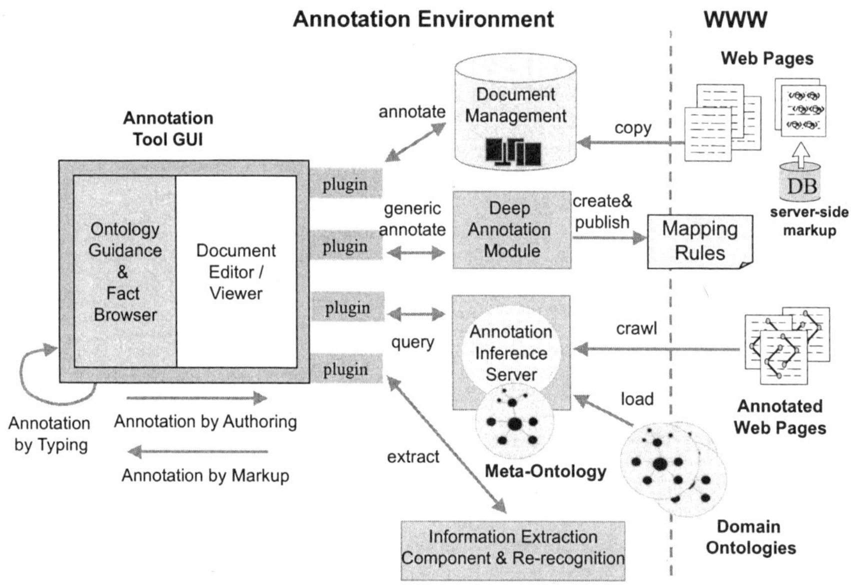

Figure 2: Architecture of CREAM

4 Modes of Interaction

The metadata creation process in OntoMat is actually supported by three types of interaction with the tool (also cf. Figure 2):

1. Annotation by Typing Statements: This involves working almost exclusively within the ontology guidance/fact browser.

2. Annotation by Markup: This mostly involves the reuse of data from the document editor/viewer in the ontology guidance/fact browser.

3. Annotation by Authoring Web Pages: This mostly involves the reuse of data from the fact browser in the document editor.

In order to clarify the different role of the three types of interaction, we here describe how they differ for generating three types of metadata:

1. Generating instances of classes

2. Generating attribute instances

3. Generation relationship instances

4.1 Annotation by Typing

Annotation by typing is almost purely based on the ontology guidance/fact browser (cf. Section 3). The user generates metadata (class instances, attribute instances, relationship instances) that are completely independent from the Web page currently viewed.

In addition, the user may drag-and-drop around instances that are already in the knowledge base in order to create new relationship instances (cf. arrow #0 in Figure 3).

4.2 Annotation by Markup

The basic idea of annotation by markup is the usage of marked-up content in the document editor/viewer for instance generation.

1. Generating class instances: When the user drags a marked up piece of content onto a particular concept from the ontology, a new class instance is generated. A new URI is generated and a corresponding property is assigned the marked up text (cf. arrow #1 in Figure 3).

   For instance, marking "Siegfried Handschuh" and dropping this piece of text on the concept PhDStudent creates a new URI, instantiates this URI as belonging to PhDStudent and assigns "Siegfried Handschuh" to the swrc:name slot of the new URI.

2. Generating attribute instance: In order to generate an attribute instance the user simply drops the marked up content into the corresponding table entry (cf. arrow #2 in Figure 3). Depending on the setting the corresponding XPointer or the content itself is filled into the attribute.

3. Generating relationship instance: In order to generate a relationship instance the user simply drops the marked up content onto the relation of a pre-selected instance (cf. arrow #3 in Figure 3). Like in "class instance generation" a new instance is generated and connected with the pre-selected instance.

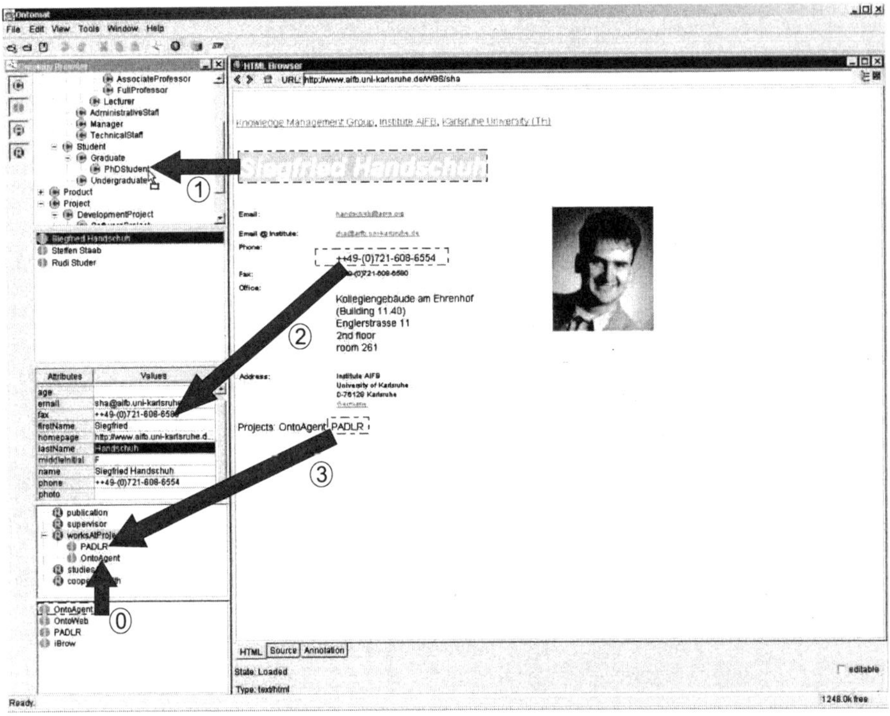

Figure 3: Annotation example

4.3 Annotation by Authoring

The third major process is authoring Web pages and metadata together. There are two modi for authoring: *(i)*, authoring by using ontology guidance and fact browser for content generation and, *(ii)*, authoring with the help of metadata re-recognition or — more general — information extraction. As far as authoring is concerned, we have only implemented *(i)* so far. However, we want to point out that already very simple information extraction mechanisms, i.e. metadata re-recognition (cf. Section 3) may help the author to produce consistent metadata.

Authoring with Content Generation By inverting the process of markup (cf. Figure 2), we may reuse existing instance description, like labels or other attributes:

1. Class instances: Dropping class instances from the fact browser into the document creates text according to their labels and — if possible — links (cf. arrow #1 in Figure 4).

2. Attribute instances: Dropping attribute instances from the fact browser in the document (cf. arrow #2 in Figure 4) generates the corresponding text or even linked text.

3. Relationship instances: Dropping relationship instances from the fact browser in the document generates simple "sentences". For instance, the dropping of the relationship COOPERATES-WITH between the instances corresponding to Rudi and Steffen triggers the creation of a small piece of text (cf. arrow #3 in Figure 4). The text corresponds to the instance labels plus the label of the relationship (if available), e.g. "Rudi Studer cooperates with Steffen Staab". Typically, this piece of text will require further editing.

Further mechanisms, like the creation of lists or tables from selected concepts (e.g. all Persons), still need to be explored.

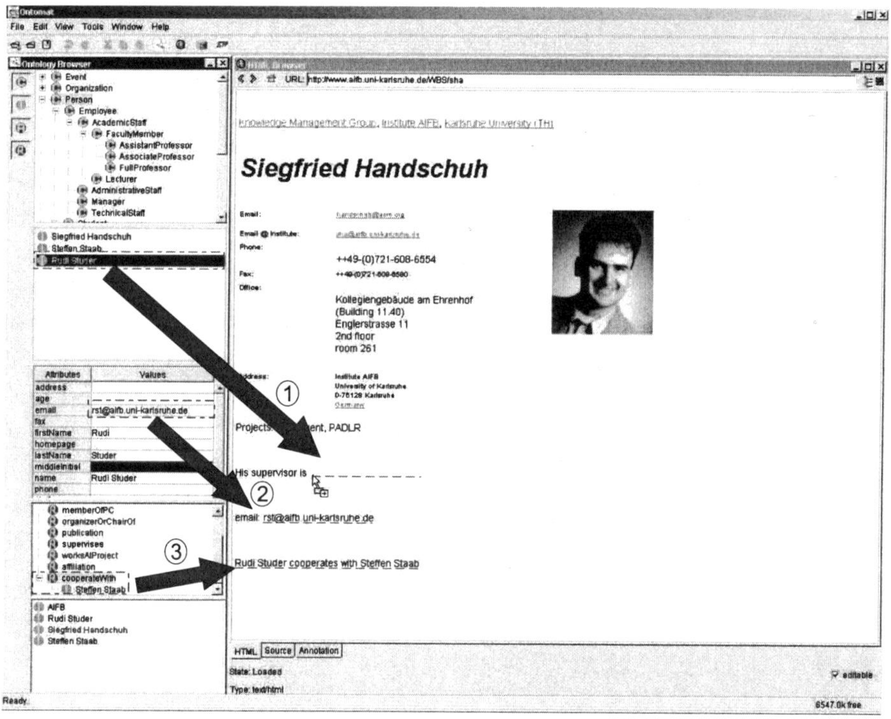

Figure 4: Annotation by Authoring example

5 Semi-automatic Creation of Metadata

Providing plenty of relational metadata by manual annotation, i.e. conceptual mark-up of text passages, is a laborious task.

In Section 2 we described the idea that wrappers and information extraction components could be used to facilitate the work. Hence, we have developed S-CREAM (Semi-automatic CREAtion of Metadata), an annotation framework (cf. [17]) that integrates a learnable information extraction component (viz. Amilcare [4]).

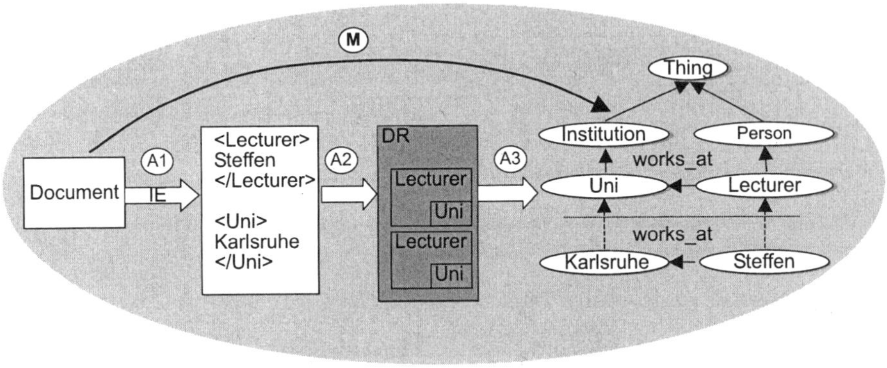

Figure 5: Manual and Automatic Annotation

Amilcare is a system that learns information extraction rules from manually marked-up input. S-CREAM aligns conceptual markup, which defines relational metadata, (such as provided through OntoMat-Annotizer) with semantic and indicative tagging (such as produced by Amilcare).

Synthesizing S-CREAM: In order to synthesize S-CREAM out of the existing frameworks CREAM and Amilcare, we consider their core processes in terms of input and output, as well as the process of S-CREAM. Figure 5 surveys the three processes. The first process is indicated by a circled M. It is manual annotation of metadata, which turns a document into relational metadata that corresponds to the given ontology. The second process is indicated by a circled A1. It is information extraction, e.g. provided by Amilcare. When comparing the desired relational metadata from manual markup and the semantic tagging provided by information extraction systems, one recognizes that the output of this type of systems is underspecified for the purpose of the Semantic Web. In particular, the nesting of relationships between different types of concept instances is undefined and, hence, more comprehensive graph structures may not be produced. In order to overcome this problem, we introduce a new processing component, viz. a lightweight module for discourse representation. This third process is given in Figure 5 is indicated by the composition of A1, A2 and A3. It bridges from the tagged output of the information extraction system to the target graph structures via an explicit discourse representation. Our discourse representation is based on a very lightweight version of Centering.

6 On Deep Annotation

A large percentage of Web pages are not static documents. Rather the majority of Web pages are dynamic.[5] For dynamic web pages (e.g. ones that are generated from the database that

[5]It is not possible to give a percentage of dynamic to static web pages in general, because a single Web site may use a simple algorithm to produce an infinite number of, probably not very interesting, web pages. Estimations, however, based on web pages actually crawled by existing search engines estimate that dynamic web pages outnumber static ones by 100 to 1.

contains a catalogue of books) it does not seem to be useful to annotate every single page. Rather one wants to "annotate the database" in order to reuse it for one's own Semantic Web purposes.

For this objective, approaches have been conceived that allow for the construction of wrappers by explicit definition of HTML or XML queries [30] or by learning such definitions from examples [24, 4]. Thus, it has been possible to manually create metadata for a set of structurally alike Web pages. The wrapper approaches come with the advantage that they do not require cooperation by the owner of the database. However, their disadvantage is that the correct scraping of metadata is dependent to a large extent by data layout rather than by the structures underlying the data.

While for many web sites, the assumption of non-cooperativity may remain valid, we assume that many web sites will in fact participate in the Semantic Web and will support the sharing of information. Such web sites may present their information as HTML pages for viewing by the user, but they may also be willing to describe the structure of their information on the very same web pages.

Dynamic web sites with an cooperative owner may present their information as HTML pages for viewing by the user, but they may also be willing to describe the structure of their information on the very same web pages. Thus, they give their users the possibility to utilize:

1. information proper,
2. information structures, and
3. information context.

A user may then exploit these three in order to create mappings into his own information structures (e.g., his ontology) — which may be a lot easier than if the information a user gets is restricted to information structures [29] and/or information proper only [8].

We define "deep annotation" as an annotation process that utilizes information proper, information structures and information context in order to derive mappings between information structures. The mappings may then be exploited by the same or another user in order to query the database underlying a web site in order to retrieve semantic data — combining the capabilities of conventional annotation and databases.

6.1 Process

The process of deep annotation consists of the following four steps (depicted in Figure 6):

Input: A Web site[6] driven by an underlying relational database.

Step 1: The database owner produces server-side web page markup according to the information structures of the database.

Result: Web site with server-side markup.

Step 2: The annotator produces client-side annotations conforming to the client ontology and the server-side markup.

[6]Cf. Section 8 on other information sources.

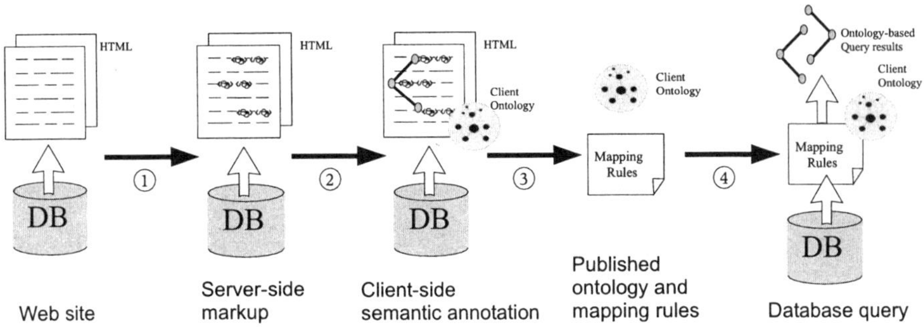

Figure 6: The Process of Deep Annotation

Result: Mapping rules between database and client ontology

Step 3: The annotator publishes the client ontology (if not already done before) and the mapping rules derived from annotations.

Result: The annotator's ontology and mapping rules are available on the Web

Step 4: The querying party loads second party's ontology and mapping rules and uses them to query the database via the web service API.

Result: Results retrieved from database by querying party

Obviously, in this process one single person may be the database owner and/or the annotator and/or the querying party.

For example, the annotator might annotate a organization entry from ontoweb.org according to his own ontology. Then, he may use the ontology and mapping to instantiate his own syndication services by regularly querying for all recent entries the titles of which match to his list of topics.

6.2 Scenario and Roles

Our scenario for deep annotation consists of three major pillars corresponding to the three different roles (database owner, annotator, querying party) as described in the process.
Database and Web Site Provider. At the web site, we assume that there is an underlying database (cf. Figure 7) and a server-side scripting environment, like Zope, JSP or ASP, used to create dynamic Web pages. Furthermore, the web site may also provide a Web service API to third parties who want to query the database directly.
Annotator. The annotator uses an extended version of the OntoMat in order to manually create relational metadata, which correspond to a given client ontology, for some Web pages. The extended OntoMat takes into account problems that may arise from generic annotations required by deep annotation (see Section 6.3). With the help of OntoMat, we create mapping rules from such annotations that are later exploited by an inference engine.
Querying Party. The querying party uses a corresponding tool to visualize the client ontology, to compile a query from the client ontology and to investigate the mapping. In our

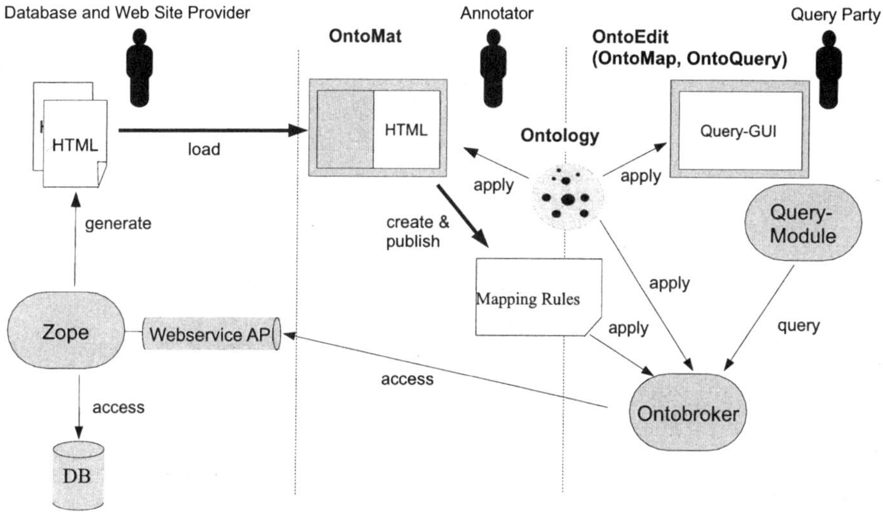

Figure 7: Scenario for Deep Annotation

case, we use OntoEdit [31] for those three purposes. In particular, OntoEdit also allows for the investigation, debugging and change of given mapping rules. For this purpose, OntoEdit integrates and exploits the Ontobroker [12] inference engine (see Figure 7).

6.3 Annotation

To enable deep annotation one must consider an additional kind of annotation, viz. *generic annotation*. In a *generic annotation*, a piece of text that corresponds to a database field and that is annotated is only considered to be a place holder. I.e. a variable must be generated for such an annotation and the variable may have multiple relationships allowing for the description of general mapping rules.

Annotation Process: An annotation process of server-side markup (generic annotation) is supported by the user interface as follows:

1. The user opens in the browser a server-side marked up web page.
2. The server-side markup is handled individually by the browser, e.g. it provides graphical icons on the page wherever a markup is present, so that the user can easily identify values which come from a database.
3. The user can select one of server-side markups to either create a new *generic instance* and map its database field to an generic attribute, or map a database field to an *generic attribute* of an existing *generic instance*.
4. The database information necessary to query the database in a later step is stored along-with the *generic instance*.

The reader may note that *literal annotation* is still performed when the user drags a marked up piece of content, that is not a server-side markup.

Create Generic Instances of Classes: When the user drags a server-side markup onto a particular concept of the ontology, a new generic class instance is generated (cf. arrow #1 in Figure 8). The application displays a dialog for the selection of the instance name and the attributes to map the database value to. Attributes which resemble the column name are preselected (cf. dialog #1a in Figure 8). If the user clicks OK, database concept and instance checks are performed and the new generic instance is created. Generic instances will appear with a database symbol in their icon.

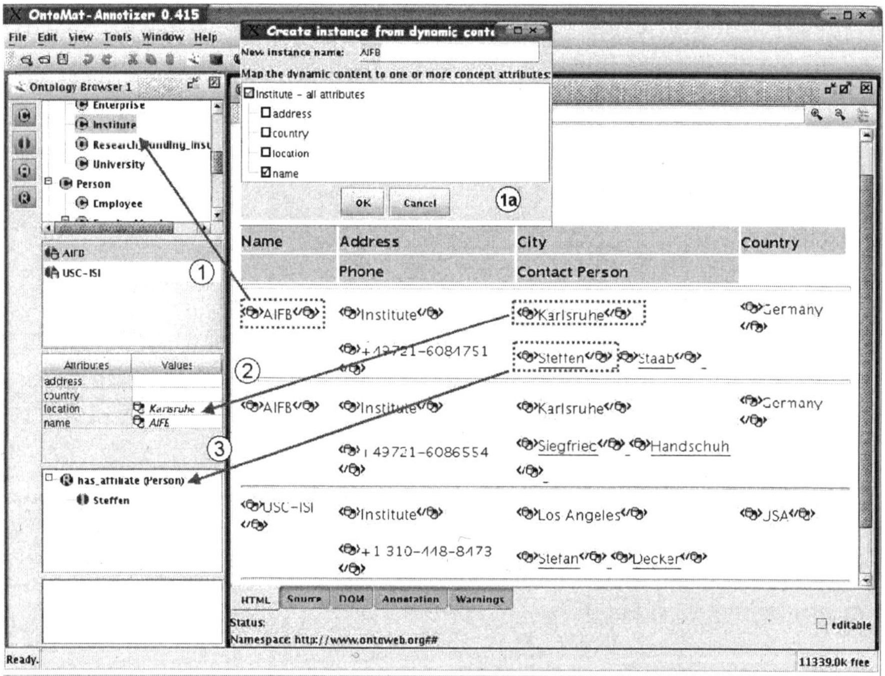

Figure 8: Screenshot of Providing Deep Annotation with OntoMat

Create Generic Attribute Instances: In order to create a generic attribute instance the user simply drops the server-side markup into the corresponding table entry (cf. arrow #2 in Figure 8). Generic attributes which are mapped to database table columns will also show a special icon and their value will appear in italics. Such generic attributes cannot be modified, but their value can be deleted.

When the generic attribute is filled the following steps are performed by the system:

1. Checking database definition integrity.

2. All attributes of the selected generic instance (except the generic attribute to be pasted to) are examined. The following conditions apply to each attribute:
   - The attribute is empty or
   - The attribute does not hold server-side markup or
   - The attribute holds markup, the database name and the query ID of the content on the current selection must be the same. This must be checked to ensure that result fields come from the same database and the same query. If this is not checked, unmatching information (e.g. publication titles and countries) could be queried for.
3. The generic attribute contains the information given by the markup, i.e. which column of the result tuple delivered by a query represents the value.

Create Generic Relationship Instances: To create a generic relationship instance the user simply drops the selected server-side markup onto the relation of a pre-selected instance (cf. arrow #3 in Figure 8). As in Section 6.3 a new generic instance is generated. In addition, the new generic instance is connected with the preselected generic instance.

6.4 Mapping and Querying

The results of the annotation are mapping rules between the database and the client ontology. The annotator publishes[7] the client ontology and the mapping rules derived from annotations. This enables third parties (querying party) to access and query the database on the basis of the semantics that is defined in the ontology. The user of this mapping description might be a software agent or a human user.

Querying the Database: OntoQuery is a Query-by-Example user interface. One creates a query by clicking on a concept and selecting the relevant attributes and relationships. The underlying Ontobroker system transforms the ontological query into a corresponding SQL query. Ontobroker uses the mapping description, which are internal represented as F-Logic Axioms, to transform the query. The SQL query will be send as an RPC call to the web service, where it will be answered in the form of a set of records. These records are transformed back to an ontological representation. This task will be executed automatically, so that no interaction with the user is necessary.

After the creation of all instances we start computing the values of the instance relationships and attributes. The way the values are assigned is determined by the mapping rules. Since the values of an attribute or a relationship have to be computed from both the relational database and the ontology, we generate two queries per attribute/relationship, one SQL query and one Ontobroker query. Each query is invoked with an instance key value (corresponding database key in SQL-queries) as a parameter and returns the value of the attribute/relationship.

Note that the database communication takes place through binding variables. The corresponding SQL query is generated, and if this is the first call, it is cached. A second call would

[7] Here, we used the Ontobroker OXML format to publish the mapping rules.

try to use the same database cursor if still available, without parsing the respective SQL statement. Otherwise, it would find an unused cursor and retrieve the results. In this way efficient access methods for relations and database rules can be maintained throughout the session.

7 Comparison with Related Work

Creating ontology-based semantic annotation for the shallow and the deep Web as we have presented it here is a cross-sectional undertaking.[8] By this we mean that there are a number of communities that have contributed towards reaching the objective of semantic annotation. So far, we have identified communities for Semantic Web, knowledge acquisition, annotation, information extraction (cf. [5]), information integration, mapping frameworks and wrapper construction (cf. [1]).

In the following we mention only briefly some of the related work, for a more elaborate comparison the interested reader may turn to [16, 19] as well as to the corresponding contributions in this book.

We know of three major systems that use knowledge markup intensively in the Semantic Web, viz. SHOE [20], Ontobroker [6], and WebKB [27]. All three rely on markup in HTML pages. They all started with providing manual markup by editors. However, our experiences (cf.[11]) have shown that text-editing knowledge markup yields extremely poor results, viz. syntactic mistakes and improper references.

The approaches from this line of research that are closest to *CREAM* are the SHOE Knowledge Annotator[9], WebKB, and the MnM annotation tool.

The SHOE Knowledge Annotator is a Java program that allows users to mark-up web pages with the SHOE ontology. The SHOE system [26] defines additional tags that can be embedded in the body of HTML pages. The SHOE Knowledge Annotator is rather a little helper (like our earlier OntoPad [12], [6]) than a full fledged annotation environment.

WebKB [27] uses conceptual graphs for representing the semantic content of Web documents. It embeds conceptual graph statements into HTML pages. Essentially they offer a Web-based template like interface.

A more recent development was the system from The Open University [25] and the corresponding MnM [32] annotation tool. MnM [32] also uses the Amilcare information extraction system. It allows the semi-automatic population of an ontology with metadata. So far, they have not dealt with relational metadata, authoring concerns or deep annotation.

Annotea (Amaya) [23, 21] is a tool that shares the idea of creating a kind of user comment about Web pages. The term "annotation" in these frameworks is understood as a remark to an existing document. But Annotea actually goes one step further. It allows reliance on an RDF schema as a kind of template that is filled in by the annotator. For instance, Annotea users may use a schema for Dublin Core and fill the author-slot of a particular document with a name. The user may also decide to use complex RDF descriptions instead of simple strings for filling in such a template.

The authoring of hypertexts and the authoring with concepts are topics in the COHSE project [2, 14]. They allow for the automatic generation of metadata descriptions by analysing the content of a Web page and comparing the tokens with concept names described in a lexicon.

[8] Just like the Semantic Web overall!

[9] `http://www.cs.umd.edu/projects/plus/SHOE/KnowledgeAnnotator.html`

8 Conclusion

CREAM is a comprehensive framework for creating semantic metadata, relational metadata in particular — the foundation of the future Semantic Web. CREAM supports annotation on the Shallow and the Deep Web. In order to avoid problems with syntax, semantics and pragmatics, CREAM employs a rich set of modules including inference services, crawler, document management system, ontology guidance/fact browser, and document editors/viewers.

Nevertheless, the general problem of metadata creation remains interesting. Questions like "how do you annotate multimedia items?" or "what happens if there are 100,000 people known in your annotation inference server?" affect the scalability to more and larger dimensions, respectively. Some of them are currently approached by other research — as will be seen, e.g., in this book — others such as "what is the appropriate methodology for annotation?" await for further research.

9 Acknowledgements

Research for this paper has been funded by the projects DARPA DAML OntoAgents and EU IST project DOT.KOM (Designing adaptive InfOrmation exTraction from text for KnOwledge Management). We gratefully thank Dirk Wenke (Ontoprise) and Leo Meyer for implementations that contributed toward the prototype described in this paper. Further, the research presented in this paper has profited from discussions with our colleagues at University of Karlsruhe, Stanford University and Ontoprise GmbH. In particular, we want thank Stefan Decker (now: Information Science Institute, USC), Alexander Maedche (now: FZI Research Center for Information Technologies) and Mika Maier-Collin (Ontoprise).

References

[1] R. Baumgartner, S. Eichholz, S. Flesca, G. Gottlob, and M. Herzog. Semantic Markup of News Items with Lixto. In this book, 2003.

[2] S. Bechhofer, C. Goble, L. Carr, W. Hall, S. Kampa, and D. De Roure. COHSE: Conceptual Open Hypermedia Service. In this book, 2003.

[3] R. Benjamins, D. Fensel, and S. Decker. KA2: Building Ontologies for the Internet: A Midterm Report. *International Journal of Human Computer Studies*, 51(3):687–713, 1999.

[4] F. Ciravegna. Adaptive information extraction from text by rule induction and generalisation. In *Proceedings of the 17th International Joint Conference on Artificial Intelligence (IJCAI)e*, Seattle, Usa, August 2001.

[5] F. Ciravegna and Y. Wilks. Designing Adaptive Information Extraction for the Semantic Web in Amilcare. In this book, 2003.

[6] S. Decker, M. Erdmann, D. Fensel, and R. Studer. Ontobroker: Ontology Based Access to Distributed and Semi-Structured Information. In R. Meersman et al., editors, *Database Semantics: Semantic Issues in Multimedia Systems*, pages 351–369. Kluwer Academic Publisher, 1999.

[7] S. DeRose, E. Maler, and R. Daniel. XML Pointer Language (XPointer). Technical report, W3C, 2001. Working Draft 16 August 2002.

[8] A. Doan, J. Madhavan, P. Domingos, and A. Halevy. Learning to map between ontologies on the semantic web. In *Proceedings of the World-Wide Web Conference (WWW-2002)*, pages 662–673. ACM Press, 2002.

[9] Dublin core metadata initiative, April 2001. http://purl.oclc.org/dc/.

[10] Dublin Core Metadata Template, 2001. http://www.ub2.lu.se/metadata/DC_creator.html.

[11] M. Erdmann, A. Maedche, H.-P. Schnurr, and S. Staab. From Manual to Semi-automatic Semantic Annotation: About Ontology-based Text Annotation Tools. In *P. Buitelaar & K. Hasida (eds). Proceedings of the COLING 2000 Workshop on Semantic Annotation and Intelligent Content*, Luxembourg, August 2000.

[12] D. Fensel, J. Angele, S. Decker, M. Erdmann, H.-P. Schnurr, S. Staab, R. Studer, and Andreas Witt. On2broker: Semantic-based access to information sources at the WWW. In *Proceedings of the World Conference on the WWW and Internet (WebNet 99), Honolulu, Hawaii, USA*, pages 366–371, 1999.

[13] Reference description of the DAML+OIL (March 2001) ontology markup language, March 2001. http://www.daml.org/2001/03/reference.html.

[14] C. Goble, S. Bechhofer, L. Carr, D. De Roure, and W. Hall. Conceptual Open Hypermedia = The Semantic Web? In S. Staab, S. Decker, D. Fensel, and A. Sheth, editors, *The Second International Workshop on the Semantic Web*, CEUR Proceedings, Volume 40, http://www.ceur-ws.org, pages 44–50, Hong Kong, May 2001.

[15] T. R. Gruber. A Translation Approach to Portable Ontology Specifications. *Knowledge Acquisition*, 6(2):199–221, 1993.

[16] S. Handschuh and S. Staab. Authoring and annotation of web pages in cream. In *Proceedings of the 11th International World Wide Web Conference, WWW 2002, Honolulu, Hawaii, May 7-11, 2002*, pages 462–473. ACM Press, 2002.

[17] S. Handschuh, S. Staab, and F. Ciravegna. S-CREAM — Semi-automatic CREAtion of Metadata. In *EKAW02, 13th International Conference on Knowledge Engineering and Knowledge Management*, LNCS/LNAI 2473, pages 358–372, Sigüenza, Spain, October 2002. Springer.

[18] S. Handschuh, S. Staab, and A. Maedche. CREAM —Creating relational metadata with a component-based, ontology-driven annotation framework. In *Proceedings of K-Cap 2001*, pages 76–83. ACM Press, 2001.

[19] S. Handschuh, S. Staab, and R. Volz. On deep annotation. In *Proceeding of the WWW2003 - The Twelfth International World Wide Web Conferenceb (to appear)*, Budapest, HUNGARY, May 2003.

[20] J. Heflin and J. Hendler. Searching the Web with SHOE. In *Artificial Intelligence for Web Search. Papers from the AAAI Workshop. WS-00-01*, pages 35–40. AAAI Press, 2000.

[21] J. Kahan, M. Koivunen, E. Prud'Hommeaux, and R. Swick. Annotea: An Open RDF Infrastructure for Shared Web Annotations. In *Proceedings of the Tenth International World Wide Web Conference, WWW 10, Hong Kong, China, May 1-5, 2001*, pages 623–632. ACM Press, 2001.

[22] Klarity – automatic generation of metadata based on concepts within the document, 2001. Klarity white paper. http://www.klarity.com.au.

[23] Marja-Riitta Koivunen and Ralph R. Swick. Collaboration through Annotations in the Semantic Web. In this book, 2003.

[24] N. Kushmerick. Wrapper Induction: Efficiency and Expressiveness. *Artificial Intelligence*, 118(1-2):15–68, 2000.

[25] Y. Lei, E. Motta, and J. Domingue. An Ontology-Driven Approach to Web Site Generation and Maintenance. In *EKAW02, 13th International Conference on Knowledge Engineering and Knowledge Management*, LNCS/LNAI 2473, Sigüenza, Spain, October 2002. Springer.

[26] S. Luke, L. Spector, D. Rager, and J. Hendler. Ontology-based Web Agents. In *Proceedings of the First International Conference on Autonomous Agents, Marina del Rey, CA, USA, February 5-8, 1997*, pages 59–66, 1997.

[27] P. Martin and P. Eklund. Embedding Knowledge in Web Documents. In *Proceedings of the 8th Int. World Wide Web Conf. (WWW'8), Toronto, May 1999*, pages 1403–1419. Elsevier Science B.V., 1999.

[28] *MUC-7 — Proceedings of the 7th Message Understanding Conference*, 1998. http://www.muc.saic.com/.

[29] N. F. Noy and M. A. Musen. PROMPT: Algorithm and Tool for Automated Ontology Merging and Alignment. In *Proc. of AAAI-2000*, pages 450–455, 2000.

[30] A. Sahuguet and F. Azavant. Building intelligent Web applications using lightweight wrappers. *Data and Knowledge Engineering*, 3(36):283–316, 2001.

[31] Y. Sure, J. Angele, and S. Staab. Guiding Ontology Developement by Methodology and Inferencing. In K. Aberer and L. Liu, editors, *ODBASE-2002 — Ontologies, Databases and Applications of SEmantics. Irvine, CA, USA, Oct. 29-31, 2002*, LNCS, pages 1025–1222. Springer, 2002.

[32] M. Vargas-Vera, E. Motta, J. Domingue, M. Lanzoni, A. Stutt, and F. Ciravegna. MnM: Ontology Driven Semi-Automatic and Automatic Support for Semantic Markup. In *EKAW02, 13th International Conference on Knowledge Engineering and Knowledge Management*, LNCS/LNAI 2473, pages 379–391, Sigüenza, Spain, October 2002. Springer.

[33] M. Vargas-Vera, E. Motta, J. Domingue, S. Buckingham Shum, and M. Lanzoni. Knowledge Extraction by using an Ontology-based Annotation Tool. In *Proceedings of the Knowledge Markup and Semantic Annotation Workshop 2001 (at K-CAP 2001)*, pages 5–12, Victoria, BC, Canada, October 2001.

Annotation for the Semantic Web
S. Handschuh and S. Staab (Eds.)
IOS Press, 2003

Collaboration through Annotations in the Semantic Web

Marja-Riitta Koivunen and Ralph R. Swick
{marja,swick}@w3.org
World Wide Web Consortium MIT/LCS,
200 Tech. Square,
Cambridge, MA 02139

Abstract. Shared annotations on the Web offer an important means to support collaboration between co-workers, students, or any other group wanting to write and read each others comments in the context of Web documents. As each group's working habits are different it is useful to be able to tailor the annotations to the needs of the group.

Annotea is a metadata based annotation infrastucture that supports information sharing through annotations attached to any XML-based document, such as XHTML, MathML, and SVG documents, as well as to annotations themselves. No write access is needed to the annotated documents as they are not modified.

Annotea is completely open and is built on top of standard W3C technologies. The annotations are modelled as RDF metadata and XPointer and XPath are used to attach the annotations to documents. Annotations can be shared by storing them into annotation servers and queried by using annotation capable clients, such as the W3C Amaya editor/browser. The HTTP protocol is used for the data exchange between a client and servers.

Because Annotea uses W3C Semantic Web technologies, specifically RDF and RDFS, it can be easily extended to support many kinds of annotations and annotation-like collaborative applications on the schema level. The data that comprises an annotation, by virtue of being RDF/XML, is available to other applications.

In this paper, we describe three user scenarios and discuss how they benefit from our metadata based annotation infrastructure. We explain how a basic annotation schema can be extended and describe other modifications that are useful when implementing these scenarios. Currently the most laborious part in the scenarios is the design and implementation of the user interface to accompany the schema changes. The data store has proven to be very flexible, requiring very few changes as we incorporate new data into our annotations.

1 INTRODUCTION

Shared annotations enhance collaboration within a group of co-workers, between students preparing a report, or any other group wanting to write and read each others comments. However, in today's World Wide Web, the act of commenting on each other's content is usually performed through clumsy conventions on e-mail or discussion lists. Users can seldom write back to the documents they read even when they are members of a closed collaborative group.

Annotea [10] is a metadata based annotation infrastucture that can support very rich communications about the Web documents without requiring write access to the annotated document. A user can attach an annotation to a Web document and a collaborator will see the

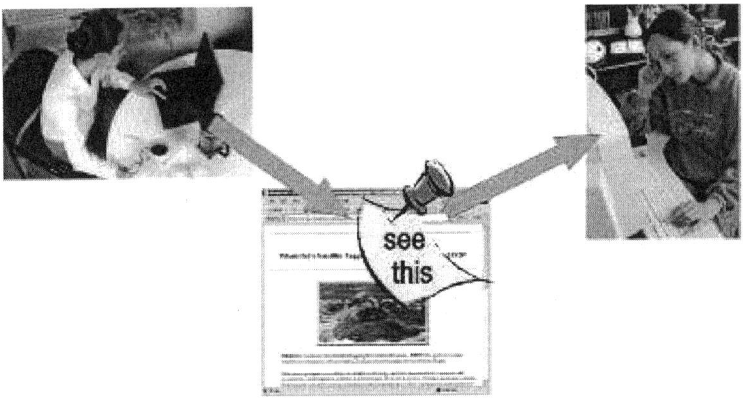

Figure 1: A user shares a comment with another user by annotating a Web document.

annotation when he or she retrieves the same Web document (see Figure 1) as long as they share a common annotation server. Because Annotea uses Semantic Web technologies it can be easily extended to support the evolving annotation needs of a group and to support other collaborative applications similar to annotations that share metadata about Web documents.

Annotea annotations are metadata associated with a Web document or parts of a Web document. This metadata uses vocabularies grounded in semantically rich ontologies that are themselves published in the Web. In addition, the association between the metadata and the Web document is itself described through extensible semantics. By enabling collaborative groups to declare their own specializations of a generic "annotates" relationship, Annotea encourages the recording and sharing of explicit semantics. The Annotea metadata infrastructure opens many possibilities that can be extended beyond the basic annotation capabilities [11].

Section 2 of this paper describes a simple scenario demonstrating how basic annotations support collaboration and then introduces two additional scenarios illustrating extensions. Section 3 explains the basic Annotea metadata infrastructure in more detail and then explains the features that are needed to support the additional scenarios in Section 2. Finally Section 4 explains the current implementation status and possible future work.

2 SCENARIOS

The following subsections describe three annotation scenarios. The first scenario explains the use of annotations for basic collaboration, the second scenario uses annotations as shared bookmarks, and the last scenario examines the use of annotations for communicating evaluation results. Currently, Annotea offers implementations for the annotations and replies discussed in the basic collaboration scenario; the other scenarios describe possible extensions that we are in the process of implementing or with which we have done some preliminary experimenting.

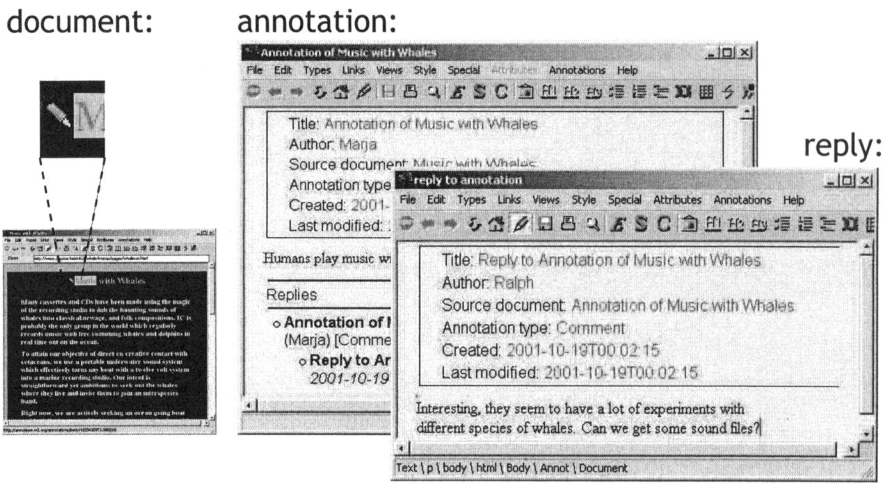

Figure 2: A selected annotation is first opened in an annotation window showing a reply thread view at the bottom. Then a selected reply is opened in a reply window.

2.1 Scenario: Using Annotations for Collaboration

A group of students in a seminar course are writing a report on the communication of whales. They collaborate by using the Web to publish new material they create themselves and to share hypertext links to existing reference material they find on the Web. They also annotate the material they uncover without regard to read-only or read-write access rights as long as they share the same annotation (metadata) server dedicated for the seminar.

Only users subscribing to the seminar annotation servers can see the students' annotations. It is easy for the users to select a particular server when they want to work on the course material. As they visit an annotated document their browsers show annotation icons embedded in the document. They can open these annotations and add replies to them if they wish. Figure 2 presents one of the annotations made by the group using the Amaya client. The annotation is presented to other students with a pencil icon in the context of the original document. Each icon can be opened to an annotation window containing the content of the annotation and any replies it might have. The replies can also be opened from the reply thread view to show their content in a reply window.

As the students read reference documents they find in the Web, they use annotations to mark or question unclear text, reply to these questions, point out interesting perspectives, add keywords or categories, and share other general comments with each other. They use the available Annotea annotation and reply types with some new annotation types they have defined themselves. Replies often start fruitful discussions in the context of the reference documents.

When the students create a summary document they cite interesting reference documents based on the annotations they created and add discussions about interesting problems based on the reply threads. Naturally, this summary document can be annotated as well. When a citation to a reference document is added to the summary document the cited document is

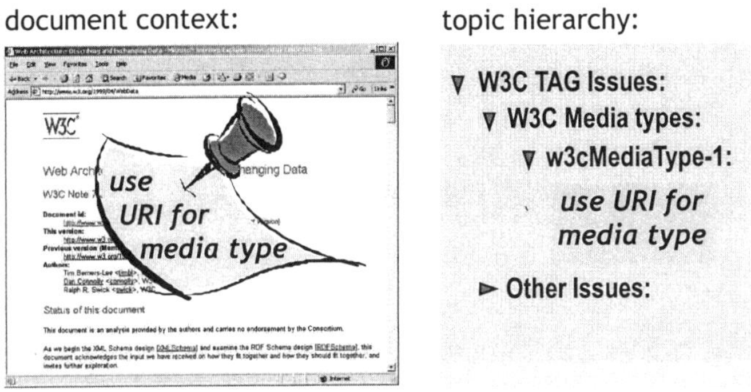

Figure 3: Annotations can be used to attach topics to Web documents and offer a) a document context view or a b) a topic hierarchy view to a list of annotated documents.

annotated by using a special annotation type and an icon defined by the group. The idea is that when a student looks at the reference document later he or she can immediately see from the presence of the annotation that a citation to this document has already been included in the summary.

2.2 *Scenario: Using Annotations for Shared Bookmarks*

A W3C Working Group (AWG [1]) is a geographically distributed group of people collaborating to develop a specification for a new or improved piece of core Web technology. The group develops working drafts of documents, maintains a list of open issues and their explanations, and collects background material and develops discussion material about the issues before they are solved and incorporated into the working drafts. As the discussions about the issues advance some issues may be divided into subissues so that the issues form a hierarchy.

Annotations can support the discussions by letting AWG members easily mark and comment the material related to each issue. When other AWG members visit the documents annotated by their peers they easily see in the document's context what controversial parts exist. In addition, the group can file the annotated documents or the annotations themselves under certain topics related to an issue hierarchy and offer an alternative view of the annotations.

Annotations with topics can be automatically presented in a topic hierarchy based on topic metadata. The users may select a view of the AWG comments that are sorted automatically under the AWG issues as illustrated in Figure 3b or 4. There is no need for an AWG member to sort and edit manually a shared document of links under selected topics or send e-mail to a dedicated editor.

In a sense, the annotations with topics can be thought of as bookmarks as they also mark interesting documents or parts of documents and catalog them. Therefore the view of topic hierarchies can be very similar to the views used for bookmark or "favorites" hierarchies in today's browsers (see Figure 4).

Topic is just one of a variety of such extensions that the group could decide to store with their annotation metadata. The AWG members could also benefit from adding some status

[1] Although AWG might resemble a real W3C group it is used here as an imaginary group.

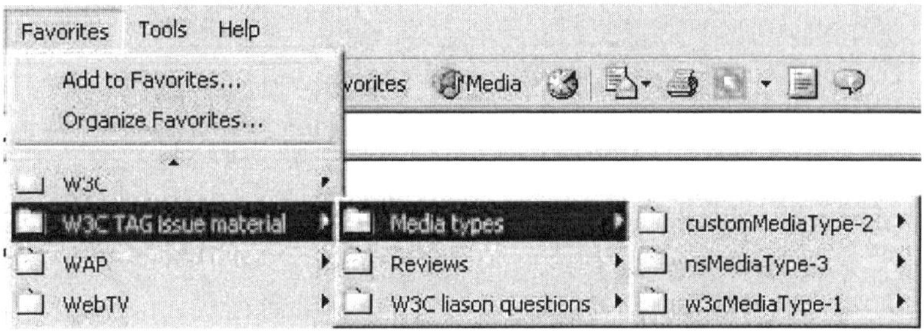

Figure 4: A sample hierarchical presentation of bookmark categories.

Figure 5: Anna marks the accessibility defects in developers' draft document by using annotations.

information about an issue to the comments related to issues. It is also possible to annotate an annotation or a reply comment, for example, with a link to one or more messages in a mail archive containing further discussion of the issue.

2.3 Scenario: Using Annotations to Present Evaluation Results

Annotations can also be used to attach either machine-generated or manually-generated evaluations to a document. Anna, an accessibility specialist in her company, uses annotations to remind the developers that the physical and cognitive abilities of the readers of her company's Web documents may vary and therefore it is important that they are accessible.

Anna assesses the markup used in her company's Web documents by applying the Web Accessibility Initiative [16] guidelines and some automatic accessibility evaluation tools that rely on EARL [13]. EARL is a metadata language that can express accessibility problems in a document, citing by URI the specific guideline that describes the accessibility issue. In Figure 5 Anna has attached an annotation to an image stating that the document does not have alternative text for the image and therefore is not accessible to users who cannot see the

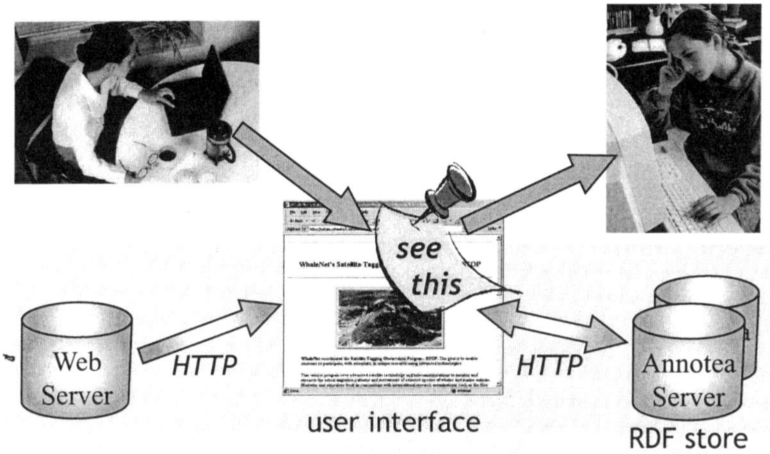

Figure 6: Annotea infrastucture

image.

Anna stores the EARL analysis of each document in her company's annotation server and adds to the server some inferencing rules that represent a transformation from the EARL vocabulary to the annotation vocabulary. As a result of processing the inferencing rules the developers can see the EARL report items as annotations in the document context and can use replies to address the issues and mark them as fixed.

3 ANNOTEA METADATA INFRASTRUCTURE

The basic Annotea infrastructure, as we have implemented it, is presented in Figure 6. When a user attaches an annotation to a Web document the annotation metadata is stored on one or more annotation servers. When the annotated Web document is visited by a user using an Annotea capable client the client queries annotations related to the Web document from the annotation servers to which the user subscribes.

Annotations are written to the server using the HTTP POST and PUT requests and queried using the HTTP GET request for all queries [15]. The simple and most common query is a request for "all" annotations of a document or for a complete reply thread starting from a given annotation. This query is implemented as a simple HTTP GET with a URI parameter giving the name of the Web document or the root annotation. More complex queries are specified through a generic RDF query language named 'Algae'. Algae queries are themselves passed to an Annotea server by URI-encoding them into an HTTP GET.

After the annotations are retrieved from the server they can be presented to the user in several ways. In our Amaya [1] client they appear in the context of the Web document as icons that, when selected by the user, render the annotation content in a separate pop-up window. Another client could query and present the same metadata information in other ways; for example, embedding the annotation content in-line in the document [4].

Annotea uses W3C technologies when possible. Each Annotea server is a generic RDF

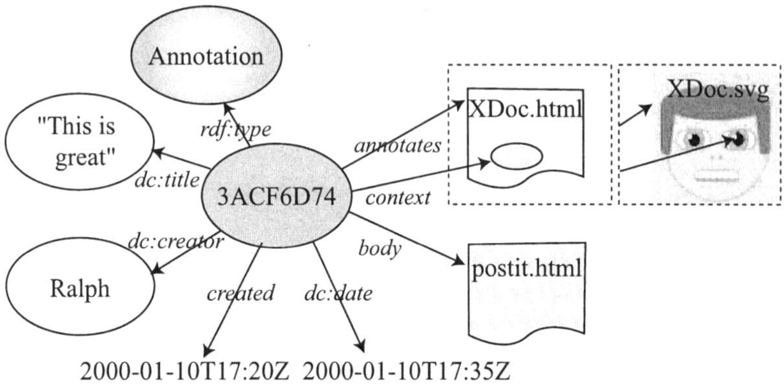

Figure 7: An instance of an annotation using the basic Annotea annotation schema while annotating an XHTML or a SVG document

store. The HTTP protocol is used to store and retrieve the RDF/XML [12] metadata describing annotations from the Annotea servers. The XPointer syntax is used to refer to the part of the document being annotated. Our Amaya client also uses XLink technology to present annotations as linked icons in a Web document.

The metadata infrastructure of the Annotea project makes it easy to support a wide variety of annotation related scenarios. In many scenarios new subclasses are defined or new properties are added to the chunk of metadata needed by an application. RDF and RDF Schema provide the basic mechanism to declare new properties and classes. In addition, the DAML+OIL [8] and OWL [6] ontology construction vocabularies provide a framework for describing new properties with precise semantics and for publishing those semantics in the Web. The basic annotation schema and the extensions needed for the annotation scenarios presented above are discussed in the following sections in more detail.

3.1 Basic Annotea Annotations

In the first scenario, the students annotate Web documents and use reply threads as supported by the Annotea infrastructure. The annotations and the replies in these scenarios are metadata described with RDF. From the Annotea application point of view the annotation metadata as well as the reply metadata forms a natural basic chunk of information that is needed for creating an annotation and presenting a sensible view of it to the user.

Figure 7 presents an instance of an annotation using a basic annotation schema. It includes properties from multiple RDF schemas [5] e.g. Dublin Core (***dc:)*** [7]. Annotations can apply to a whole document or just to a part of it and the document being annotated can be any XML document e.g. an XHTML document (illustrated by the first dotted-outline region in Figure 7) or an SVG image (as illustrated by the second dotted-outline region). The ***annotates*** property relates an instance of an annotation to the annotated document and the ***context*** property refers to the actual location of the annotation within the annotated document. The prose forming the annotation content written by the user is stored in the ***body*** property and a descriptive annotation title is stored in the ***dc:title*** property. The other properties further describe the annotation.

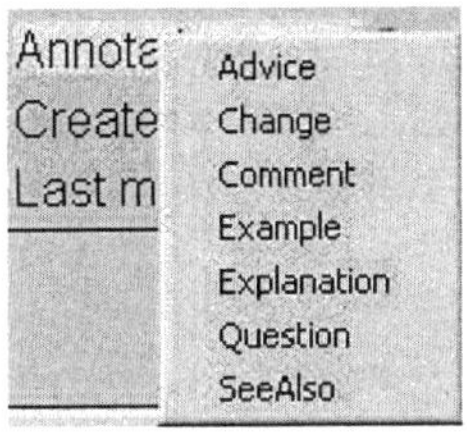

Figure 8: Predefined ***Annotation*** subtypes in a menu

3.2 Adding annotation types

From the document annotator's point of view it is often meaningful to separate annotations that are meant to initiate different actions by the viewer of the annotation. This is done by defining distinct annotation classes and associating one or more of these classes with annotation instances by means of the **rdf:type** property. The root annotation class is ***Annotation*** and the user may choose a special annotation type from a schema defining seven annotation subclasses: ***Advice***, ***Change***, ***Comment***, ***Example***, ***Explanation***, ***Question***, and ***SeeAlso***. By default our Amaya client creates annotations of type ***Comment***.

The annotation types used in Annotea are not fixed to these predefined types. A collaborating group can easily extend Annotea and define their own **Annotation** subtypes by writing a new RDF schema. To inform the client of the new annotation types the schema is added to the client's list of preloaded annotation schemas. The client reads the schema definitions and presents all annotation types in a menu in the user interface (see Figure 8). These annotation types are used in addition to the predefined types. If the predefined annotations are not needed the schema defining them can be commented out on the preload list.

In the future, we would like to let users easily use and manipulate new properties associated with the annotation types. We would like users to be able to create user interface profiles that an application can use to learn what properties form a meaningful chunk together and how new properties should be presented without requiring any programming of the application.

3.3 Adding an icon for an annotation type

When annotations are presented as icons added to a document it makes sense to be able to indicate different annotation types visually by using different icons. In Annotea it is possible to extend the annotation definitions by adding a different icon for each annotation type. For instance, Figure 9 presents an instance of an annotation type ***Question*** with an added icon definition. When this icon definition is processed by the Amaya client, the user interface changes so that it uses the new icons instead of the generic pencil icon.

The current implementation of Amaya only presents the icons associated with the annotation types but in the future we expect to define RDF rules that evaluate which icon to use in which context. For example, the user may want to use a different icon for all annotations

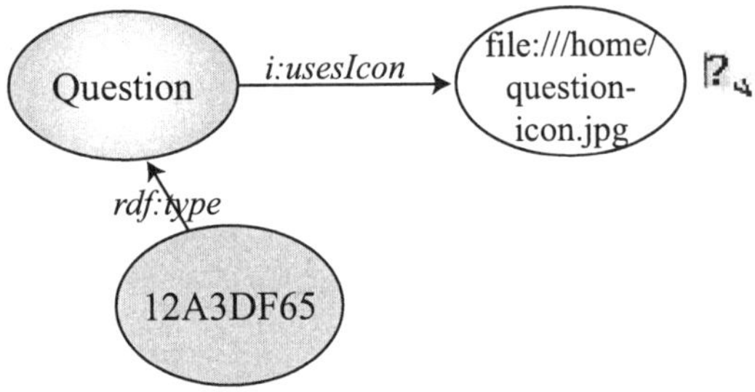

Figure 9: Adding an icon for all annotations of type ***Question***.

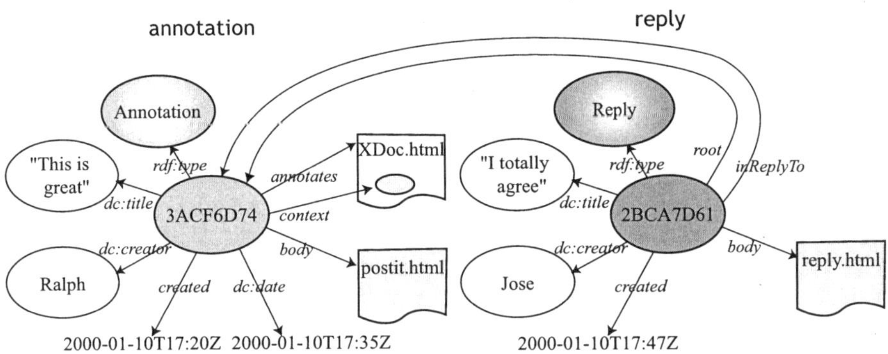

Figure 10: An instance of a reply using the Annotea reply schema attached to an annotation

from a specific server or a special icon for a selected user and otherwise use the generic icons for annotation types.

3.4 Extending the Annotation Schema for Reply Threads

Many users want to be able to add replies to annotations and see the replies presented as a discussion thread. For that purpose Annotea is extended to include a reply concept that can be attached to an annotation or to another reply. The discussion threads consisting of replies always start from an annotation.

Figure 10 presents (on the right hand side) an instance of a reply using the Annotea reply schema. The figure illustrates two new properties, the ***inReplyTo*** and ***root*** property. The **inReplyTo** property declares the annotation or reply that is the previous one in the thread. The **root** property points to the first annotation in the thread. The **root** property is used for performance optimization; it permits us to find replies related to a particular annotation more easily without having to do more chaining in the query processor.

The reply schema looks very similar to our annotation schema and in a way the ***Reply*** type could be defined as an ***Annotation*** subtype. However, a reply has enough of its own characteristics from the user's point of view that it makes sense to define it as a totally new

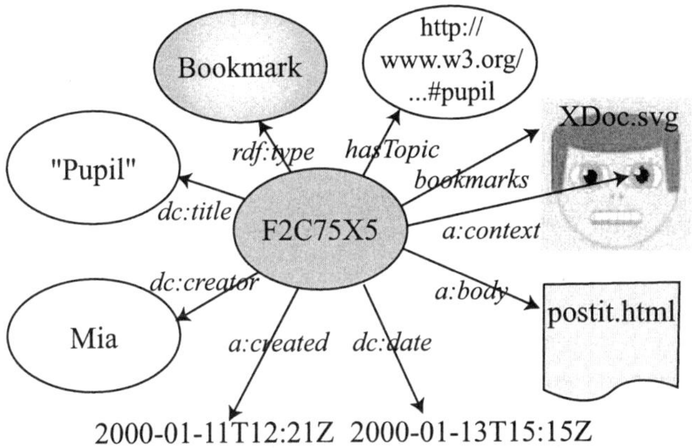

Figure 11: An instance of a bookmark using the bookmark schema attached to an SVG document.

concept with its own subtypes that only reuses the **Annotation** properties. For instance, we don't want to list the subtypes of reply in the same menu as the annotation subtypes. If further deployment experience shows that it would be useful to declare ***Reply*** to be a subclass of ***Annotation*** or some other common parent class it will be easy to add the subtype information to the reply schema.

The generic metadata-based design of our annotation server and the query language has made it easy to incorporate the additional reply properties; the bulk of the work is in extending the user interface capabilities so that our Amaya client will know how to present the reply thread in the end of the annotation window and how to present the reply in a reply window. In the future, we could have a method in a library that knows how to present thread-like objects with a parent and a root property and just map our reply schema to that presentation in a similar way that presentation of collections is done in Haystack [9].

3.5 Using Annotea for Shared Bookmark Annotations

When a user wishes to categorize documents by topic, it is quite straightforward to do this by extending our annotation framework. We can add a new property, ***hasTopic,*** for assigning a topic within our annotation model. The generic metadata approach naturally supports such additions and our existing Annotea server will store and retrieve this new property with no problems when the property is included as part of the annotation metadata. The client shows these annotations as any other annotations in the document view and more advanced clients may even know how to present this additional property within the annotation view and let the user modify its value.

However, our current expectation is that from the user point of view the concept of adding topics is not quite the same as adding annotations. It does have many of the same aspects but it is closer to the metaphor of bookmark implementations in many of the browsers. In our case the bookmarks can be shared on the Web. The user interface for presenting shared bookmarks can be very flexible; the data can be viewed as similar to annotations in the context of a bookmarked document or as a hierarchical view arranged by topic with bookmark-style

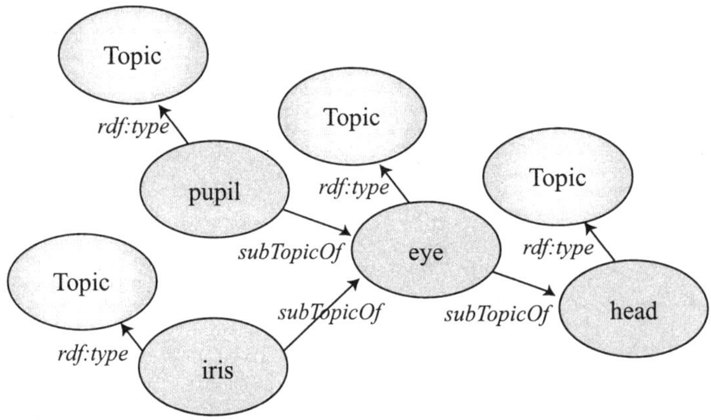

Figure 12: An instance of a sample topic hierarchy describing animal heads.

links to the bookmarked documents.

While we see annotations and bookmarks as separate concepts they still have nearly identical implementations within the data store. This separation of concepts primarily helps to simplify the user interface. Figure 11 illustrates an instance of a bookmark, citing a document (a diagram in this case) via the **bookmarks** property instead of the **annotates** property and using the **hasTopic** property to categorize the bookmark (and, by inference, the document). Other metadata about the bookmark is described using the same properties that are used for annotations. Figure 12 illustrates a topic hierarchy in which the specific topic of Figure 11 might reside. A traditional topic view would reproduce the graph of Figure 12 in a hierarchical presentation.

We separate our ***Bookmark*** class from our ***Annotation*** class for the same reasons that we separated our ***Reply*** class. While bookmarks share many metadata properties with annotations (and replies), we propose that one is not a superset of the other. This can be changed in the future when we learn more about the clients' needs for the user interface and learn to dynamically adjust the user interface when new metadata is added.

3.6 Adding Topic Hierarchy Rules to Server

To be able to present resources, such as bookmarks, under the topic hierarchies we need to be able to define topic hierarchies. Users need to be able to query all the resources under a certain topic, whether the document is annotated explicitly as having that topic or is annotated as having a subtopic one or more levels below the requested topic. For instance, when an AWG participant (from scenario 2.2) is looking for background material related to a certain issue he might want to also get the material related to the subissues of that issue.

As topic hierarchies can be modified dynamically by the user, we chose to optimize the query operation by adding a simple forward-chaining inferencing mechanism to our annotation server. The following inference rule is evaluated to determine during query execution whether or not a document is associated with a general-topic:

1. IF a bookmark has the ***hasTopic*** relation to a specific-topic

AND

2. the specific-topic is a ***subTopicOf*** of a general-topic
THEN

3. the bookmark also has the ***hasTopic*** relation to the general-topic

We can also add a more general inference rule that states that a topic is associated also with its subtopics at any level:

1. IF specific-topic-1 is a **subTopicOf** specific-topic-2
AND

2. specific-topic-2 is a **subTopicOf** general-topic
THEN

3. specific-topic-1 is a **subTopicOf** general-topic

After these rules it is possible to query, for instance, all ***head*** related bookmarks associated with the topic ***eye*** and get also the bookmarks under the topics ***pupil*** or ***iris*** (see the topic hierarchy in Figure 12). Our Algae language implementation permits rules like these to be stored as RDF data in the database or used one-time for a single query and then discarded. When the rules are stored in the database they become part of the knowledge used in all subsequent queries. We have not yet implemented a mechanism for identifying the source of a fact in the database when it came from such an inference rule. This mechanism would be part of a general mechanism to exchange provenance metadata and would be the method by which a query could 'turn off' or disable certain inferences.

3.7 Accessibility Evaluation Report Items as Annotea Annotations

Annotations can be used to present automatically generated report items, such as accessibility evaluation items or markup validation items. If the report items are described in the RDF metadata format it is straight-forward to map them to an annotation schema. The annotation clients used for these purposes need to be able to present the additional properties in these evaluation or validation items or present them in the body of the annotation. For instance, an EARL report item reporting an accessibility problem has semantics that map easily into an annotation of a part or the whole of the evaluated Web document. This mapping can be expressed as a collection of inference rules over the properties produced by the EARL tools.

The generic metadata framework provides the necessary flexibility to decide on a case by case basis whether to archive, delete, or revise annotations when a document is reprocessed through the evaluation tool. A specialized evaluation or validation tool can maintain state information for successive runs in the same metadata store.

4 CURRENT IMPLEMENTATION AND FUTURE WORK

Annotea is deployed for world-wide use. The W3C runs both public and closed (work group) Annotea services. The public service is intended for demonstration purposes. Any Web user with an e-mail address can obtain permission to write to this public service. Hundreds of such users have applied for and been granted this access. The Annotea server code is freely available and other sites have installed their own workgroup servers. The basic annotation capabilities and reply threads described in Sections 3.1-3.4 have been implemented in at least one Annotea client. The user interface of this client, the W3C opensource Amaya editor/browser, is presented in Figure 2. The bookmarks and topics described in Sections 3.5-3.6 have also been implemented in the server side, however, the client user interface is still under development. We have also had some preliminary experimentations in presenting EARL-like accessibility evaluations as annotations.

Many aspects of Annotea, especially the data model and the server implementation, are easily extensible and offer interesting opportunities for future development. The extensibility of the user interface implementation lags behind and while experimenting with various user interfaces we would also like to be able to make the user interface definitions more flexible. For instance, we would like to use metadata based user interface profiles so that we can incorporate user-defined RDF schemas in the user interface without requiring changes to the client code.

As of Amaya release 7.1 we still need to code the user interfaces separately for each client. The bookmark user interface is currently high in our priority list, as are enhancements to the user interface that will help the current Annotea users. For instance, it would be nice to be able to use CSS to define some aspects of presentation style. Thanks to volunteers we currently have several Annotea client plug-ins [3],[14],[2] tailored for different browsers. Amaya is our primary development client. To let anybody easily browse the content of the annotations we also would like to have a proxy client that can be used from any Web browser.

Greater flexibility in addressing portions of documents is needed. Our current Amaya implementation relies on XPointer technology. However, XPointer is only specified for XML documents (though our implementation extends this use to HTML documents as well). The definition of the **context** property was intentionally made broad to support other forms of content identification. For instance, it would be nice to be able to use an SVG outline to define a location in an image or use a time code for a location in video or audio.

Annotea supports a subset of first order logic in limited use, such as the topic hierarchy examples given above. In the future, we would like to be able to add more logic definitions e.g. to permit the user to write rules to select the annotation icon based upon properties of the creator of the annotation, properties of the service in which the annotation is stored, or arbitrary properties of the annotation such as its age.

We also would like to offer more tools for users to easily define new annotation types with additional properties. This is in part a user interface issue; for example, the task of marking an annotation containing a 'change proposal' as 'completed' might be implemented as the creation of a ***Reply*** of a certain type. A type-specific rule could use information in the reply to adjust the presentation style of these 'completed' changes.

Finally, Annotation information could be incorporated into the rankings of search results computed by search engines, raising or lowering the ranking according to rules specified by the user or adding icons to highlight some results.

5 CONCLUSIONS

Annotea is a metadata based annotation infrastructure supporting collaborators who want to share annotations about Web documents or parts of the documents. It can support a broad range of annotation or annotation like scenarios either inherently or by using different extension mechanisms. The use of standard W3C technologies makes it possible to annotate any XML-based documents with annotations including XML content. The basic annotation schemas are easy to extend to support the annotation needs presented in the scenarios in this paper.

The generic property mechanism of RDF allows us to construct ontology-neutral data stores. The Annotea server is capable of storing new annotation schemas and responding to many kinds of queries including some limited first-order logic. Applications can use multiple ontologies simultaneously to describe different aspects of their annotations.

Currently, the most tedious work is in customizing the client user interfaces to support the new schemas and understand what properties form meaningful chunks of metadata for different applications. More research is needed to ease the presentation of the annotation metadata, especially new properties from ontologies the application (or user) may not have previously seen.

ACKNOWLEDGEMENTS

Annotea is a team effort. This paper is based on and the authors are deeply indebted to the innovative and hard work of Jose Kahan, Eric Prud'hommeaux, and Art Barstow. In addition, Eric Miller, Charles McCathieNevile, Dan Brickley, Martin Duerst and other W3C staff have contributed many ideas to Annotea. Matthew Wilson and Jim Ley have been early adopters and contributed to the work through their own client implementation efforts. Elisa Communications provided funding for a portion of the work.

Partial funding for the development of Annotea was provided by the Defense Advanced Research Projects Agency (DARPA) and Air Force Research Laboratory, Air Force Materiel Command, USAF, under agreement number F30602-00-2-0593.

References

[1] Amaya Browser/Editor home page. `http://www.w3.org/Amaya/`

[2] Annotea bookmarklet home page. (no longer under active development) `http://www.w3.org/2001/Annotea/Bookmarklet/Annotea-JavaScript.html`

[3] Annozilla home page. `http://annozilla.mozdev.org/`

[4] Niels Olof Bouvin, Polle T. Zellweger, Kaj Grønbæk, Jock D. Mackinlay. Fluid Annotations Through Open Hypermedia: Using And Extending Emerging Web Standards, in Proc. of the WWW2002 International Conference, Honolulu, Hawaii, May 2002 `http://www2002.org/CDROM/refereed/656/index.html`

[5] D. Brickley, R.V. Guha (eds.). Resource Description Framework (RDF) Schema Specification 1.0. W3C Candidate Recommendation, 27 March 2000. `http://www.w3.org/TR/2000/CR-rdf-schema-20000327`

[6] Mike Dean, Dan Connolly, Frank van Harmelen, James Hendler, Ian Horrocks, Deborah L. McGuinness, Peter F. Patel-Schneider, and Lynn Andrea Stein (eds.). Web Ontology Language (OWL) Reference Version 1.0. W3C Working Draft, 12 November 2002 `http://www.w3.org/TR/2002/WD-owl-ref-20021112/`

[7] Dublin Core Metadata Initiative, Dublin Core Metadata Element Set, Version 1.1. `http://purl.org/dc/documents/rec-dces-19990702`

[8] Frank van Harmelen, Peter F. Patel-Schneider and Ian Horrocks (eds.). Reference description of the DAML+OIL (March 2001) ontology markup language, Joint United States / European Union ad hoc Agent Markup Language Committee. http://www.daml.org/2001/03/reference.html

[9] David Huynh, Dennis Quan, Vineet Sinha, and David Karger. The Semantic User Interface Paradigm for Presenting Semi-structured Information. Student Oxygen Workshop 2002. http://www.org.lcs.mit.edu/pubs/quan-paradigm.pdf

[10] José Kahan, Marja-Riitta Koivunen, Eric Prud'Hommeaux, Ralph R. Swick. Annotea: An Open RDF Infrastructure for Shared Web Annotations, in Proc. of the WWW10 International Conference, Hong Kong, May 2001. http://www10.org/cdrom/papers/488/index.html

[11] Marja-Riitta Koivunen, and Ralph Swick. Metadata Based Annotation Infrastructure offers Flexibility and Extensibility for Collaborative Applications and Beyond, in Proc. of the KCAP 2001 workshop on knowledge markup & semantic annotation.

[12] Ora Lassila and Ralph R. Swick (eds.). Resource Description Framework (RDF) Model and Syntax Specification, W3C Recommendation, February 1999. http://www.w3.org/TR/1999/REC-rdf-syntax-19990222

[13] Sean Palmer (ed.). EARL 1.0 Specification, WAI ER WG Note 09 December 2001. http://www.w3.org/TR/EARL10/

[14] Snufkin home page. http://www.jibbering.com/snufkin/

[15] Ralph R. Swick, Eric Prud'Hommeaux,Marja-Riitta Koivunen, and José Kahan. Annotea Protocols. December 2002. http://www.w3.org/2002/12/AnnoteaProtocol-20021219

[16] Web Accessibility Initiative home page. http://www.w3.org/WAI/

Wrapping

Annotation for the Semantic Web
S. Handschuh and S. Staab (Eds.)
IOS Press, 2003

Semantic Markup of News Items with Lixto

Robert Baumgartner
DBAI, TU Wien
Favoritenstr. 9
1040 Vienna
Austria
baumgart@dbai.tuwien.ac.at

Sebastian Eichholz
Universität Münster
Leonardo Campus 3
48149 Münster
Germany
eichhos@uni-muenster.de

Sergio Flesca
DEIS, Università della Calabria
Via Pietro Bucci, 41C-42C
87030 Rende (CS)
Italy
flesca@deis.unical.it

Georg Gottlob
DBAI, TU Wien
Favoritenstr. 9
1040 Vienna
Austria
gottlob@dbai.tuwien.ac.at

Marcus Herzog
EC3
Donau-City-Str. 1
1220 Vienna
Austria
marcus.herzog@ec3.at

Abstract. Integrated information access from various Web sources is a difficult problem using the Web infrastructure of today. There is no way to aggregate data and functionalities from different sites. Wrapper technology can help to solve the problem by extracting relevant data from Web sources and prepare it to use for integration and to define an XML information flow framework.

We present techniques for supervised wrapper generation and automated Web information extraction as well as a system called *Lixto Visual Wrapper*[1] implementing these techniques. Our system can generate wrappers which translate relevant pieces of HTML pages into XML.

Lixto Visual Wrapper, of which a working beta release has been implemented, assists a wrapper designer to semi-automatically create wrapper programs by providing a fully visual and interactive user interface. *Lixto Visual Wrapper* can be used to create an "XML-Companion" for an HTML Web page with changing content, containing the continually updated XML translation of the relevant information.

Lixto wrappers can be embedded into an XML information processing framework, the so-called *Lixto Transformation Server* additionally presented in this paper. *Lixto Transformation Server*, of which a working beta release has been implemented, too, enables application designers to format, transform, merge and deliver XML data to various devices and applications. We present one particular application, semantic markup of news items on the Web to illustrate our approach.

[1]All methods and algorithms presented in this paper are covered by a pending patent. Future developments of Lixto are reported at `http://www.lixto.com`.

1 Introduction and Motivation

Nowadays Web content is mainly formatted in HTML. This is not expected to change soon, even though more flexible languages such as XML are attracting a lot of attention. While both HTML and XML are languages for representing semistructured data, the first is mainly presentation-oriented and is not really suited for database applications. XML, on the other hand, separates data structure from layout and provides a much more suitable data representation (cf. e.g. [1, 17]).

A set of XML documents can be regarded as a database and can be directly processed by a database application or queried via query languages for XML, such as XML-GL [6], XML-QL [10] and XQuery [7]. As the following example shows, the lack of accessibility of HTML data for querying has dramatic consequences on the time and cost spent to retrieve relevant information from Web pages.

Imagine you would like to monitor *Yahoo* financial news about the companies BMW and DaimlerChrysler and receive these news in emails. The *Yahoo* site does not offer the possibility to select news items based on the content and to receive them in e-mails. Other news sites do not even give possibilities to show news items covering one specific company. You have to wade through all news manually, because there is no possibility to restrict the set of news items. Another drawback is that you cannot directly collect information from different news sites (e.g. *CNN* and *Yahoo* news) into a single structured file, a difficult task of Web information integration due to the very different presentation on each site.

The solution is to use *wrapper* technology to extract the relevant information from HTML documents and translate it into XML which can be easily queried or further processed. Based on a new method of identifying and extracting relevant parts of HTML documents and translating them to XML format, we designed and implemented the efficient wrapper generation tool *Lixto Visual Wrapper* [3, 5], which is particularly well-suited for building HTML/XML wrappers. It also introduces new ideas and programming language concepts for wrapper generation. Once a wrapper is built, it can be applied automatically to continually extract relevant information from a permanently changing Web page.

In [12], the conceptual model of an application framework that provides services at the core of m-commerce applications was presented. Lixto wrappers can be embedded into this information processing framework, the so-called *Lixto Transformation Server*. *Lixto Transformation Server* enables application designers to format, transform, merge and deliver XML data to various devices. The Transformation Server specifies a set of predefined components that can be used to specify XML data flow applications. Each component features input and output channels which pass XML documents to subsequent components and receive XML documents from preceding components. The *Lixto Transformation Server* provides a mediation service to integrate various legacy applications, Web applications, and native XML data stores. From this integrated data, personalised views can be formatted according to the needs of any delivery channel such as HTML, WML and email.

The *Lixto Suite* comprising both tools (abbreviated as *Lixto*) offers the functionality to unify several Web sources into a single data resource. This helps to overcome one of the major obstacles for Web data processing which is that the Web is designed for human browsing only. It also paves the way to a "Semantic Web" at a time where most of the information is still offered solely in HTML.

The *Lixto* method and system fulfills the requirements specified in a very recent paper on e-commerce tools [22]: "These tools must be targeted at typical, non-technical content managers. In order to be usable, the tools must be graphical and interactive, so that content managers see data as it is being mapped." *Lixto*'s distinctive features are summarised in the following. *Lixto* is easy to learn and use because a fully visual and interactive user interface is provided. Neither manual fine-tuning nor knowledge of the internal language is necessary. *Lixto Visual Wrapper* uses straightforward region marking and selection procedures that allow even those developers not familiar with HTML to work with the wrapper generator.

The *Visual Wrapper* lets a wrapper designer work directly and solely on browser-displayed example pages, unlike other tools (see Section 7), that force the designer to work with other document views such as, e.g., table-views of the document or displayed HTML parse trees, or even HTML sources. After selecting example instances in the browser display, *Lixto* responds with highlighted targets in the same display (see Section 3). With *Lixto Visual Wrapper*, very expressive visual wrapper generation is possible: It allows for extraction of target patterns based on an ample set of conditions: surrounding landmarks, on the contents itself, on HTML attributes, on the order of appearance and on semantic and syntactic concepts. Extraction is not limited to tokens of some document object model, but also possible from flat strings. Multiple and single targets are treated in an uniform way. *Lixto Visual Wrapper* even allows for more advanced features such as disjunctive pattern definitions, crawling to other pages during extraction, and recursive wrapping. Moreover, the extracted data structures do not have to strictly obey the input HTML structure. Applications created with *Lixto* are robust to structural changes. Preliminary results on representative Web pages with using the current *Lixto* beta release show an excellent performance [5]. *Lixto Transformation Server* offers navigation of the "deep Web, a visual interface for manipulation and generation of stylesheets expressing, e.g. joins, and an interactive development environment for data flow based XML applications.

The above mentioned features of *Lixto Visual Wrapper* are internally reflected by a declarative extraction language called *Elog*, which uses a datalog-like logical syntax and semantics [3]. *Elog* is invisible to the user. It is ideally suited for representing and successively incrementing the knowledge about patterns described by users. This knowledge is generated in an interactive process consisting of successive narrowing (logical *and*) and broadening (logical *or*) steps. An *Elog* program is a collection of datalog-like rules containing special extraction conditions in their bodies. *Elog* is flexible, intuitive and easily extensible. Moreover, the language is very expressive: In [11], the expressive power of a kernel fragment of *Elog* has been studied, and it has been shown that it captures monadic second order logic, hence is very expressive while at the same time easy to use due to visual specification.

While *Lixto Visual Wrapper* relies on *Elog*, the components of the *Lixto Transformation Server* internally use XSLT [8] and offer a visual interface for creating a stylesheet. As the components of the *Transformation Server* are modular, new components that rely on different internal mechanisms (such as an XQuery component) can be easily added.

This paper is structured as follows. In the next section the system architecture is described. In Section 3 we give an overview of the the interactive pattern generation with the *Lixto Visual Wrapper*. Section 4 is devoted to the extensive study of one use case. Section 5 introduces the concepts of the *Lixto Transformation Server*. Section 6 presents the generation of a press clipping application by annotation of news items on various Web pages. Finally, Section 7 discusses related approaches and Section 8 highlights current research and implementation directions.

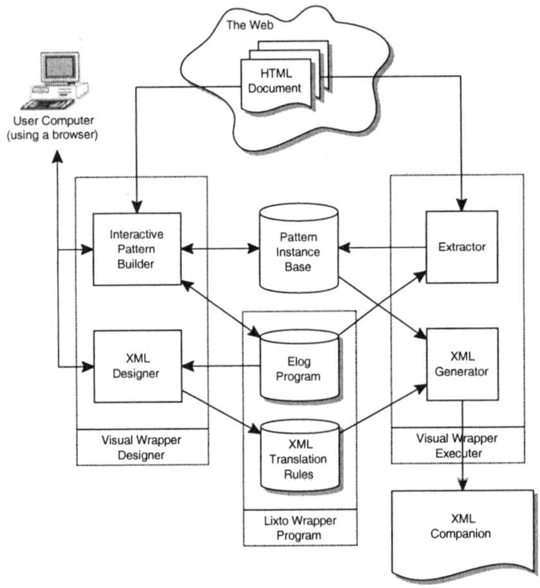

Figure 1: Overview of the implemented *Lixto Visual Wrapper*

2 Lixto Architecture

2.1 Visual Wrapper Architecture

We introduce the *Lixto Visual Wrapper* (Figure 1) by presenting its architecture. The Lixto Visual Wrapper comprises the *Wrapper Designer* and the *Wrapper Executer.*

The *Lixto Visual Wrapper Designer* assists the application designer in generating and maintaining wrapper programs, by means of interactive dialogs. The designer uses example pages to define the interesting content (so-called patterns and their pattern instances). In each step, the designer labels one sample, and after a system generalisation refines the matched instances by imposing some conditions. The *Visual Wrapper Designer* translates this into an *Elog Extraction Program.*

The *Lixto Visual Wrapper Designer* consists of the following two modules:

- The *Interactive Pattern Builder* provides the visual UI that allows a developer to specify the desired extraction patterns and the basic algorithm for creating a corresponding *Elog extraction program* as output.

- The *XML Designer* allows the developer to choose how to encode the extracted information into XML. It produces *XML translation rules* that will be used for producing the final XML output.

Once a *Lixto wrapper program* has been created on a given example page, the *Lixto Wrapper Executer* automatically executes this on desired similarly structured Web pages and

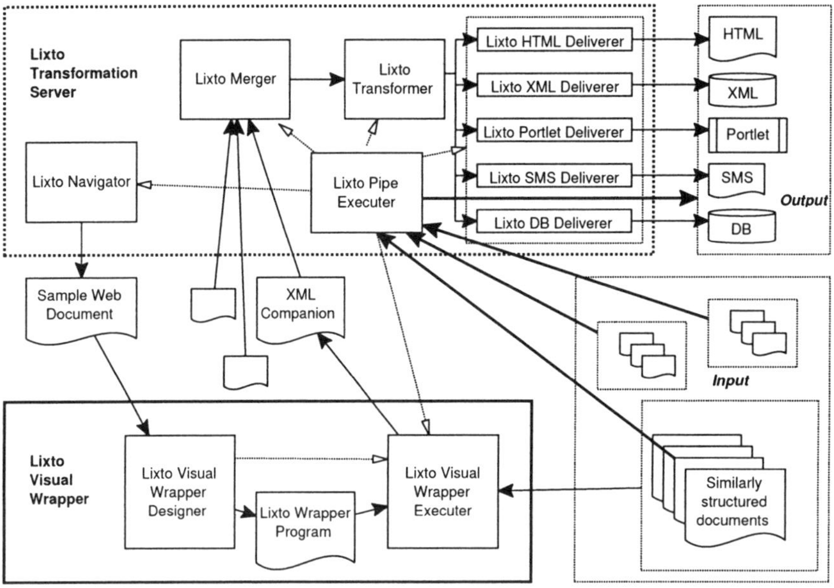

Figure 2: *Lixto* Architecture

translates the extracted data into XML. An XML Companion of the given Web page (and possibly some additionally linked Web pages) is generated. The *Lixto Visual Wrapper Executer* consists of the following two modules:

- The *Extractor* is the *Elog* program interpreter that performs the actual extraction based on a given *Elog* extraction program. The extractor, given an HTML document and a previously constructed program, generates as its output a *pattern instance base*, a data structure encoding the extracted instances as hierarchically ordered trees and strings. One program as input of the extractor can be used for continual extraction on changing pages, or to extract from several HTML pages of similar structure.
- The *XML Generator* module performs the actual translation of the extracted pattern instance base into an XML document, using the previously designed *XML translation rules*.

2.2 Transformation Server Architecture

The *Lixto Transformation Server* is a highly scalable platform to deploy XML-based data flow applications. Applications can be built from components that provide specific functionalities.

The *Lixto Transformation Server* features a Web-centric administration interface that allows application designers to visually define and test applications using the XML processing capabilities of the deployed components. So far, these components are as follows:

- *Lixto Navigator* navigates to the desired Web pages used for wrapping, dealing with get and post sequences, cookies, Java Script etc.;

- *Lixto Merger* aggregates output of various wrapper programs together;
- *Lixto Transformer* transforms, restructures and joins XML documents;
- *Lixto Deliverer* delivers information utilising various client devices.

In fact, the *Visual Wrapper* is a further component in this enumeration, but is due to its comprehensiveness treated independently.

The *Lixto Pipe Executer* can be run independently after application design is finished. It regularly extracts data from Web sites, integrates and transforms data, and syndicates the information to the specified device. The joint architecture layout of *Lixto Visual Wrapper* used in conjunction with *Lixto Transformation Server* is presented in Figure 2.

3 Interactive Wrapper Generation with Visual Wrapper

3.1 Creating Wrappers

A *Lixto* wrapper is created interactively by creating *patterns* in a hierarchical order. A pattern characterises one kind of information, e.g. all instances of prices on a page. For example, one can first define a pattern "newsitem" and then define a subpattern "headline". The subpattern relationship in this case expresses that each extracted instance of "headline" must occur within one instance of "newsitem". Pattern names act as default XML element names. The set of extracted instances of a pattern, which are either HTML elements, list of elements, or strings, depends on the current page. Each pattern is defined by one or more filters*filters*. While the pattern acts as a container for a number of filters, the filters do the extraction work: A filter e.g. allows the system to identify a set of similar nodes of the HTML parse tree, for instance a set of items internally represented as `<td>`. Filters may use various kinds of extraction techniques, e.g. operating on a parse tree representation of the HTML document, or on the HTML document treated as flat string (for details, see [5]).

A filter that exploits the HTML tree structure is created as follows: First, the wrapper designer highlights with the mouse a representative instance of the desired target pattern directly on the example page. Internally, the system associates to this instance a generalised tree path in the HTML parse tree identifying similar instances and incorporates this as main predicate of an *Elog* rule representing the filter. Second, the designer adds restrictive conditions to the filter. These are internally reflected by the system as additional predicates in the rule body describing this filter. The possible conditions include: (a) **contextual conditions** that express that the target pattern instance must (not) appear before or after some specific element. (b) **internal conditions** that express that some specific element must (not) appear inside the target pattern. (c) **range conditions** which, in case of multiple matchings, restrict the set of matched instances to a subinterval. Moreover, *Elog* permits to combine these with **pattern reference conditions**: A designer might e.g. specify that a "headline" pattern instance has to occur immediately before something which is already extracted as instance of "date".

If applied on conditions operating on the parse tree, all above mentioned kinds of conditions offer to specify attribute requirements. For these, a wrapper designer can use regular expressions or predefined concepts (and define new concepts if desired). She could e.g. require that all instances of a pattern "date" contain an english or german word for a month, or that "category" matches one instance of the predefined concept *YahooCategories*.

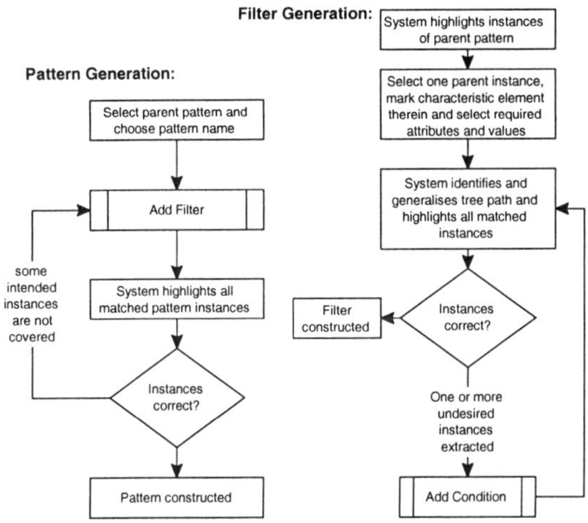

Figure 3: Pattern and Filter Generation

Adding a filter to a pattern extends the set of extracted target instances, whereas imposing a condition to a filter restricts the set of target instances. Alternately imposing conditions and adding new filters can perfectly characterise the desired information. The system creates *Elog* rules based on defined filters. The designer is never concerned with the internal language *Elog*. The interface is extremely simple and the entire wrapper construction process can be learned by an average wrapper designer in a couple of hours. The designer is guided through a supervised pattern generation as described in Section 3.2, and by simply marking relevant information items on-screen and visually setting constraints, filters and patterns are created. In Section 4 and in [4] we describe an example program construction.

3.2 Pattern Creation Algorithm

The generation of a pattern is described in Fig. 3. The designer can hierarchically define and refine patterns. She enters a pattern name, specifies the parent pattern, selects by mouse clicks one example instance of the parent pattern and marks (with the mouse) an element (e.g. one price) inside this instance on the sample page.

At the beginning, i.e. when facing a new HTML document (which is loaded into an internal browser; see screenshots of the next section) and having created a new program, the only pattern is "rootPattern" with an unique instance, the current example document. Pattern construction distinguishes interactive and automatic steps (system response steps). A pattern may consist of multiple filters. Each filter contains a number of conditions. The relationship of patterns, filters and conditions is illustrated in Figure 4: An extracted instance must satisfy all conditions of at least one filter. Two consecutive mouse clicks on different parts of the current parent instance are interpreted in the best possible way to mark an HTML element of the document parse tree or if not possible a list of elements.

In case a designer wants to delve into parts of an HTML element, we offer *string patterns*. They do not use a tree path identifier, but are based on regular expressions and predefined

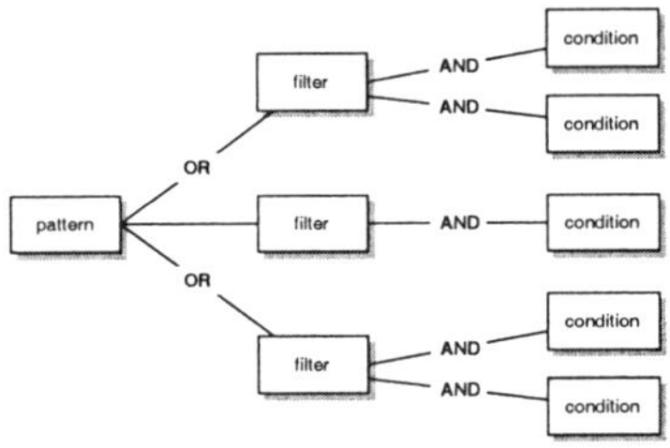

Figure 4: Pattern/Filter Relationship

concepts. For ease of description, in the following description, we assume the designer creates a tree pattern.

In the initial filter generation, the system generates a basic filter without conditions, but the designer can already state some attribute requirements (the system constructs a suitable element path definition, see [5]). Then it highlights all objects on the current example page that match these initial filter criteria (not only in the current pattern instance, but in all pattern instances) – this "visual debugging" gives immediate feedback to the designer. Sometimes a designer wants a single match within one source, sometimes multiple matches – this makes no difference in the algorithm – it just depends on the definition of filters and conditions. E.g., if the designer marks a table row, the system recognises the entity `<tr>` and highlights all table rows occurring at a comparable level in the document. At the same time the system constructs a general *Elog* rule for extracting table rows.

If the designer is satisfied with the elements identified by the system, she can confirm the pattern definition. Satisfaction, in this context, means that only desired target instances are matched. Otherwise, if the concept is too general, then she can add restricting conditions (which are reflected by *Elog* condition predicates). For each such restriction, the system adds the corresponding condition atom to the *Elog* rule defining the filter at hand. Each filter is intended to extract a subset of the desired instance set. If the current pattern is less general than intended by the user, another filter can be added, internally reflected by an additional *Elog* rule for the same pattern (several rules for the same pattern are interpreted disjunctively, as usual in Datalog). Different filters may be created based on labelling in different example parent pattern instances. By iterating restricting and generalising steps, it is usually possible to describe a desired pattern perfectly. Once a pattern has been defined, the user may use this pattern as parent for a new pattern.

In some cases, a wrapper designer does not solely want to extract information from a single Web page, but continue extraction on subsequent linked pages. *Lixto Visual Wrapper* offers to create *document patterns*, which, based on a given URL from a previous extraction step, download the respective page and continue extraction there with subsequent child patterns. Moreover, the powerful concept of *Visual Wrapper* allows for re-using patterns in such recursive steps. Designers may e.g. extract a link to a next page with the same kind of information, and apply the same patterns as used on the page before. This is possible within the framework because filters belonging to the same pattern are not required to refer to the same parent pattern (technically, a pattern graph is created).

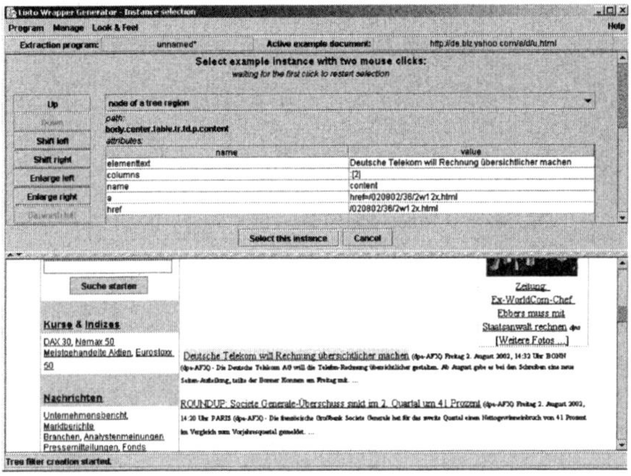

Figure 5: Visual highlighting of selected elements

3.3 Translation into XML

The output of the Extractor is well-suited for translation into XML. The interactive XML generator exploits the hierarchical structure of the pattern instance base and uses pattern names as default XML element names. The designer can interactively choose the HTML attributes that appear in the XML output. Even more important is the possibility to decide which patterns are written to XML, possibly using auxiliary patterns. Refer to Figure 8 for an example screenshot of the XML Designer.

4 Visual Wrapper Press Clipping Example

In this section we show how to create an XML representation of all current financial news from the German Yahoo Web site. The strategy is to start at the Web page with headlines of all the latest news. The *Lixto Visual Wrapper* helps to easily create a wrapper program which detects all headlines on the first page, follows every corresponding hyperlink to the detailed page for every newsitem and extracts all valuable pieces of information such as the date and time and all paragraphs of the news text.

The first step is to inspect the URL of the Web page from which we want to extract some information. In this case the application designer specifies *http://de.biz.yahoo.com/s/d/u.html* in the Document Manager of the *Lixto Visual Wrapper*. The Web page is then loaded and displayed in the bottom part of the Window while the upper part shows the current extraction program as a tree of patterns and filters. Because operation on the HTML parse tree is useful in this case, the new pattern "Link" (as subpattern of the "rootDocument") shall be a tree pattern (default value). After adding a filter to this pattern the program expects the developer to select one example instance of the elements she would like the pattern to extract. The developers selects one of the news headlines with two mouse clicks in the internal Web browser. Figure 5 shows the result of selecting one headline. The upper part of the window shows detailed information about the selected region.

The next step is the path specification. In some cases it can be useful to manually define how the path is composed. In most cases however the system default generalisation of the path of the chosen element is sufficient.

There are various methods of how the wrapper should detect attributes of the desired HTML elements. With the option "none" no attributes will be considered. Using "all exactly" will take every attribute of the selected example in account and therefore the wrapper will only detect elements with exactly the same value for every existing attribute. This is only useful for detecting one single element. In this example, the designer wants to detect all headlines and therefore chooses the method "Custom" to have full control over the attribute selection.

The *Lixto Visual Wrapper* offers a list of all attributes of the selected example headline. Here, the developer can decide which attributes have to be considered and in which way they should be considered (see Figure 6). As every headline contains a hyperlink, the designer selects the attribute "href" on the left and selects "ignore value" in the drop down menu on the right. This selects all elements which contain a hyperlink. With this selection, the wrapper would detect every hyperlink on the whole Web page, including also undesired links used for other navigations inside the Yahoo site. The attribute "columns" is given the value ":[2]", because the desired HTML elements are located in the second coloumn (of the first table). From the appearance of the Web page the designer can assume that all headlines are located in the same coloumn of the same HTML table. The developer hence selects the attribute "column" and specifies "is exactly like" in the drop down menu. The filter created based on this selection works like the following: "Select all hyperlinks with the generalised path created by the system, which are located in the second coloumn of the first table".

To immediately receive feedback for this filter and the pattern it defines the wrapper designer can test a pattern (or an individual filter). The Visual Wrapper responds by highlighting all elements which are detected by this pattern. In this example all news headlines are highlighted, but also a few hyperlinks which are no headlines (at the top and at the bottom of the page, which are also located in the second coloumn). These elements also fulfill the conditions defined with the filter. This is not an "error" of the filter, but the actual idea of this methodological approach to first define a filter which may detect too many elements and afterwards add some restrictive conditions to the filter to exclude the undesired elements.

The designer can next add a contextual condition to the filter expressing that every headline has to occur after a particular element in the Web page. In general, such a referred element shall be a stable element such as a section heading or a navigational link. With contextual conditions the developer can set the relative distance in which the referred element must appear. Adding such conditions, the undesired instances can be excluded from the set of extracted elements.

After the headlines are correctly detected, the designer wants to follow every corresponding hyperlink and extract information from the next Web page (where the details are located for each news entry). To do this, he she adds a document pattern as a child of "Link", calls it "NextPage" and adds a filter (without further specifications) to this document pattern. This filter just converts a URL to the referred document to be used for further extraction. A test of this document pattern will return every linked Web page as an instance of this pattern. Every child defined for this pattern will be executed on these Web pages.

To minimise problems with incorrectly selected HTML elements, the designer now restricts the area from which the date, time, headline and paragraphs are extracted. She defines a tree pattern "NewsItem" which starts with the date above the headline and ends with the last word of the last paragraph. During the attribute specification she only sets the attribute "elementtext" to the value "not empty content". This general pattern matches far too many

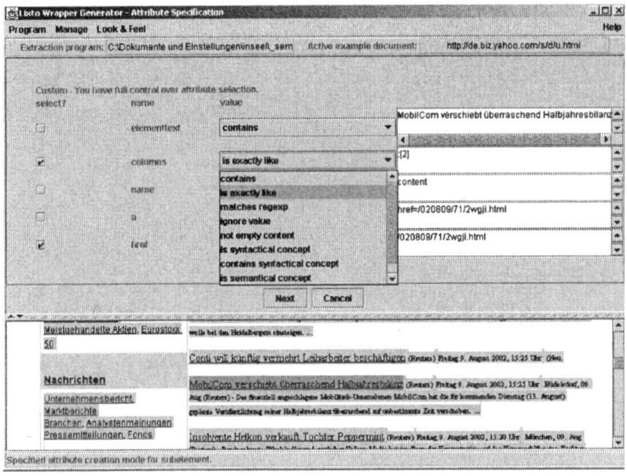

Figure 6: Attribute specification for news headline

instances and therefore she adds an internal condition which expresses that an instance of this pattern must contain an element with the name <h2>. Inside this pattern, the new subpattern "Headline" detects the headline in the same way (it is given as <h2> element). Date and time are given in a common HTML element (not depicted), which should be selected with a pattern called "DateTime" which occurs before an <h2> element. To further split this element, string patterns are required.

A string pattern can be employed on the string representation of any tree or document pattern, but in most cases it is used to further split a leaf element of the HTML parse tree (like in this example). Analysing the instance "Montag 11. April 2002, 21:11 Uhr", the designer would like to extract "11. April 2002" as the date and "21:11" as the time. Here, the wrapper designer can make use of predefined syntactical concepts. A syntactical concept is a collection of previously (user-)defined regular expressions which are alternate descriptions for a syntactically similar string. We use the concepts "date" and "time" to detect the desired parts of the string.

When it comes to defining the filter for a pattern "paragraph", the designer decides to restrict the path in the HTML parse tree. Without doing this, the included advertising information (technically: an integrated HTML table) every Yahoo news item contains would be given as a paragraph as well. She selects an example paragraph and manually defines the path *table.tr.td.p* as seen in Figure 7. To exclude paragraphs that only contain a <br> element, the designer moreover defines a negated internal condition which says that the content of this element must not be a <br> element.

The created wrapper program will extract all relevant pieces of information from the German Yahoo financial news. To define the format of the generated XML document and check the extraction the developer uses the *XML Designer*, which is an integrated part of the *Lixto Visual Wrapper*. If some elements of the XML document shall receive a name which is different from the name of the corresponding pattern, the name can be changed in the *XML Designer*. It is also possible to exclude the instances of a pattern from the XML output. In this case, she would like to exclude the patterns "NextPage" and "DateTime" from the output and give the instances of the pattern "NewsItem" the name "item". Figure 8 shows the *XML Designer* interface and the extracted information of the used sample page.

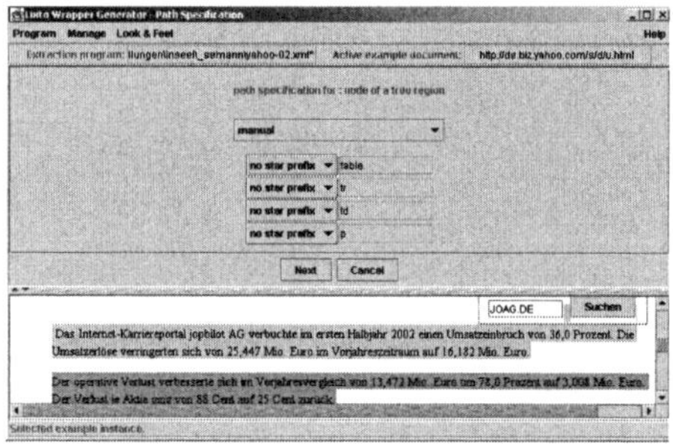

Figure 7: Manual path specification

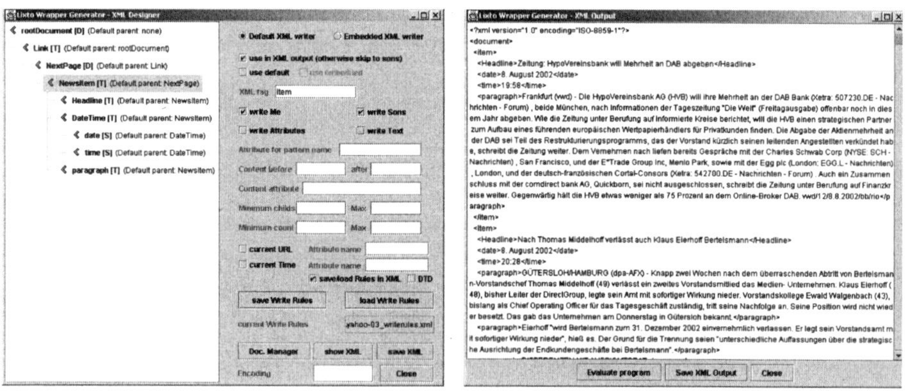

Figure 8: The XML Designer and the generated XML output

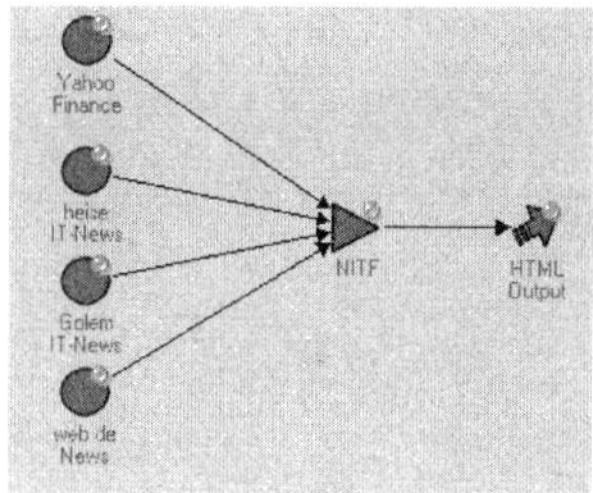

Figure 9: Information flow example

5 Lixto Transformation Server

The *Lixto Transformation Server* builds on standard technologies such as XML, XSLT and J2EE. The data processing model defines the following stages which are supported by built-in software components: Acquiring the required content from source locations using wrappers, integrating and merging the content, transforming the content and delivering the content to various devices and applications.

The *Transformation Server* supports a visual programming approach to support data processing applications utilising the functionality of the predefined processing components. By means of a visual interface complex XML processing applications can be defined and deployed. XML processing is internally based on XSLT.

An example pipe flow is visualised as shown in Figure 9. Observe that the wrapper designed in Section 4 is embedded in the Source component labeled "Yahoo Finance". Figure 9 shows an excerpt of the press clipping application developed in [9]. This example extracts news items from four different Web sites, integrates the extracted pieces of information to one collection of news items and publishes the news in a new HTML document. The full application is explained in the following section.

6 Press Clipping Application

To show the capabilities of the *Lixto Suite* we developed this demo application, which extracts news from various press Web sites, aggregates the extracted information with the latest stock quotes and creates a new Web site in both HTML and WML formats displaying this integrated information.

The Source components (represented by circle symbols) for the news items are visualised on the left-hand side of Figure 10. Notice the step-by-step integration from different Web sites to one big information pool (named "NITF ALL" as an "Integrator" component, visualised as a triangle symbol). The second class of information source represents Web sites containing the latest stock quotes. The Source "DAX Stock Quotes" extracts the latest DAX stock quotes. Furthermore, the application developer can aggregate all news items about an enterprise with corresponding stock quote. In the *Lixto Transformation Server* this can be achieved with a component of the class "Transformer" (indicated by the "join" symbol). Its functionality

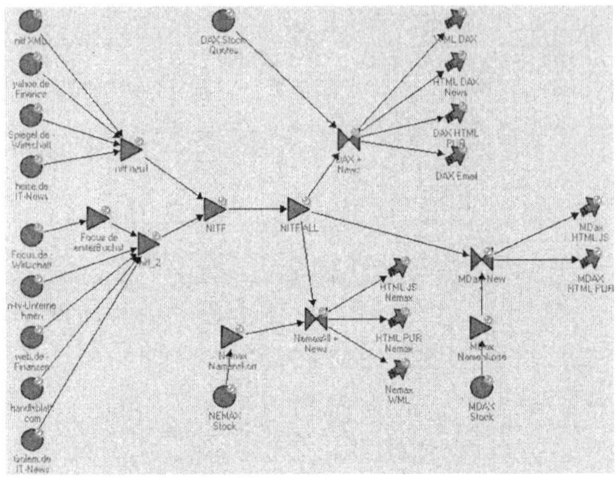

Figure 10: Information flow in the press review application

is comparable to this of inner and outer joins in the context of databases: The designer e.g. selects all data from two sources where the name of the enterprise from one source is included in the text of a news item from another source. The definition of such a transformer is visually supported by the *Transformation Server* and can be realised without detailed knowledge of the underlying transformation language XSLT.

To publish the transformed information, the developer can create items of the type "Deliverer" (visualised by an arrow symbol). This element writes the specified data either to a new HTML Web page, a WML site or even an e-mail. In fact, every XML based output (e.g. SVG, VoiceXML) format is supported.

Once activated, the application extracts the desired information periodically and writes the output data to the defined end device. In this demo scenario, a complete Web portal is created which presents news about all companies from the DAX. In Figure 11, a screenshot of the portal integrating various news sources and stock quotes is given. Notice that the content of generated WML documents is identically to the content of the HTML Web pages.

A specific feature in this scenario is the chosen XML structure of the news items. As the XML structure of every component is completely user-defined, we chose to use the standard format NITF (News Industry Text Format), which is a part of the NewsML (News Markup Language) specification. NITF and NewsML are generally used to save, exchange, and display news information. If somebody (e.g. a content provider) is running a system with NewsML, the integration of the NITF data delivered by the *Lixto Transformation Server* can be realised very easily as additional XML deliverer.

7 Related Work

Related work in the area of wrapper generation can be structured in several subareas: *Standalone wrapper programming languages* (such as Araneus[2], Florid [19], and Jedi [13]) do not provide any visual support and hence are difficult to use for laypersons. *Machine learning approaches* rely on learning from examples and counterexamples of a large number of Web pages (e.g. WIEN [15] and Stalker [20]). In general, drawbacks of machine-learning ap-

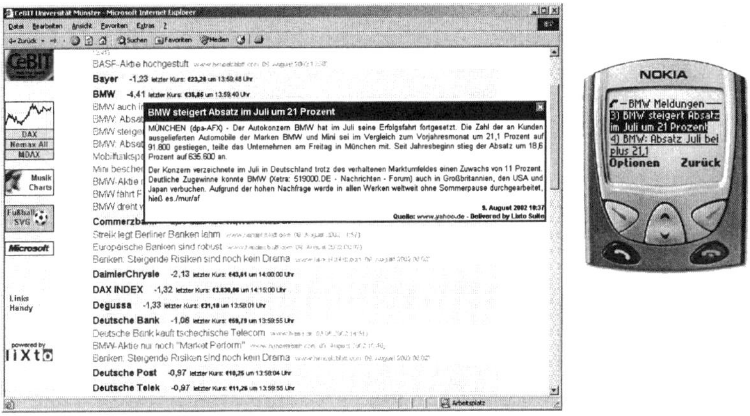

Figure 11: HTML and WML output of the Transformation Server on a Web browser and a WAP device

proaches are limited expressive power, a number of incorrect results, and the large number of required example pages. *Lixto Visual Wrapper* belongs to the category of *supervised wrapper generation tools* such as e.g. *W4F* [21] and *XWrap* [18]. In general, other supervised wrapper generation tools require manual postprocessing and do not offer the browser-displayed document for labelling. Moreover, their extraction language and the visual expressivity is limited in respect to *Elog*. A detailed comparison of academical wrapper generation tools can be found in [16], and a very good survey on commercial and non-commercial wrapper generation tools is given in [14].

Related work in the area of XML information processing and mediation is manifold, especially in the commercial domain, they do however not offer such an integrated solution as the *Lixto* framework.

8 Conclusion and Current Work

Lixto is an easily accessible Web technology based on a solid theoretical framework and a visual approach that allows application designers to extract data from any HTML page on the internet, and map the extracted data in a machine readable format.

Many functions that will be tangible only in the future "Semantic Web" are turning into reality already today with *Lixto*. *Lixto* applications collect data, transform the information into a common structure and syndicate it to applications or devices. Typical scenarios include the presented online press clipping, and other scenarios in the areas of competitive intelligence, mobile applications and portal integration.

Current work includes adding support for various other semistructured document formats, developing a publish-subscribe mechanism for end users, integrating feature- and concept learning techniques, adding predefined templates for typical scenario settings, and interacting with relational databases as well as with native XML data stores.

References

[1] S. Abiteboul, P. Buneman, and D. Suciu. *Data on the Web - From Relations to Semistructured Data and XML.* Morgan Kaufmann, 2000.

[2] P. Atzeni and G. Mecca. Cut and paste. In *Proc. of PODS*, 1997.

[3] R. Baumgartner, S. Flesca, and G. Gottlob. Declarative information extraction, web crawling and recursive wrapping with Lixto. In *Proc. of LPNMR*, 2001.

[4] R. Baumgartner, S. Flesca, and G. Gottlob. Supervised wrapper generation with Lixto. In *Proc. of VLDB (Demonstration Session)*, 2001.

[5] R. Baumgartner, S. Flesca, and G. Gottlob. Visual web information extraction with Lixto. In *Proc. of VLDB*, 2001.

[6] S. Ceri, S. Comai, E. Damiani, P. Fraternali, S. Paraboschi, and L. Tanca. XML-GL: a graphical query language for querying and restructuring XML documents. In *Proc. of WWW Conf.*, 1999.

[7] D. Chamberlin and al. (Eds.). XQuery: A query language for XML. http://www.w3.org, 2001.

[8] James Clark (Ed.). XSL Transformations. http://www.w3.org/TR/xslt.

[9] Sebastian Eichholz. Aspekte der Wrapper-Entwicklung im Umfeld von HTML und XML. Master's thesis, University of Münster, March 2002.

[10] D. Florescu, A. Deutsch, A. Levy, D. Suciu, and M. Fernández. A query language for XML. In *Proc. 8th Intern. WWW Conference*, 1999.

[11] G. Gottlob and C. Koch. Monadic datalog and the expressive power of languages for Web Information Extraction. In *Proc. of PODS*, 2002.

[12] M. Herzog and G. Gottlob. InfoPipes: A flexible framework for M-Commerce applications. In *Proc. of TES workshop at VLDB*, 2001.

[13] G. Huck, P. Fankhauser, K. Aberer, and E.J. Neuhold. JEDI: Extracting and synthesizing information from the web. In *Proc. of COOPIS, IEEE CS Press*, 1998.

[14] Stefan Kuhlins and Ross Tredwell. Toolkits for generating wrappers. In *Net.ObjectDays (to appear)*, 2002.

[15] N. Kushmerick, D. Weld, and R. Doorenbos. Wrapper induction for information extraction. In *Proc. IJCAI*, 1997.

[16] Alberto H.F. Laender, Berthier A. Ribeiro-Neto, Altigran S. da Silva, and Juliana S. Teixeira. A brief survey of web data extraction tools. In *Sigmod Record 31/2*, 2002.

[17] A.Y. Levy and D.S. Weld. Intelligent internet systems. *Artificial Intelligence*, 118(1-2), 2000.

[18] L. Liu, C. Pu, and W. Han. XWrap: An extensible wrapper construction system for internet information. In *Proc. of ICDE*, 2000.

[19] W. May, R. Himmeröder, G. Lausen, and B. Ludäscher. A unified framework for wrapping, mediating and restructuring information from the web. In *WWWCM*. Sprg. LNCS 1727, 1999.

[20] I. Muslea, S. Minton, and C. Knoblock. A hierarchical approach to wrapper induction. In *Proc. of 3rd Intern. Conf. on Autonomous Agents*, 1999.

[21] A. Sahuguet and F. Azavant. Building light-weight wrappers for legacy web data-sources using W4F. In *Proc. of VLDB*, 1999.

[22] M. Stonebraker and J. Hellerstein. Content integration for e-business. In *Proc. of Sigmod*, 2001.

Using RDF Schema to interpret XML documents meaningfully

Michel Klein
Vrije Universiteit Amsterdam
De Boelelaan 1081a
1081 HV Amsterdam, the Netherlands
Michel.Klein@cs.vu.nl

Abstract. Much data on the web is — or can be — represented in XML. However, the XML data model does not specify the meaning of data, something that is required for its use on the "Semantic Web". This chapter presents a procedure that can be used to turn existing XML documents into knowledge structures, by interpreting them as RDF data via an RDF Schema specification. This allows semantic annotation of XML documents via external RDF Schema specifications. The procedure could potentially multiply the availability of semantically annotated data.

1 The Semantic Web requires structure and meaning

In the vision of the "Semantic Web", computers will be able to use the data on the web not just for display purposes, but for automation, integration and reuse of data across various applications[1]. This will enable several new types of applications, ranging from advanced information retrieval systems, to e-business integration, to automatically configured web services. In general, this requires two things. First, the data should somehow be *structured*, in order to allow machines to distinguish and identify pieces of data. Second, it is necessary that these pieces of data are described in such a way that the *meaning* of it can be exploited by machines. This meaning is often described by relating data to general concepts, which are, in their turn, characterized by their properties and relations to other concepts. These specifications of relevant concepts and their relations are often called "ontologies".[2]

When we look at the current status of the Web, we can make several observations. With respect to the structure, we find a lot of data that is only slightly structured. For example, one could think of the large number of HTML pages that contain information which is only structured for rendering purposes. In such pages, pieces of text are structured by labelling them with their role in the document, for example *title*, *paragraph* or *list item*. This often implies that the structure has a very coarse granularity. In many cases, wrapping techniques are used to translate these poorly structured data sources into a more structured format that can be used by machines. The previous chapter described a number of techniques for generating such wrappers.

[1]As explained at http://www.w3.org/2001/sw/

[2]Note that we use the word "meaning" here in an informal way: we refer to the interpretation of data, not to the formal semantics of the ontology.

Many wrappers transform unstructured data into XML. XML is a general mechanism for adding user-defined tags to textual data. These tags allow to structure and label data with a very fine granularity. XML is becoming very popular, and not only as output of wrapper techniques. There are already a few web-sites represented in XML and formatted via an XSL stylesheet[3]. Also, what is more significant, XML is being used by industry. Many companies publish product information in XML or use XML for the communication in their business processes. All together, this gives us a vast amount of well structured data.

We can also make a few observations about the current status of meaning descriptions. We see that — as a result of the enthusiasm about the idea of a Semantic Web — the interest in the use and development of ontologies is increasing. The concept of ontology is becoming clear to more and more people and tool support is growing, too. Ontology development is slowly evolving from an expert-task to a task that can be performed by arbitrary web publishers.

However, although there are already a number of ontologies available, there is not yet much data on the web that is related to it. RDF Schema [3] and DAML+OIL [4] — examples of languages to specify ontologies on the internet — rely on the data model of the Resource Description Framework (RDF) for the representation of instance data. RDF data is not yet abundantly available, and if available, it is often very coarse-grained, for example, describing complete web pages instead of specific pieces of data on it.

Based on these observations, we can conclude that there is an important link missing: the connection between the existing (structured) data on the web and the domain knowledge as represented in ontologies. In this chapter, we will present a procedure to interpret general XML documents as RDF data via an RDF Schema, i.e. an ontology. This allows people to describe the content of structured documents via an ontology. Machines can than interpret the XML document unambiguously as a set of statements in the RDF data model.

The rest of this chapter is organized as follows. In the next section, we will explain necessity and the goal of our procedure. We also introduce the RDF framework and the RDF Schema ontology language. Section 3 explains the procedure itself and illustrates it with an example. Section 4 discusses some open issues and compares our approach to other approaches that relate XML with RDF. Finally, section 5 concludes the chapter.

2 Using an ontology to interpret XML

The main purpose of XML is to provide a mechanism that can be used to mark-up and structure documents. This allows machines to identify pieces of data in a document by their label. For example, an XML document might contain the markup `<price currency="EUR">45,38</price>`. This string assigns a label "price" with the text "45,38" and a label "currency" with the text "EUR". However, these labels themselves don't bear any formal meaning, there is only the associations that humans have with them.

On the other hand, the labelling and structuring in XML documents is often based on some interpretation of the meaning behind it. It is thus important to make this implicit meaning explicit when the data is used on the "Semantic Web". This is exactly the goal of the procedure that we present in this chapter: the "meaningless" mark-up labels in XML are connected with meaning by humans that specify their implicit interpretation via an RDF Schema ontology. This can not be done automatically, but it is a creative process where humans interpret and specify the implicit assumptions that underlay an XML document.

[3]See `http://www.w3.org/Style/XSL/`.

It is a common misconception that XML-Schema [7] documents can be used to add meaning to XML documents. As XML is mainly a structuring mechanism, the goal of XML Schema is to provide structure prescriptions for XML documents. That is, XML Schema can be used to specify restrictions of what can be in between the labels in XML documents, e.g. they can specify that the content of a "price" label should be a rational number. It cannot be used to specify the meaning of tags, despite the feature to build hierarchies of *element types*. This hierarchy doesn't contain conceptual knowledge, but only functions as a syntactic shortcut to allow reuse of complex definitions. A more elaborate comparison of XML Schema with conceptual hierarchies can be found in [8].

2.1 Different interpretations of XML data

To actually associate meaning with XML documents, it is necessary to relate the tags in the document with something that carries meaning. Concepts and properties in ontologies can be used for that, because ontologies formally specify the understanding of concepts in a particular domain. The naive way of relating ontologies with XML documents is to match the labels in an XML document syntactically with the names of concepts and properties in the ontology that is associated with it. This indeed relates tags to meaningful concepts, but it only solves part of the problem. The relation between the tags, the attributes and the data is still unspecified.

For example, consider two pieces of XML, `<price>45,38</price>` and `<miles>62,14</miles>`, which are structurally equivalent. In the first case, "45,38" is the *value* of "price", in the second case the tag specifies the *data type* of "62,14". Similarly, attributes can have different roles, too. In `<price currency="EUR">45,38</price>`, the attribute ("currency") gives some information about the data type of the value. However, in `<address type="billing">...</address>` the attribute ("type") tells something about the kind of address. The interpretation of the meaning of nested labels is even more complicated. For example, consider the following piece of XML:

```
<name>
  <surname>Smith</surname>
  ...
</name>
```

If we ignore our common sense knowledge about "names", we could interpret "surname" as a specific type of a name, or a part of a name (which is the intended meaning in this example), or even a specific instance of a name. In [6, chapter 6], six different examples are shown which illustrate six possible interpretations of a nesting relation, for example, a concept-instance relation, an aggregation, or an object-attribute relation.

2.2 The RDF data model

For reliable use on the Semantic Web, it is necessary that the data can be unambiguously interpreted. The Resource Description Framework (RDF) [9] is a data model that provides such an unambiguous interpretation of data. The data model is quite simple: basically, it consist of statements of the form `subject, predicate, object`, where statements can be linked by using the object of one statement as the subject of another. The things that are being described (as subject of statements) are called *resources*. The object of a statement can either be another resource or a literal string value. In this way, RDF gives some meaning to the terms that are used in statements, i.e. it is clear whether a term functions as the subject of a statement or as a property of something.

The RDF data model makes it thus possible to distinguish between the different interpretations that we showed in the previous paragraph. Below are two sets of statements that specify two different interpretations of the relation between tags and values in `<price>45,38</price>` and `<miles>62,14</miles>`, respectively.

subject	predicate	object
Price	value	"45,38"

subject	predicate	object
something	data-type	Miles
something	value	"62,14"

Our goal is to use a domain ontology to associate meaning with an ambiguous XML document, so that it results in an unambiguous set of RDF triples. To do so, we need an algorithm that determines how the ontology specifies an interpretation of XML labels and their data. Once we have such an algorithm, we can specify the *interpretation* of XML data unambiguously by an ontology. This will allow us to describe the meaning of XML data remotely, resulting in data that is useable on the Semantic Web. This procedure to annotate syntactic data doesn't require any change or addition to XML or RDF itself. Therefore, it can be used immediately.

2.3 RDF Schema ontologies

For the representation of the ontologies that specify the interpretation of XML data, we use RDF Schema. Basically, RDF Schema is a simple type system for RDF. It provides a mechanism to define domain-specific properties and classes of resources to which you can apply those properties.

The basic modelling primitives in RDF Schema are Class definitions and subClassOf statements (which together allow the definition of class hierarchies), Property definitions and subPropertyOf statements (to build property hierarchies), domain and range statements (to restrict the possible combinations of properties and classes), and type statements (to declare a resource as an instance of a specific class). With these primitives you can build a simple ontology for a specific domain. RDF Schema is quite simple compared to full-fledged knowledge representation languages. However, in the remainder of this chapter we will show that a simple language like RDF Schema is already sufficient for our goal.

3 Specification of the procedure

The procedure that we propose uses an ontology that specifies which concepts are relevant, how they are related, and which properties they might have. The baseline of our procedure is that we use the ontology to specify *which* labels in the XML document are interesting, and what role they have, i.e., whether they specify a property or a class. This implies that we do not convert every syntactic structure into an statement in the RDF data model. This is intended: our experiences show that many syntactic structures do not have much meaning from a human point of view.

The nesting relation between two elements in an XML document is not automatically interpreted as a named property between resources. Instead, the ontology decides whether a label is interpreted as the name of a class, or as the name of a property. Based on this, our procedure specifies which RDF statements should be created. Our algorithm has to take care of a few special cases. One of them is the situation when two directly connected labels in XML are both identified as classes. In this case, a new property has*Classname* is defined to connect the two in the RDF data. This means that our default interpretation of nesting relation is the "object-attribute" relation [6]. Another special case is the treatment of XML *attributes*. Our procedure treats them in exactly the same way as sub-elements: this is in agreement with the data model of XML, which is a ordered tree in which attributes and subelements are equivalent (except for the order: this is not important for attributes) [2]. Finally, our procedure ignores comments.

We have introduced one new RDF property in our procedure, which is called rdfx:describes. This property is used to connect the resource of the XML document itself (its URI) to the classes that are used to describe its own properties. This property is not required when the top-level elements are identified as properties instead of classes. For example, if there is an element `<date>01-01-2002</date>` that tells something about the document, we create a statement that connects document and date directly:

subject	**predicate**	**object**
document_URI	date	"01-01-2002"

The benefit of having a specific property in this case is that we can define a fixed meaning for it: the object of a statement with rdfx:describes as a predicate tells something about the subject. Applications can exploit this fixed meaning, e.g. for retrieval. Dynamically generated properties (the has*Classname* properties explained above) do not have a fixed meaning; therefore, they cannot be exploited directly by general applications.

Besides the rdfx:describes property, the procedure also uses the rdf:value property from the RDF specification. This property is necessary when an XML element that is identified as a class has a literal value, e.g. `<price>45,38</price>`, where "price" is a class. In the RDF data model, it is not possible to connect a class directly with a literal string, because only properties can have literal values. To solve this, we connect the the class with a value via the rdf:value property.

3.1 Detailed description

The procedure is described in detail below. To make clear which classes and properties are defined in the ontology that describes the document, we prefix these names with the semi namespace-qualifier "onto:". Further, we prefix the standard properties from the RDF specification with "rdf:" and the property we introduced ourselves with "rdfx:".

1. make the document itself the "active resource", i.e., the URI of the document will be used as subject for the first statement;

2. traverse all elements (including attributes) of the XML document tree in a depth-first order, starting form the root element;

3. for each element, look in the describing ontology for a property or class definition with a syntactically equal name; if it is not found, continue with the next element;

4. when the element is associated with a property Prop

   (a) if there is no "unfinished statement" (a statement of which only two of the three elements are filled in), create the first part of a triple (i.e. an unfinished statement):

subject	predicate	object
"active_resource"	onto:Prop	...

   (b) else, if there is an unfinished statement, finish it with a new anonymous resource and create a new unfinished statement:

subject	predicate	object
...	...	*anon_1*
anon_1	onto:Prop	...

5. if the element is associated with a class Cls

   (a) if there is an unfinished statement, finish it and create the following new triple:

subject	predicate	object
...	...	*anon_1*
anon_1	rdf:type	onto:Cls

   and make *anon_1* the new "active resource".

   (b) else, if the document itself is the active resource, create the following triples:

subject	predicate	object
URI_of_document	rdfx:describes	*anon_1*
anon_1	rdf:type	onto:Cls

   and make *anon_1* the new "active resource".

   (c) else, define a property has*Cls* (based on the name of the class) and create the following triples:

subject	predicate	object
active_resource	onto:hasCls	*anon_1*
anon_1	rdf:type	onto:Cls

   and make *anon_1* the new "active resource".

6. if the element has textual content (called PCDATA or CDATA in XML)

   (a) if there is an unfinished statement, finish it by giving it the content as *literal* value:

subject	predicate	object
...	...	*"textual_content"*

   (b) else, add the following statement:

subject	predicate	object
active_resource	rdf:value	*"textual_content"*

7. continue traversing the XML tree; when backtracking behind an element that has matched a class, make the previous active resource the active resource.

3.2 Example of use

To show how this procedure can be used to transform XML data into RDF statements, we will now give an example. We will describe the data in a piece of XML by an ontology and show how our procedure transforms this in a set of useful RDF statements. We use a part of a cXML purchase order. cXML[4] is an XML langauge for the communication of data related to electronic commerce in B2C situations.

A sample cXML purchase order might look like this:

```
<cXML>
  <IndexItem>
    <ItemDetail>
      <UnitPrice>
        <Money currency="USD">1000</Money>
      </UnitPrice>
      <Description xml:lang="en">Armada M700 PIII 500 12GB</Description>
      <UnitOfMeasure>EA</UnitOfMeasure>
      <Classification domain="SPSC">C43171801</Classification>
      <ManufacturerPartID>140141-002</ManufacturerPartID>
      <ManufacturerName>Florsheim</ManufacturerName>
      <URL>http://www.compaq.com</URL>
    </ItemDetail>
    <IndexItemDetail>
      <LeadTime>10</LeadTime>
      <ExpirationDate>2000-06-01</ExpirationDate>
      <EffectiveDate>2000-01-01</EffectiveDate>
      <SearchGroupData>
        <Name xml:lang="en">Notebook</Name>
        <SearchDataElement name="Processor Speed" value="500MHZ"/>
      </SearchGroupData>
      <TerritoryAvailable>USA</TerritoryAvailable>
    </IndexItemDetail>
  </IndexItem>
</cXML>
```

The ontology in which we described our interpretation of the meaning of this data is given below (for reasons of clarity, we do not use the RDF Schema syntax in the example, but use a trivial textual syntax instead). This ontology describes the most important concepts and properties in an intuitive way, using the tag names that are used in the XML document.

```
Class ItemDetail

Class Money

Class Classification

Property UnitPrice

Property currency
 - rdfs:domain Money

Property description
```

---

[4] http://www.cxml.org/

```
Property domain
 - rdfs:domain Classification
```

When we now use this ontology to apply our procedure to the sample XML document, we will get the set of RDF triples that is shown below. A graph-representation of these triples is shown in Figure 1. In both representations, we assume that the document is identified with the URI "http://mybus.com/order#1223".

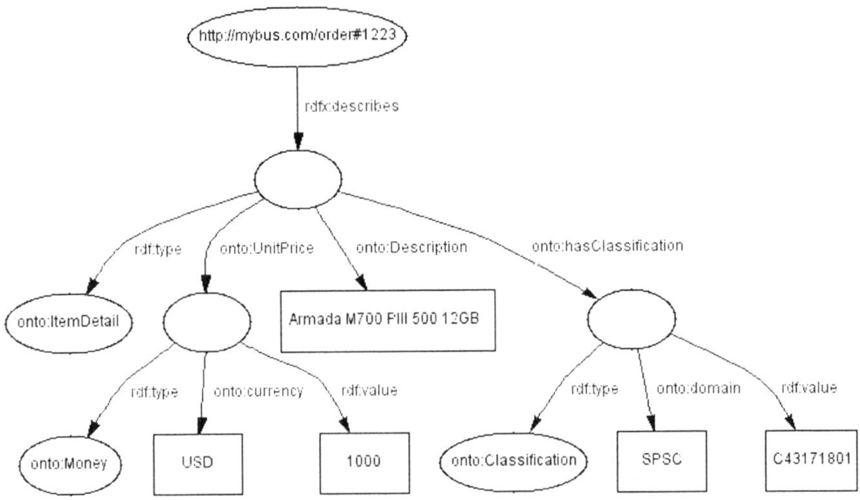

Figure 1: The graph representation of the RDF statements that resulted from the procedure

subject	**predicate**	**object**
http://mybus.com/order#1223	rdfx:describes	*anon_1*
anon_1	rdf:type	onto:ItemDetail
anon_1	onto:UnitPrice	*anon_2*
anon_2	rdf:type	onto:Money
anon_2	onto:currency	"USD"
anon_2	rdf:value	"1000"
anon_1	onto:Description	"M700 PIII 500 12GB"
anon_1	onto:hasClasssification	*anon_3*
anon_3	rdf:type	onto:Classsification
anon_3	onto:domain	"SPSC"
anon_3	rdf:value	"C43171801"

The resulting RDF statements represents meaningful information that can be accessed via the ontology. This accessibility can be further improved by extending the ontology. For example, to make clear that what is called "ItemDetail" in the example should be considered as a "Product", one could state in the ontology that "ItemDetail" is a subclass of "Product".

The procedure can also help to harmonize differently structured information. For example, in xCBL[5], price information is encoded as follows:

[5]XML Common Business Library. Another set of specifications of XML business document and their com-

```
<ProductPrice>
  <Amount>1000</Amount>
  <Currency>
    <CurrencyCoded>USD<CurrencyCoded>
  </Currency>
</ProductPrice>
```

This is structurally different from the cXML encoding, although it represents the same information. If we apply our procedure to this piece of XML with an "ontology" consisting of a class ProductPrice and the two properties amount and currencyCoded, it results in the following triple-set:

subject	predicate	object
anon_1	rdf:type	onto:ProductPrice
anon_1	onto:amount	"1000"
anon_1	onto:currencyCoded	"USD"

This triple-set is completely equivalent with the corresponding triples from the cXML encoding. The only difference is the name of the properties and classes, but this can easily be solved by defining equivalent properties and classes.[6] Thus, when the meaning of different XML representations is specified via associated ontologies, information can be integrated via mapping ontologies. The normalization is already done by the procedure that interprets the documents via the ontology. Of course, the creation and specification of mapping ontologies far from trivial. However, a discussion if this is beyond the scope of this chapter.

4 Discussion

In this section, we will discuss some of the choices we made in the procedure, and compare our approach with other approaches that relate ontologies and XML, or XML and RDF.

First, in our procedure, we deliberately chose to transform only those elements into RDF statements that match with a construct (class or property) in the ontology. This results in a smaller set of triples than when all structural constructs are transformed into statements. We made this choice because we think that it depends on the *use* whether structural constructs are meaningful enough to be retained. Moreover, this also allows us to steer the transformation of the data. An example is the transformation of "ProductPrice" in the previous paragraph. The triples would not have been similar to the cXML result if we were not able to ignore the `<Currency>` tag.

Second, there is still an important problem left: how to transform knowledge that is entirely encoded in the *content* of elements or attributes. An example of this type of knowledge is shown in the depicted cXML purchase order:

```
<SearchDataElement name="Processor Speed" value="500MHZ"/>
```

This element has two attributes of which the *values* represent the name and value of the property. Ideally, this would be transformed in a statement with a predicate Processor_Speed and object "500MHZ". To specify this, we could use "PropertyIdentifier" and "ValueIdentifier" pairs in our ontology. These pairs then specify which textual content should be interpreted as name of a property, and which content as the value of that property. However, this would

ponents, but is targeted at B2B e-commerce. See `http://www.xcbl.org/`.

[6]In RDFS, however, equivalent statements are not supported. RDFS extensions like DAML+OIL have this possibility.

break the feature that we use a pure domain ontology for the interpretation of data. Things like "PropertyIdentifier" and "ValueIdentifier" specify information about the *representation*, not about the domain.

A third point to discuss is the choice for RDF Schema, Of course, other ontology languages than RDF Schema could be used to describe the meaning of the data, too. However, we took RDF Schema as an example because it is currently the most prominent ontology language on the web. Also, there are already a number of tools available that help users to create RDF Schema ontologies.[7] Even this basic ontology language is already powerful enough to be used for our purpose.

Our approach is notably different from other approaches that relate XML and RDF. Generally speaking, there are two approaches. The first provides a new XML syntax for RDF data, preferable simpler than the current one [8]. This approach uses XML to define a language to represent the triples. An example is the "strawman syntax" of Tim Berners-Lee[9], or Jonathan Borden's syntax[10]. It should be clear by now that our procedure does not provide an XML syntax for triples, but uses an ontology to extract RDF statements from XML documents.

A second approach comes closer to our method. This approach "harvests" RDF triples from general XML documents. For example, Sergey Melnik has described such a procedure [11]. However, these procedures transform every element into RDF statements, and do not exploit ontological information about the domain. This thus results in statements that closely follow the structure and sometimes have only little meaning.

In the C-Web project[12], an approach with goals comparable to ours is developed [1]. They created a mapping language to map XPath location paths to schema paths in the ontology. This approach allows to make more specific mappings, but requires an additional resource, i.e. the specification of rules. Our approach only depends on XML source and the ontology.

Finally, there are also methods to relate ontologies to XML. In [5], for example, a procedure is described to derive DTD's (document structure prescriptions) for XML documents. In [8], a similar procedure is described to derive XML Schema prescription from a ontology. Both procedures start with an ontology and result in an XML structure to represent instance data. The method described in this chapter starts from the XML document and uses the ontology to describe what is represented.

5 Conclusion

In this chapter, we pointed out the problem that much data on the web is, or will be, represented in XML, but that this data cannot directly be used on the Semantic Web. XML provides structure, but leaves the interpretation open. To use the XML data in a Semantic Web, we proposed a procedure that transforms ambiguous XML data into useful RDF statements. This procedure depends on an ontology that describes the meaning of the data.

Our procedure has several advantages. First of all, it can directly be used without any alteration or addition to either XML, RDF, or RDF Schema. Also, all languages are used in

[7]For example, both Protégé (`http://protege.stanford.edu`) and OilEd (`http://oiled.man.ac.uk/`) have built-in support for RDF Schema.

[8]Note that we didn't show the official RDF syntax in this chapter; we only showed tables with statements

[9]`http://www.w3.org/DesignIssues/Syntax`

[10]`http://www.openhealth.org/RDF/RDFSurfaceSyntax.html`

[11]`http://www-db.stanford.edu/~melnik/rdf/fusion.html`

[12]See `http://cweb.inria.fr`

agreement with their original purpose: XML is used to allow syntactic structuring of data, RDF to provide a uniform underlying data model, and RDF Schema to specify conceptual knowledge about data. Moreover, with our procedure, it is possible to describe the data remotely, i.e., no write-access to the XML document is needed. This has the additional advantage that different people can access the data via different viewpoints. The ontology is used to superimpose a specific perspective on the data, which results in a particular set of statements. This also gives the possibility to ignore specific parts of the data.

The specification of the intended interpretation of XML data is a creative process. Therefore, the procedure cannot be automated completely, but it will always require human intervention.

We are currently developing an interpreter that implements the procedure that is described in this chapter. This online tool will be able to transform XML documents into RDF files. This could make a lot of existing syntactic data sources available as meaningful knowledge structures and will give XML documents a role in the Semantic Web.

References

[1] B. Amann, I. Fundulaki, M. Scholl, C. Beeri, and A. M. Vercoustre. Mapping XML fragments to community web ontologies. In *Proceedings Fourth International Workshop on the Web and Databases (WebDB'2001)*, 2000.

[2] Tim Bray, Jean Paoli, and C. M. Sperberg-McQueen. Extensible markup language (XML) 1.0 W3C recommendation. `http://www.w3.org/TR/REC-xml`, 1998.

[3] D. Brickley and R. V. Guha. Resource Description Framework (RDF) Schema Specification 1.0. Candidate recommendation, World Wide Web Consortium, March 2000.

[4] Dan Connolly, Frank van Harmelen, Ian Horrocks, Deborah L. McGuinness, Peter F. Patel-Schneider, and Lynn Andrea Stein. DAML+OIL (March 2001) Reference Description. W3C Note, World Wide Web Consortium, March 2001.

[5] Michael Erdmann and Rudy Studer. How to structure and access XML documents with ontologies. *Data & Knowledge Engineering*, 36(3):317–335, March 2001.

[6] Michael Erdmann. *Ontologien zur konzeptuellen Modellierung der Semantik von XML.* PhD thesis, University of Karlsruhe, Norderstedt, 2001. Book on Demand.

[7] David C. Fallside. XML schema part 0: Primer. `http://www.w3.org/TR/xmlschema-0/`, May 2001. W3C Recommendation.

[8] Michel Klein, Dieter Fensel, Frank van Harmelen, and Ian Horrocks. The Relation between Ontologies and XML Schemas. *Linköping Electronic Articles in Computer and Information Science*, 6(4), 2001.

[9] O. Lassila and R. R. Swick. Resource Description Framework (RDF): Model and Syntax Specification. Recommendation, World Wide Web Consortium, February 1999. See http://www.w3.org/TR/REC-rdf-syntax/.

Information Extraction and Linguistics

Linguistic Annotation for the Semantic Web

Paul Buitelaar and Thierry Declerck
DFKI GmbH, Language Technology Department
Stuhlsatzenhausweg 3, D-66123 Saarbruecken, Germany

Abstract. Establishing the semantic web on a large scale implies the widespread annotation of web documents with ontology-based knowledge markup. For this purpose, tools have been developed that allow for semi-automatic annotation of web documents with ontology-based metadata. However, given that a large number of web documents consist either fully or at least partially of free text, language technology tools will be needed to support this authoring process by providing an automatic analysis of the semantic structure of textual documents. In this way, free text documents will become available as semi-structured documents, from which meaningful units can be extracted automatically (*information extraction*) and organized through clustering or classification (*text mining*). Obviously, this is of importance for both knowledge markup and ontology development, i.e. the dynamic adaptation of ontologies to evolving applications and domains. In this paper we present the following linguistic analysis steps that underlie both of these: *morphological analysis, part-of-speech tagging, chunking, dependency structure analysis, semantic tagging*. Examples for each are given in the context of two projects that use linguistic and semantic annotation for the purpose of cross-lingual information retrieval and content-based multimedia access.

1 Introduction

Establishing the semantic web on a large scale implies the widespread annotation of web documents with ontology-based knowledge markup. For this purpose, tools have been developed that allow for semi-automatic annotation of web documents with ontology-based metadata. However, given that a large number of web documents consist either fully or at least partially of free text, language technology tools will be needed to support this authoring process by providing an automatic analysis of the semantic structure of textual documents. In this way, free text documents will become available as semi-structured documents, from which meaningful units can be extracted automatically (*information extraction*) and organized through clustering or classification (*text mining*). Obviously, this is of importance for both knowledge markup and ontology development, i.e. the dynamic adaptation of ontologies to evolving applications and domains.

Information extraction and text mining are handled in more detail in other chapters of this volume. Here we will focus on the following linguistic analysis steps that underlie both of these: *morphological analysis, part-of-speech tagging, chunking, dependency structure analysis, semantic tagging*. Examples for each are given in the context of two projects that use linguistic and semantic annotation for the purpose of cross-lingual information retrieval and content-based multimedia access.

2 Morphological Analysis

Morphological analysis is concerned with the inflectional, derivational, and compounding processes in word formation in order to determine properties such as stem and inflectional information. Together with part-of-speech (PoS) information this process delivers the morpho-syntactic properties of a word. As a crucial pre-processing step, morphological analysis is used in virtually all fields of natural language processing and in applications such as information retrieval[1]. Some well-known systems are `PC-KIMMO` [1], `GERTWOL` [2], Morphix [3], Mmorph [4], ChaSen [5], the Xerox `MLTT` system [6], and `MULTEXT` [7].

Morphological analysis gives information on the stem of a word, possible parts-of-speech (substantive, adjective, verb, etc.), its inflectional properties (information on *gender: male, female, neuter; number: plural, singular; case: nominative, accusative, dative, etc.*) and possible compound analysis (specifically for languages such as German and Dutch). For example, for the German word Häusern (houses) the following morphological information should be analysed:

```
[PoS=N NUM=PL CASE=DAT GEN=NEUT STEM=HAUS]
```

The stem of the word is Haus, with PoS 'noun' (N). The inflectional properties are `NUM` (number) with value plural, `CASE` with value dativ and `GEN` (gender) with value neuter. Similarly, for the compound word Wintergarten (*winter garden*), a morphological analysis system should return the available morpho-syntactic information for each of its compound words: Winter and Garten.

Morphological analysis is based on the existence of an available lexicon for the language under consideration. Since words are very often highly ambiguous with respect to PoS and inflection, some disambiguation steps are needed. Consider for example the German word Gewinn (*profit*), which is associated with:

a verb reading - imperative singular of gewinnen (*to win*):

```
[POS=V FORM=IMP NUM=SG]
```

a noun reading - singular nominative, dative or accusative of Gewinn (*profit*):

```
[POS=N NUM=SG CASE=(Nom, Dat, Acc)]
```

Morphological disambiguation interacts with PoS tagging (see next section) as well as with chunking (see section 4), which is putting words together in one fragment and thus provides an indirect morphological and PoS disambiguation.

3 Part-of-Speech Tagging

Part-of-Speech (PoS) tagging is the process of determining the correct syntactic class (a part-of-speech, e.g. noun, verb, etc.) for a particular word given its current context. For instance, the word `works` in the following sentences will be either a verb or a noun:

```
He  works  the whole day for nothing.
His  works  have all been sold abroad.
```

[1]For example, [8] shows that adding morphological information (lemma) improves accuracy of a German document retrieval task up to 6%.

As illustrated by this example, PoS tagging involves disambiguation between multiple part-of-speech tags, next to guessing of the correct part-of-speech tag for unknown words on the basis of context information. Currently available tools for PoS tagging are based either on rule-based or stochastic methods to disambiguate and to tag unknown words (this overview based on [9]).

3.1 Rule-Based

Rule-based approaches use hand crafted or automatically extracted rules that use contextual information to assign tags to unknown or ambiguous words (see for instance: [10] [11] [12]). For example, such a rule could describe the fact that if a word is preceded by a determiner and followed by a noun, is should be tagged as an adjective. In addition, many rule-based systems use morphological information to aid in the disambiguation process. For instance, a morphological rule could state that a word, which is preceded by a verb and ends on *-ing* should be tagged as a verb.

3.2 Stochastic

Stochastic PoS taggers are based on statistical models, incorporating frequency or probability (see for instance: [13] [14] [15]). A simple stochastic tagger disambiguates words solely on the probability that a word occurs with a particular tag in a given training set. In other words, the most frequent tag in the training set will be the one assigned to an ambiguous instance of that word. A more advanced alternative to this is to calculate the probability of a given sequence of tags (a so-called *n-gram*), i.e. the probability that a tag occurs with the *n* previous tags. The most common algorithm for implementing an n-gram approach is *Viterbi*, a breadth-first search algorithm [16].

4 Chunking

The concept of chunks has been introduced originally in relation with so-called *performance structures* that reflect the intuitive subdivision of sentences as uttered by a speaker. Such structures, which have been experimentally verified, can sometimes be different from purely linguistically motivated constituent analysis of sentences that reflect the *competence* of a speaker [17]. Based on this observation, [18] defines chunks as the non-recursive parts of core phrases, such as nominal, prepositional, adjectival and adverbial phrases, and verb groups.

4.1 Chunk Parsing

Chunk parsing is an important step towards making natural language processing robust, since the goal of chunk parsing is not to deliver a full analysis of sentences, but to extract just the linguistic fragments that can be surely identified as a reflection of the linguistic performance. This parsing method is said to be robust, since it delivers always some linguistic information, whereas full parsers would fail to deliver any (even partial) linguistic information if the whole utterance cannot be completely analysed in accordance with some competence model of the particular language.

4.2 Partial Parsing

The concept of partial parsing is closely related to chunk parsing. Basic chunks are the results of a first analysis that detects linguistic fragments in a very accurate way, since it is based on secure local information. On the base of this analysis, rules for the combination of partial results are defined and this process can go through further cycles, called *cascades* [19]. This ensures a higher accuracy of the analysis, since problems are only then handled when it can be reasonably assumed that enough linguistic information has been generated during previous cascades. However, even if this strategy fails to produce an analysis for the whole sentence, the partial linguistic information gained so far will still be useful for many applications, such as information extraction and text mining.

4.3 Named Entities

Related to chunking is the recognition of so-called *named entities* (names of institutions and companies, date expressions, etc.). The extraction of named entities is mostly based on a strategy that combines look up in gazetteers (lists of companies, cities, etc.) with the definition of regular expression patterns. Named entity recognition can be included as part of the linguistic chunking procedure. So for example, the following sentence fragment:

```
...the secretary-general of the United Nations, Kofi Annan,...
```

will be annotated as a nominal phrase, including two named entities: `United Nations` with named entity class: organization, and `Kofi Annan` with named entity class: person[2].

5 Annotation in MuchMore: PoS, Morphological Analysis, Chunks

In this section we present an example of linguistic annotation as used in the MuchMore project on concept-based, cross-lingual information retrieval [20]. The MuchMore annotation format integrates multiple levels of linguistic analysis in a multi-layered XML-based DTD, which organizes each level as a separate track with options of reference between them via indices [21]. Linguistic annotation in MuchMore is based on *ShProT*, a shallow processing tool that consists of a tokenizer [22], the TnT part-of-speech tagger [23], a morphological analyser based on Mmorph and Chunkie [24] for chunk parsing. In addition, MuchMore also covers semantic tagging of terms and relations using EuroWordNet [25] and UMLS (Unified Medical Language System) [26] as primary semantic resources (see section 8).

5.1 Part-of-Speech

Part-of-Speech tagging is performed by TnT, which is an HMM-based part-of-speech tagger trained on general language corpora (the NEGRA corpus for German [27], the SUSANNE corpus for English [28]). In order to perform in an optimal way, TnT needs to be adapted to a specific domain. Two approaches may be considered: 1. Retrain TnT on an annotated domain-specific corpus, or 2. Update the underlying TnT lexicon.

As part-of-speech annotated medical corpora are difficult to obtain, we decided in the context of MuchMore to extend the existing TnT lexicon with information from a medical

[2]See also [56] [57] [59] for more details on named entity recognition in the context of information extraction.

lexicon. Because of a similar syntax for general language and the medical language of the MuchMore corpus of scientific abstracts, we obtained good results without retraining.

5.2 Morphological Analysis

Morphological analysis is based on a full-form lexicon generated by Mmorph. Each token is looked up for a matching entry that will provide its morphological information. If no valid word form has been matched, the token is analysed as a potential compound. Initial decompounding experiments produced poor results. However, after adapting the existing Mmorph lexicon to the medical domain results rather improved. Adaptation proceeded according to the following two steps. First, the Mmorph lexicon was updated with additional morphological information from medical lexicons for both German and English. This enabled us to avoid incorrect decompositions like:

```
Zoonoses    ->   zoo + nose
Epicillin   ->   epic + ill + in
Endoral     ->   end + oral
```

Secondly, general-language word forms that function as prefixes in the medical domain (e.g. `auto`) were removed from the Mmorph lexicon, avoiding incorrect decompositions like:

```
Autoimmune          ->   auto + immune
Postinflammatory    ->   post + inflammatory
Radiogram           ->   radio + gram
```

5.3 Chunks

Chunk analysis is performed by Chunkie, which is an HMM-based partial parser that is capable of recognizing not only the boundaries, but also the internal structure of simple as well as complex phrases. On the basis of the PoS and morphological information, Chunkie is able to determine noun phrases (NP), adjectival phrases (AP) and prepositional phrases (PP). Similar with TnT, the performance of Chunkie can be improved by adaptation to a specific domain. For this purpose however, a domain-specific tree bank should be available.

5.4 Example

Linguistic annotation of PoS, morphology and chunking may be illustrated with an analysis of the following sentence:

```
Balint syndrom is a combination of symptoms including simultanagnosia,
a disorder of spatial and object-based attention, disturbed spatial
perception and representation, and optic ataxia resulting from bilateral
parieto-occipital lesions.
```

In the MuchMore annotation format, each sentence contains a <text> block that holds the tokens as XML content, and both lemma and part-of-speech information as XML attributes:

```
<text>
   <token id="w1" pos="NN">Balint</token>
   <token id="w2" pos="NN">syndrom</token>
   <token id="w3" pos="VBZ" lemma="be">is</token>
   <token id="w4" pos="DT" lemma="a">a</token>
   <token id="w5" pos="NN" lemma="combination">combination</token>
```

```
    <token id="w6" pos="IN" lemma="of">of</token>
    <token id="w7" pos="NNS" lemma="symptom">symptoms</token>
    ...
    <token id="w20" pos="JJ" lemma="spatial">spatial</token>
    <token id="w21" pos="NN" lemma="perception">perception</token>
    <token id="w22" pos="CC" lemma="and">and</token>
    <token id="w23" pos="NN" lemma="representation">
     representation</token>
    ...
</text>
```

Each phrase is annotated by use of indices over tokens. In the current example an NP is found that covers the tokens w1,w2 (`Balint syndrom`) and a more complex NP that covers the tokens w20-w23 (`spatial perception and representation`):

```
<chunks>
    <chunk id="c1" from="w1" to="w2" type="NP"/>
    <chunk id="c7" from="w20" to="w23" type="NP"/>
</chunks>
```

6 Dependency Structure

In information extraction, which is concerned with the detection of complex relations or events[3], there is a need to analyse the internal dependency structure of sentences or chunks. Dependency structure may be illustrated by the following simple example:

```
computer terminal switch
```

This noun phrase consists of three nouns that have a semantic dependency to each other: *switch* depends on `terminal`, whereas `terminal` depends on `computer`. At the same time, either `terminal switch` depends on `computer`, or `switch` depends on `computer terminal`. In other words, we are either dealing with a 'switch' for a 'computer terminal', or a 'terminal switch' for a 'computer'. Identifying the appropriate dependency structure is a linguistic analysis task that takes into account the information supplied by the shallow processing tasks mentioned before, as well as the semantic class of individual words and phrases (i.e. *semantic tagging*) that will be discussed in more detail in section 8 and 9.

A *dependency structure* consists of two or more linguistic units that immediately dominate each other in a syntax tree. Therefore, shallow processing (i.e. *chunking*) is insufficient since this typically does not consider such structures. There are two main types of dependencies that are relevant for the kind of applications under consideration. On the one hand, so-called *grammatical functions* (like subject and direct object) for each of the linguistic chunks in the sentence and which allows to identify the actors involved in certain events. So for example in the following sentence, the syntactic subject is the constituent `the shot by Christian Ziege`:

```
The shot by Christian Ziege goes over the goal.
```

However, in order to detect the actor of the event 'goal scene', it is also necessary to analyse its internal dependency structure. In linguistic analysis, for this we use the terms *head*, *complements* and *modifiers*, where the head is the dominating node in the syntax tree of a phrase, complements are necessary qualifiers thereof, and modifiers are optional qualifiers.

[3]See for example [56] [57] [59] [60].

In the example above, the prepositional phrase `by Christian Ziege` (containing the named entity `Christian Ziege`) depends on (and *modifies*) the noun `shot`, whereas the nominal phrase `the shot` depends on (and *complements*) the verb `goes`. Only through the detection of this particular dependency structure, a system would be able to extract the semantic and domain specific information that a player was involved in a 'goal scene'[4].

7 Annotation in MUMIS: PoS, Morphological Analysis, Chunks, Named Entities, Grammatical Functions and Dependency Structure

In this section we present linguistic annotation of PoS, morphology, chunks, named entities, grammatical functions and dependency structure as performed in the MUMIS project on content-based multimedia access [58]. MUMIS uses an integrated set of linguistic tools - SCHUG: Shallow and Chunk based Unification Grammar, which implements a rule-based system of cascades [29]. This system will not be described in detail here (for details see the chapter on *Content-based Indexing and Searching of Multimedia Documents* in this volume). The application defined by the MUMIS scenario implies annotation of named entities, grammatical functions and head-modifier structure, in addition to the shallow processing information also covered by MuchMore. SCHUG has adopted the annotation schema developed in this project, which enables easier performance comparison, and also allows for a smooth integration of the various annotation layers provided by these two systems. Therefore, it is possible to include dependency structure information in this annotation format and also to add a new annotation layer that provides information on grammatical functions.

7.1 Morphological Analysis and Part-of-Speech

For morpho-syntactic information, SCHUG integrates parts of the system described in [22] and maps the results to the MuchMore format (see section 5.4 above), as shown in the following example:

```
Industrie, Handel und Dienstleistungen werden in der ersten Liste
aufgefuehrt, wobei die in Klammern gesetzten Zahlen auf die
Mutterfirmen hinweisen.
(Industry, trade and services are shown in the first list, where
the numbers in brackets point to the parent company.)

<text>
   <token id="w1" pos="NN" lemma="Industrie">Industrie</token>
   <token id="w2" pos="PUNCT">,</token>
   <token id="w3" pos="NN" lemma="Handel">Handel</token>
   <token id="w4" pos="CONJ">und</token>
   <token id="w5" pos="NN" lemma1="Dienst" lemma2="Leistung">
    Dienstleistungen </token>
   ...
</text>
```

[4]See for more details on dependency structure, for instance the introduction to parsing strategies in [62]. More elaborated discussions on relevant syntactic theories and on head grammars are given in [63] [64] [65] [66].

7.2 Chunking and Dependency Structure Analysis

SCHUG implements a modular strategy for the recognition of domain specific named entities. For MUMIS in particular, the task is to detect soccer relevant named entities (e.g. `player, team, trainer, referee, time code, specific-event`). This information will be encoded on the chunk annotation level, with an index pointing to the distinct tokens that correspond to each individual named entity.

The chunking procedure of SCHUG consists of a rule-based sequence of cascades, which produces a richer linguistic representation than the MuchMore tools. So, for example, also (complex) verb groups are annotated (chunks are put into square brackets):

```
[NP Industrie, Handel und Dienstleistungen] [VG werden] [PP in der ersten
Liste] [VG aufgefuehrt], wobei [NP die in Klammern gesetzten Zahlen]
[PP auf die Mutterfirmen] [VG hinweisen].
```

The MuchMore annotation format allows for a straightforward mapping of this information in the chunk layer as shown below. Note that now also information on heads, modifiers and complements are represented. In the case of the first NP, which is*coordinated*, all nouns are considered to be heads. In the case of a PP, the head is always the preposition and its complement is always an NP. The internal structure of the complement NP is not given here.

```
<chunks>
    <chunk id="c1" from="w1" to="w5" type="NP" head="w1,w3,w5"/>
    <chunk id="c2" from="w6" to="w6" type="VG"/>
    <chunk id="c3" from="w7" to="w10" type="PP" head="w7"
     complement="w8,w9,w10"/>
    <chunk id="c4" from="w11" to="w1" type="VG"/>
    ....
</chunks>
```

Next, also grammatical functions are annotated. In order to detect these accurately, an analysis of the *clauses* of a sentence is required. Clauses are the subparts of a sentence that correspond to a (possibly complex) semantic unit, each of which contains a main verb with its complements (grammatical functions) and possibly other chunks (modifiers). For the same example this would produce:

```
<clauses>
  <clause id="cl1" from="c1" to="c4" pred_struct="c2 c4" GF_Subj="c1"/>
  <clause id="cl2" from="c6" to="c9" pred_struct="c9" GF_Subj="c6"/>
</clauses>
```

The annotation identifies two clauses, each with a span of several chunks (pointed to by an index), with information on its predicative structure (pred_struct) and grammatical function (e.g. GF_Subj). Predicative structure can be complex as with the first clause, where the predicate corresponds to a discontinuous verb group with a an auxiliary verb - `werden` (to be) and a main verb - `aufführen` (perform).

8 Semantic Tagging

In the semantic web context, web documents are marked up with metadata, using manual annotation with web-based knowledge representation languages such as RDF and DAML+OIL for describing the content of the document. Some ongoing projects along these lines are SHOE [30], COHSE [31], and OntoAnnotate [32], all of which aim at motivating people to richly annotate electronic documents in order to turn them into a machine-understandable format, and at developing and spreading annotation-aware applications such as content-based information presentation and retrieval.

From a somewhat different angle, automatic semantic annotation has developed within language technology in recent years in connection with more integrated tasks like information extraction. Natural language applications, such as information extraction and machine translation, require a certain level of semantic analysis. An important part of this process is semantic tagging: the annotation of each content word with a semantic category. Semantic categories are assigned on the basis of a semantic lexicon like WordNet for English [33] or EuroWordNet, which links words between many European languages through a common inter-lingua of concepts.

Especially from a domain specific point of view, these separate developments now seem to converge on a common goal of relating textual units in documents to information organized in structured ways. In the following sections we will take a closer look at some of the semantic resources that are available and their use in semantic tagging. Special emphasis is given also to the important subtask of sense disambiguation, which is needed if a word or term corresponds to more than one possible semantic class. Finally, semantic tagging of terms (and of relations between terms) is illustrated by an example from the MuchMore annotation.

8.1 Semantic Resources

Semantic knowledge is captured in resources like dictionaries, thesauri, and semantic networks, all of which express, either implicitly or explicitly, an ontology of the world in general or of more specific domains, such as medicine. They can be roughly distinguished into the following three groups:

- Thesauri: Semantic resources that group together similar words or terms according to a standard set of relations, including broader term, narrower term, sibling, etc.
- Semantic Lexicons: Semantic resources that group together words (or more complex lexical items) according to lexical semantic relations like synonymy, hyponymy, meronymy, and antonymy
- Semantic Networks: Semantic resources that group together objects denoted by natural language expressions (terms) according to a set of relations that originate in the nature of the domain of application.

8.1.1 Thesauri

Roget is a thesaurus of English words and phrases. It groups words in synonym categories or concepts. Besides synonyms also antonyms are covered. A sample categorization (for the concept Feeling) is:

```
I.   Words Expressing Abstract Relations
II.  Words Relating To Space
III. Words Relating To Matter
IV.  Words Relating To The Intellectual Faculties;
     Formation and Communication of Ideas
V.   Words Relating To The Voluntary Powers;
     Individual And Intersocial Volition
VI.  Words Relating To The Sentiment and Moral Powers

I. AFFECTIONS IN GENERAL
   Affections.
      Feeling.
        warmth, glow, unction, gusto, vehemence;
        fervor, fervency;
        heartiness, cordiality;
        earnestness, eagerness;
        empressment, gush, ardor, zeal, passion, ...
```

MeSH (Medical Subject Headings) is a thesaurus for indexing articles and books in the medical domain, which may then be used for searching MeSH-indexed databases [34]. MeSH provides for each term a number of term variants that refer to the same concept. It currently includes a vocabulary of over 250,000 terms. The following is a sample entry for the term gene library (MH is the term itself, ENTRY are term variants):

```
MH     =   Gene Library
ENTRY  =   Bank, Gene
ENTRY  =   Banks, Gene
ENTRY  =   DNA Libraries
ENTRY  =   Gene Banks
ENTRY  =   Gene Libraries
ENTRY  =   Libraries, DNA
ENTRY  =   Libraries, Gene
ENTRY  =   Library, DNA
ENTRY  =   Library, Gene
```

8.1.2 Semantic Lexicons

WordNet has primarily been designed as a computational account of the human capacity of linguistic categorization. It therefore covers a rather extensive set of semantic classes (called *synsets*), currently over 90.000. Synsets are collections of synonyms, grouping together lexical items according to meaning similarity. For instance, a board and a plank are similar lexical items and can thus be grouped together in the synset: {board, plank}. At the same time, however, board also refers to a group of people, which may be represented by the synset {board, committee}. So, in fact synsets are actually not made up of lexical items, but rather of lexical meanings (i.e. senses). Observe, that synsets define lexical meaning in an implicit way, contrary to using explicit definitions.

Synsets range from the very specific to the very general. Very specific synsets typically cover only a small number of lexical items, while very general ones tend to cover many. The following example for 'tree' illustrates how in WordNet the hyponymy relation is used. The word 'tree' has two meanings that roughly correspond to the classes of plants and that of diagrams, each with their own hierarchy of classes that are included in more general superclasses:

```
09396070 tree 0
 09395329 woody_plant 0 ligneous_plant 0
  09378438 vascular_plant 0 tracheophyte 0
   00008864 plant 0 flora 0 plant_life 0
    00002086 life_form 0 organism 0 being 0 living_thing 0
     00001740 entity 0 something 0

10025462 tree 0 tree_diagram 0
 09987563 plane_figure 0 two-dimensional_figure 0
  09987377 figure 0
   00015185 shape 0 form 0
    00018604 attribute 0
     00013018 abstraction 0
```

EuroWordNet is a multilingual semantic lexicon for several European languages and is structured in similar ways to WordNet. Each language specific (Euro)WordNet is linked to all others through the Inter-Lingual-Index (ILI), which is based on WordNet1.5. Via this index the languages are interconnected, so that it is possible to move from a word in one language to similar words in any of the other languages in the EuroWordNet semantic lexicon.

8.1.3 Semantic Networks

UMLS is one of the most extensive semantic resources available. It is based in part on the MeSH thesaurus and is specific to the medical domain. UMLS integrates linguistic, terminological and semantic information in three corresponding parts: the Specialist Lexicon, the Metathesaurus and the Semantic Network.

The Metathesaurus is a multilingual thesaurus that groups term variants together that correspond to the same concept, for instance the following term variants in several languages for the concept `C0019682` (`HIV`):

```
C0019682   ENG   HIV
C0019682   ENG   HTLV-III
C0019682   ENG   Human Immunodeficiency Virus
C0019682   ENG   Virus, Human Immunodeficiency
C0019682   FRE   VIRUS IMMUNODEFICIENCE HUMAINE
C0019682   GER   HIV
C0019682   GER   Humanes T-Zell-lymphotropes Virus Typ III
```

The Semantic Network organises all concepts in the Metathesaurus into 134 semantic types and 54 relations between semantic types. Relations between semantic types are represented in the form of triplets, with two semantic types linked by one or more relations:

```
Pharmacologic Substance   affects       Pathologic Function
Pharmacologic Substance   causes        Pathologic Function
Pharmacologic Substance   complicates   Pathologic Function
Pharmacologic Substance   diagnoses     Pathologic Function
Pharmacologic Substance   prevents      Pathologic Function
Pharmacologic Substance   treats        Pathologic Function
```

CYC is a semantic network of over 1,000,000 manually defined rules that cover a large part of common sense knowledge about the world [35]. For example, CYC knows that trees are usually outdoors, or that people who died stop buying things. Each concept in this semantic network is defined as a constant, which can represent a collection (e.g. the set of all people), an individual object (e.g. a particular person), a word (e.g. the English word `person`), a quantifier (e.g. `there exist`), or a relation (e.g. a predicate, function, slot, attribute). Consider for instance the entry for the predicate #$mother:

```
#$mother :
   (#$mother ANIM FEM)
       isa: #$FamilyRelationSlot #$BinaryPredicate
```

This says that the predicate #$mother takes two arguments, the first of which must be an element of the collection #$Animal, and the second of which must be an element of the collection #$FemaleAnimal.
Further semantic networks used in semantic tagging are: **Mikrokosmos** [36] and **Sensus** [37].

9 Sense Disambiguation

Words mostly have more than one interpretation, or *sense*. If natural language were completely unambiguous, there would be a one-to-one relationship between words and senses. In fact, things are much more complicated, because for most words not even a fixed number of senses can be given. Therefore, only in certain circumstances and depending on what we mean exactly with sense, can we give restricted solutions to the problem of *Word Sense Disambiguation* (WSD.)

9.1 Methods

WSD involves two parts, a semantic lexicon that associates words with sets of possible semantic classes (i.e. *senses*) and a method of associating (annotating, tagging) occurrences of these words with one or more of its senses. The systems and algorithms that have been developed for this cover the full spectrum of methods developed in natural language processing, artificial intelligence and more recently also of machine learning. For our purposes here, we may group these as follows: *Knowledge-based*, *Hybrid*, and *Empirical*.

In knowledge-based approaches, the construction of the tag set (the senses used and their association with word types in the semantic lexicon) and the tagging (disambiguation between possible senses and association of the preferred sense with a given word token) are both supervised. These approaches use small, but deep, handcrafted lexicons to analyse a small number of examples in a non-robust way, that is, the systems can handle only certain input (see for instance: [38] [39] [40] [41]). All of these rely on pre-coded, domain-specific knowledge, which is the heaviest cost factor in work on WSD, yet indispensable (*knowledge acquisition bottleneck*). Typically, handcrafted rules are constructed, according to given examples. There is no automatic training of the system.

In hybrid approaches, the construction of the tag set is supervised, but the training for the tagging can be either supervised or unsupervised. In the first case, corpora that have been manually annotated are used for training. In the second case, corpora that have not been annotated are used for training. These approaches combine hand-crafted knowledge bases with empirical data derived from large corpora. These approaches use large scale, more shallow, hand-crafted lexicons (WordNet, Roget, lexical database versions of standard English dictionaries like LDOCE, OALD, etc.) to analyse text in a robust way, that is, the systems can handle free, naturally occurring text. Most of these systems became possible thanks to technological advances, using large-scale, machine-readable dictionaries [42], thesauri such as Roget's [43], and computational dictionaries like WordNet [44], [45].

In empirical approaches, the construction of the tag set and the training for the tagging are both unsupervised. These approaches use no external knowledge base at all, but instead derive the tag set itself from the corpus as well. This might be called *self-organizing* WSD. It seeks to do without the pre-defined set of alternative senses, inferring them instead by working, as it were, in the opposite direction: A corpus is used to classify words based solely on patterns of occurrence. The resulting clusters are presumed to represent senses. The two stages that this process consists of are (1) clustering the occurrences of a word into a number of categories and (2) assigning a sense to each category. This idea was first discussed in [46]. It can dispense with the sense-labeling step if the results are only used machine-internally. To stress this subtle but important difference, the method is called *Word Sense Discrimination* in [47]. However, a notable problem with such methods is the close dependence of the resulting classification on the training corpus and the choice of clustering granularity.

9.2 Evaluation

A problem with the various methods proposed for WSD is the lack of a standardized evaluation metric. Publications often focus on only a few words. In a special issue on WSD of the journal for *Computational Linguistics* two out of four articles concentrate exclusively on the three words `line`, `serve`, and `hard`, while many other papers use some other small set of words [48]. In hand-tagged corpora, disagreement between human judges invariably introduces considerable noise [49] [50]. Moreover, it is difficult to draw comparisons across domains. These problems motivated the SENSEVAL [51] and SENSEVAL2 [52] competitions, aimed at developing a standardized evaluation metric for WSD systems.

10 Annotation in MuchMore: Terms and Relations

In addition to the annotation of corpora with shallow processing information as discussed in section 2.4, also semantic information is annotated in the context of the MuchMore project. This includes semantic tagging with EuroWordNet synsets as well as semantic tagging with UMLS concepts and relations as specified in the Metathesaurus and Semantic Network.

10.1 UMLS

A major objective of the MuchMore project is to explore techniques for enhancing cross-lingual information retrieval (CLIR) through automatic semantic annotation of domain-specific terms and relations. For this purpose, the publicly available medical language resource UMLS is used. At the level of terms, the following semantic information is used in annotation:

- Concept Unique Identifier (CUI): maps a term to a concept in the Metathesaurus
- Type Unique Identifier (TUI): maps a concept to one or more semantic types in the Semantic Network
- Medical Subject Headings (MeSH id): maps a CUI to one or more MeSH codes

- Preferred Term: a term that is marked as preferred for a given set of terms and a corresponding concept

Semantic relations are currently annotated between semantic types (TUIs) that co-occur within a sentence. This means that we can only annotate relations between items that were previously identified as terms. The semrel element thus refers to the level of UMLS terms by specifying the pair of terms and the type of relation found. Due to the generic nature of semantic types, the number of possible semantic relations specified between them in UMLS can be considerable. However, through term disambiguation and relevance-based selection of relations it is possible to prune them.

10.2 EuroWordNet

In addition to UMLS, terms are annotated with EuroWordNet to compare domain-specific and general language use. We annotate both single- and multi-word EWN terms, whereby each possible sense of a term represents a separate XML element `sense` with the attribute `offset` (EWN code of the sense). For the purpose of cross-lingual information retrieval we limit the annotation with EWN to senses for nouns only.

10.3 Example

For the example sentence of section 5.4, the words w20-w21 (spatial perception) point to the concept `Space Perception` in the UMLS Metathesaurus, which corresponds to the CUI code C0037744 and TUI code T041 (`Mental Process`) and to two MeSH codes. Word w26 (optic) triggered the concept Optics with corresponding CUI, TUI and MeSH codes.

```
<umlsterm id="t7" from="w20" to="w21">
   <concept id="t7.1" cui="C0037744" preferred="Space Perception"
    tui="T041">
       <msh code="F2.463.593.778"/>
       <msh code="F2.463.593.932.869"/>
   </concept>
</umlsterm>
<umlsterm id="t8" from="w26" to="w26">
    <concept id="t8.1" cui="C0029144" preferred="Optics" tui="T090">
       <msh code="H1.671.606"/>
    </concept>
</umlsterm>
```

The UMLS Semantic Network further defines that `Space Perception` is an issue in `Optics` (expressed by the relation: issue_in), which is coded as follows (note that attributes t7.1 and t8.1 point to the UMLS concepts introduced in the example above):

```
<semrel id="r7" term1="t7.1" term2="t8.1" reltype="issue_in"/>
```

In EuroWordNet annotation, word w21 (perception) has the following senses:

```
<ewnterm id="e2" from="w7" to="w7">
   <sense offset="0487490"/>
   <sense offset="3955418"/>
   <sense offset="4002483"/>
</ewnterm>
```

corresponding to the following synsets:

```
0487490 perceiving, perception, sensing
3955418 perception
4002483 percept, perception, perceptual experience
```

We are currently working on a word sense disambiguation module to cut down on ambiguities concerning EuroWordNet senses, based on unsupervised training as described in [53] [54]. Evaluation of the disambiguation module is undertaken as part of the CLIR evaluation task (comparing disambiguated and non-disambiguated versions of the annotated document collection), as well as separately by using a manually tagged lexical sample corpus [55].

11 Annotation in MUMIS: Entities, Relations and Events

The primary goal of the MUMIS project is to generate formal annotation of multimedia documents that allows for content-based indexing of soccer videos. The project provides highly structured domain-specific annotation of relevant entities, relations and events that can be extracted from transcribed audio and video broadcasts of specific soccer games and corresponding on-line textual documents. The linguistic annotation of these documents as provided by the SCHUG tools are associated with domain-specific information that is encoded in a ontology on the soccer domain. The ontology represents in a hierarchical fashion the main events, relations and entities relevant to the domain (see also [29] and the chapter on multimedia annotation in this volume).

One of the main text types that MUMIS is dealing with is the *on-line ticker* (short descriptions of interesting soccer events, each event indicated by a time-code), for example:

```
7. Ein Freistoss von Christian Ziege aus 25 Metern geht ueber das Tor.
(A 25-meter free-kick by Christian Ziege goes over the goal.)
```

In this example, various entities, relations and events that are relevant to the soccer domain occur (e.g. the artefact: `Tor`, person-player: `Ziege` and two events: the first one expressed by a nominalization (corresponding to an np chunk: `free-kick: Freistoss`) and the second one by a verbal phrase (`goal-scene: geht ueber das Tor`). Some relations are not explicitly mentioned, but can still be inferred by the MUMIS system. For example, the team for which `Ziege` is playing can be inferred from the ontological information that a player is part of a team and the instance of this particular team can be extracted from additional texts. So information not present in the text directly can be added by additional information extraction and reasoning (see also [29]).

```
<chunks>
   <chunk id="c1" from="w1" to="w2" type="NP" head="w1"/>
   <chunk id="c2" from="w3" to="w7" type="NP" head="w4"/>
   <chunk id="c3" from="w8" to="w10" type="PP" head="w8"
    complement="w9 w10"/>
   <chunk id="c4" from="w11" to="w11" type="VG"/>
   <chunk id="c5" from="w12" to="w14" type="PP" head="w12"
    complement="w13 w14"/>
</chunks>
```

```
<clauses>
   <clause id="cl1" from="c1" to="c5" pred_struct="c3"
    GF_Subj="c2"/>
</clauses>

<events>
   <event id="e1" clause="cl1" event-name="free-kick">
      <relations>
        <relation id="r1" reltype="player" player-name="Christian
         Ziege" in-team="Germany"/>
        <relation id="r2" reltype="location" loc-from="25-meter"/>
        <relation id="r3" reltype="time" time-val="07:00"/>
      </relations>
   </event>
    <event id="e2" clause="cl1" event-name="goal-scene-fail">
      <relations>
        <relation id="r1" reltype="player" player-name="Christian
         Ziege" in-team="Germany"/>
        <relation id="r2" reltype="location" loc-from="25-meter"
         loc-to="goal-area"/>
        <relation id="r3" reltype="time" time-val="07:00"/>
      </relations>
   </event>
</events>
```

12 Conclusions: From Language to Semantics to Information Structure

In this paper we showed how to connect language with knowledge as encoded in ontologies through an integration of linguistic and semantic annotation. This touches an important point of discussion in linguistic semantics, namely if it should cover knowledge of language or knowledge of the world. In a way, it should cover both, as what is expressed in language tells us about the worlds built up in our memory. It is therefore not so much a question about what constitutes the meaning of a text, but rather what constitutes a particular world about which a particular text is saying something. This, of course, has also always been a central question in much of philosophy of language, as only through language and most importantly, through categorization in language, we can talk about the world, or the worlds that we imagine. Especially also in the context of emerging semantic web technology this is an important observation, as the information structure that is built up by such an entity (i.e. a domain or organization specific semantic web) reflects the world of a particular organization or group of organizations. A particular semantic web then functions as the collective memory of an organization and the corresponding information structure is the image of the world that it has access to.

13 Acknowledgements

This research has in part been supported by EC/NSF grant IST-1999-11438 for the MuchMore project, EC grant IST-1999-10651 for the MUMIS project.
Many thanks to Spela Vintar, Diana Raileanu and Bogdan Sacaleanu (MuchMore), Mihaela Hutanu and Claudia Crispi (MUMIS).

References

[1] Koskenniemi K. Two-level morphology: a general computational model for word-form recognition and production. Publication No. 11. Helsinki: University of Helsinki Department of General Linguistics. 1983.

[2] http://www.lingsoft.fi/doc/gertwol/

[3] Finkler W. and Neumann G. Morphix: A Fast Realization of a Classification-Based Approach to Morphology. Proceedings of the 4th Austrian Artificial Intelligence Conference. 1988.

[4] Petitpierre, D. and Russell, G. MMORPH - The Multext Morphology Program. Multext deliverable report for the task 2.3.1, ISSCO, University of Geneva. 1995.

[5] Matsumoto Y., Kitauchi A., Yamashita T., Hirano Y., Matsuda H., Asahara M. Japanese Morphological Analysis System ChaSen, version 2.0, Manual 2nd edition. 1999. http://chasen.aist-nara.ac.jp/

[6] http://www.xrce.xerox.com/research/mltt/fsnlp/morph.de.html

[7] http://www.issco.unige.ch/projects/MULTEXT.html

[8] Volk M., Vintar S., Buitelaar P., Raileanu D., Sacaleanu B. Semantic Annotation for Concept-Based Cross-Language Medical Information Retrieval. To appear in the International Journal of Medical Informatics.

[9] http://www.georgetown.edu/cball/ling361/tagging_overview.html

[10] Brill E. A simple rule-based part of speech tagger. Proceedings of the Third Annual Conference on Applied Natural Language Processing, ACL. 1992.

[11] Brill E. Unsupervised learning of disambiguation rules for part of speech tagging. Proceedings of the third ACL Workshop on Very Large Corpora. 1995.

[12] Tapanainen, P., Voutilainen, A. Tagging accurately: don't guess if you don't know. Technical Report, Xerox Corporation. 1994. http://www.ling.helsinki.fi/ tapanain/cg/index.html

[13] Cutting D., Kupiec J., Pedersen J., Sibun P. A Practical Part-of-Speech Tagger. In Proceedings of the 3rd conference on Applied Natural Language Processing (ANLP). 1992. ftp://parcftp.xerox.com/pub/tagger/

[14] Schmid H. Probabilistic Part-of-Speech Tagging Using Decision Trees. In International Conference on New Methods in Language Processing. Manchester. 1994. (http://www.ims.uni-stuttgart.de/projekte/corplex/TreeTagger/DecisionTreeTagger.html)

[15] Brants, T. TnT - A Statistical Part-of-Speech Tagger. In: Proceedings of 6th ANLP Conference, Seattle, WA. 2000.

[16] Brill E., Marcus M. Tagging an unfamiliar text with minimal human supervision. ARPA Technical Report. 1993. (ftp://ftp.cs.jhu.edu/pub/brill/Programs/UNSUP_TAGGER_V0.8.tar.gz)

[17] Chomsky N. Aspects of the Theroy of Syntax. The MIT Press, Cambridge, MA, 1965.

[18] Abney S. Chunks and Dependencies: Bringing Processing Evidence to Bear on Syntax. In: Computational Linguistics and the Foundations of Linguistic Theory. CSLI. 1995.

[19] Abney S. Partial Parsing via Finite-State Cascades. Journal of Natural Language Engineering, 2(4): 337-344. 1996.

[20] http://muchmore.dfki.de

[21] Vintar S., Buitelaar P., Ripplinger B., Sacaleanu B., Raileanu D., Prescher D. An Efficient and Flexible Format for Linguistic and Semantic Annotation In: Proceedings of LREC2002 , Las Palmas, Canary Islands - Spain, May 29-31, 2002.

[22] Piskorski J., G. Neumann. An Intelligent Text Extraction and Navigation System. Proceedings of the 6th International Conference on Computer-Assisted Information Retrieval (RIAO). 2000.

[23] http://www.coli.uni-sb.de/ thorsten/tnt/

[24] Skut W. and Brants T. A Maximum Entropy partial parser for unrestricted text. In: Proceedings of the 6th ACL Workshop on Very Large Corpora (WVLC), Montreal. 1998.

[25] Vossen, P. 1997. EuroWordNet: a multilingual database for information retrieval. In: Proceedings of the DELOS workshop on Cross-language Information Retrieval, March 5-7, 1997.

[26] http://umls.nlm.nih.gov

[27] http://www.coli.uni-sb.de/sfb378/negra-corpus/

[28] http://www.cogs.susx.ac.uk/users/geoffs/Rsue.html

[29] Declerck T. A set of tools for integrating linguistic and non-linguistic information. Proceedings of SAAKM 2002, ECAI 2002, Lyon.

[30] Hefln J., Hendler J., and Luke S. SHOE: A Knowledge Representation Language for Internet Applications. Technical Report CS-TR-4078. Department of Computer Science, University of Maryland, 1999.

[31] Bechhofer S. and Goble C. Towards Annotation using DAML+OIL Communications of the ACM, 2000.

[32] Staab S., Maedche A., Handschuh S. An Annotation Framework for the Semantic Web. In The First International Workshop on Multimedia Annotation, Tokyo, Japan, 2001.

[33] Miller, G.A. WordNet: A Lexical Database for English. Communications of the ACM 11. 1995.

[34] http://www.nlm.nih.gov/mesh/meshhome.html

[35] http://www.cyc.com

[36] Kavi Mahesh and Sergei Nirenburg. A situated ontology for practical NLP. In Proceedings of IJCAI-95 Workshop on Basic Ontological Issues in Knowledge Sharing. 1995.

[37] Knight, K., Luk . Building a Large Knowledge Base for Machine Translation. Proceedings of the American Association of Artificial Intelligence Conference AAAI-94. Seattle, WA. 1994.

[38] Small, S.L. Word Expert Parsing: A Theory of Distributed Word-based Natural Language Understanding. Ph.D. thesis, The University of Maryland, Baltimore, MD. 1980.

[39] Small, S.L. Parsing as cooperative distributed inference. In King, M. (ed.): Parsing Natural Language. Academic Press, London. 1983.

[40] Hirst, G. Semantic Interpretation and the Resolution of Ambiguity. Cambridge University Press. 1988.

[41] Adriaens, G., and S.L. Small. Word expert revisited in a cognitive science perspective. In Small, S., G.W. Cottrell, and M.K. Tanenhaus (eds.): Lexical Ambiguity Resolution: Perspectives from Psycholinguistics, Neuropsychology, and Artificial Intelligence. Morgan Kaufmann, San Mateo, CA, pages 13-43. 1988.

[42] Lesk, M.E. Automated sense disambiguation using machine-readable dictionaries: How to tell a pine cone from an ice cone. In Proceedings of the SIGDOC Conference. 1986.

[43] Yarowsky, D. Word-sense disambiguation using statistical models of Roget's categories. In Proceedings of COLING-92, Nantes, France. 1992.

[44] Resnik, P. Using information content to evaluate semantic similarity in a taxonomy. In Proceedings of the 14th International Joint Conference on Artificial Intelligence (IJCAI). 1995.

[45] Ng, H.T., and H.B. Lee. Integrating multiple knowledge sources to disambiguate word sense: An exemplar-based approach. In Proceedings of ACL96. 1996.

[46] Schtze, H. Context space. In Goldman, R., P. Norvig, E. Charniak, and B. Gale (eds.): Working Notes of the AAAI Fall Symposium on Probabilistic Approaches to Natural Language, AAAI Press, Menlo Park, CA, pages 113-120. 1992.

[47] Schtze, H. Automatic word sense discrimination. Computational Linguistics, 24(1):97-123. 1998.

[48] Ide N., Veronis J. Introduction to the special issue on word sense disambiguation: The state of the art. Computational Linguistics, 24(1):1–40. 1998.

[49] Kilgariff, A. 1998. Gold standard datasets for evaluating word sense disambiguation programs. Computer Speech and Language 12(4), Special Issue on Evaluation.

[50] Vonis, J. 1998. A study of polysemy judgements and inter-annotator agreement. In Programme and advanced papers of the Senseval workshop, Herstmonceux Castle (England), pages 2-4.

[51] Kilgariff, A., and M. Palmer. 2000. Introduction to the special issue on SENSEVAL. Computers and the Humanities 34(1/2):1-13.

[52] http://www.sle.sharp.co.uk/senseval2/

[53] Buitelaar P., Alexandersson J., Jaeger T., Lesch S., Pfleger N., Raileanu D., von den Berg T., Klckner K., Neis H., Schlarb H. An Unsupervised Semantic Tagger Applied to German. In: Proceedings of Recent Advances in NLP (RANLP) , Tzigov Chark, Bulgaria. 2001.

[54] Buitelaar P., Sacaleanu B. Ranking and Selecting Synsets by Domain Relevance. In: Proceedings of WordNet and Other Lexical Resources: Applications, Extensions and Customizations. NAACL 2001 Workshop, Carnegie Mellon University, Pittsburgh. 2001.

[55] Raileanu D., Buitelaar P., Bay J., Vintar S. An Evaluation Corpus for Sense Disambiguation in the Medical Domain. In: Proceedings of LREC2002, Las Palmas, Canary Islands. 2002.

[56] Appelt D.E. An Introduction to Information. AI Communications, 12. 1999.

[57] Cunningham H. Information Extraction: A user Guide. Research Report CS-9907,Department of Computer Science, University of Sheffield. 1999.

[58] Declerck T., Wittenburg P., Cunningham H. The Automatic Generation of Formal Annotations in a Multimedia Indexing and Searching Environment. Proceedings of the Workshop on Human Language Technology and Knowledge Management, ACL-2001.

[59] MUC-7: Seventh Message Understanding Conference. http://www.muc.saic.com/, SAIC Information Extraction. 1998.

[60] Neumann G., Backofen R., Baur J., Becker M., Braun C. An Information Extraction Core System for Real World German Text Processing. Proceedings of the 5th Conference on Applied Natural Language Processing, ANLP-97, 209-216. 1997.

[61] Lappin, S., Shih H-H. A generalized Algorithm for Ellipsis Resolution. Proceedings of the 16th International Conference on Computational Linguistics, COLING-96. 1996.

[62] Hellwig P. NATURAL LANGUAGE PARSERS A "Course in Cooking. COLING-ACL '98– Pre-Conference Tutorial. 1998.

[63] Balari S. Information-Based Linguistics and Head-Driven Phrase Structure. In Miguel Filgueiras and Lu Damas and Nelma Moreira and Ana Paula Tom, editor(s), Natural Language Processing. 55-101. Berlin: Springer-Verlag. 1991.

[64] Borsley R. D. Modern Phrase Structure Grammar. Blackwell textbooks in linguistics, number 11. : Blackwell Publishers. 1996.

[65] Borsley R. D. Heads in HPSG. In Greville Corbett and N. Fraser and S. McGlashan, editor(s), Heads in Grammatical Theory. Forthcoming.

[66] Pollard C., Sag. Head-Driven Phrase Structure Grammar. Chicago: University of Chicago Press. 1994.

Annotation for the Semantic Web
S. Handschuh and S. Staab (Eds.)
IOS Press, 2003

Designing Adaptive Information Extraction for the Semantic Web in Amilcare

Fabio Ciravegna and Yorick Wilks
Department of Computer Science, University of Sheffield,
Regent Court, 211 Portobello Street,
Sheffield, S1 4DP, UNITED KINGDOM

1 Introduction

A crucial aspect of creating the Semantic Web (SW) is to enable users to create machine-readable Web content. Emphasis in the research community has till now been put on building tools for manual annotation of documents (e.g. [18]), but only recently has the problem of producing automatic or semi-automatic methods for annotating documents become an issue [17, 27]. The main problem with manual annotation is that it is a difficult, slow, time-consuming and tedious process that involves high costs and very often a large number of errors as well (up to 25% in some cases [24]). The latter is especially true in case of user with no experience of document annotation (naive annotators), while it slightly improves with expert annotators (about 15%). Manual annotation of documents by naive Web users is quite unlikely to be correct or even performed at all. The semantics of ontologies (generally used as reference for annotation) can be opaque to a layman, selecting the correct concepts or even the correct ontology could be out of reach for such users. Some type of support is needed to make the annotation process feasible. According to some researchers, the future of the SW will not rely on few large, complex, consistent ontologies shared by great numbers of users. The SW will instead be dynamic and based on a great number of small ontological components [19]. These components will be continuously extended, merged or created, and therefore the annotation services associated to them will have to be constantly adjusted or revised according to these changes. This poses a number of obvious constraints and requirements on the technology to support annotation in terms of usability, portability and maintainability.

Information Extraction from texts (IE) is an automatic method for locating important facts in electronic documents for successive use, e.g. for document annotation or for information storing (such as populating an ontology with instances). IE can provide support in document annotation either in an automatic way (unsupervised extraction of information) or semi-automatic way (e.g. as support for human annotators in locating relevant facts in documents, via information highlighting). IE was defined in the past years mainly as a technology created by the MUC conferences, which were comparative evaluations sponsored by DARPA[24]. The main requirements for the technology have been, in the MUC context, effectiveness with respect to quite complex tasks and reduced porting time by IE experts [9]. So far, only limited application to the Web has been attempted, especially for the Semantic Web [21]. Its use has been generally intended as a technology providing generic support to annotation (e.g. recognising Named Entities [11]). When it has been used as support to more specific tasks, IE experts are generally involved in the development cycle in order to develop

IE grammars or knowledge bases. As mentioned above, we believe that if we really want to use IE as support for annotation for the SW, we have to develop a new kind of technology where issues such as usability (e.g. by naive Web users), cost of new applications, portability and maintainability are the main design issues. Note that other application areas, such as Knowledge Management, are currently posing similar requirements to IE: interestingly, these are areas in which the SW could play (or is already playing) a major role [5].

Porting (and or maintaining) IE systems actually means coping with four (overlapping) main tasks:

- Adapting to new domain information: implementing (or modifying) lexica, knowledge bases, etc., designing new templates, so that the system is able to manipulate domain-specific concepts;
- Adapting to sublanguage features: modifying grammars and lexica in order to cope with specific linguistic constructions that are typical of the application;
- Adapting to different text genres: specific text genres (e.g. medical abstracts, scientific papers, police reports) may have their own lexis, grammar or discourse structure.
- Adapting to different text types: Web-based documents can vary from rigidly structured XML documents (e.g. tables) to free texts. Each different text type can have different requirements in term of language analysis.

IE experts are quite rare in industry and therefore, if IE is to be used, it must be adaptable using knowledge only of the domain (e.g. via text annotation only). This is quite a shift from the classic MUC-oriented technology (e.g. [20, 1]) which relies strongly on IE experts. Also, adaptive technology that requires linguistic (not domain) annotation (e.g. [23]) is not suitable in this context. Moreover, in terms of amount of annotated material for training, the need must be reduced in order to minimize the burden on the user side (lower cost, reduced development/maintenance time).

Concerning porting across text types, in classical Natural Language Processing (NLP) adapting to new text types has been generally considered as a task of porting across different types of free texts [3]. The use of IE for the SW requires an extension of the concept of text types to new, unexplored, dimensions. Linguistically-based methodologies used for free texts can be difficult to apply or ineffective on highly structured texts such as web pages produced by data bases. They are not able to cope with the variety of extralinguistic structures (e.g. XML tags, document formatting, and stereotypical language) that are used to convey information in such documents. On the other hand, wrapper-like algorithms designed for highly structured HTML/XML pages [22, 25] are largely ineffective on unstructured texts (e.g. free texts). This is because such methodologies make scarce (or no) use of NLP, avoiding any generalization over the flat word sequence, and tending to be ineffective on free texts, for example, because of data sparseness [6]. The challenge is to develope methodologies able to fill the gap between the two approaches in order to cope with different text types. This is particularly important for the SW, as Web pages can contain documents of any type and even a mix of text types, e.g., they can contain both free, semi-structured and structured texts at the same time (see Figure 1 for an example). Even methodologies that require the selection of alternative grammars or methodologies for specific texts types (e.g. [11, 26]) are not suitable when a mixture of texts types is present, because the type mixture would rather

Figure 1: The cnn.com page as example of mixed text types page

require mixing such grammars, rather than selecting one of them; non-IE experts simply cannot merge grammars. The IE methodology for the SW must be adaptive also in this sense, of being able to recognise what linguistic resources are useful for analysing a specific context, sometimes even a context local to specific information: e.g. if a piece of information is in a table, a deep linguistic method relying on a parser's results is unlikely to be effective, but when the information is in a free text zone, the same method is likely to work). To our knowledge none of the classic IE methods is adaptive in this sense, but we believe that this is a main requirement for the application for the SW.

In this paper we present Amilcare, an adaptive IE system designed as support to document annotation in the SW framework. It is based on an adaptive methodology that meets most of the requirements mentioned above and in particular:(1) portability by a wide range of users, from naive users to IE experts; (2) ability to cope with different types of texts (including mixed ones); (3) possibility to be inserted in the usual user annotation environment providing minimum disruption to usual annotation activities; (4)portability with reduced number of texts. In this paper we describe Amilcare, the learning algorithm, the details of the human-system interaction. Finally we describe a number of experiments that show its effectiveness and its usability.

2 Amilcare

Amilcare is an adaptive IE system, i.e. it uses machine learning to adapt to new applications/domains. It is rule based, i.e. its learning algorithm induces rules that extract information. Rules are learnt by generalising over a set of examples found in a training corpus annotated with XML tags. The system learns how to reproduce such annotation via Information Extraction. Amilcare is based on the $(LP)^2$ algorithm [4], a supervised algorithm that falls into a class of Wrapper Induction Systems (WIS) using LazyNLP [6]. Unlike other WIS

[22, 25, 15, 16], LazyNLP WIS use linguistic information. They try to learn the best (most reliable) level of language analysis useful (or effective) for a specific IE task by mixing deep linguistic and shallow strategies. The learner starts inducing rules that make no use of linguistic information, like in classic wrapper-like systems. Then it progressively adds linguistic information to its rules, stopping when the use of linguistic information becomes unreliable or ineffective. Linguistic information is provided by generic NLP modules and resources defined once for all and not to be modified by users to specific application needs. Pragmatically, the measure of reliability here is not linguistic correctness (immeasurable by incompetent users), but effectiveness in extracting information using linguistic information as opposed to using shallower approaches. Unlike previous approaches where different algorithm versions with different linguistic competence are tested in parallel and the most effective is chosen [26], lazy NLP-based learners learn which is the best strategy for each information/context separately. For example they may decide that using parsing is the best strategy for recognising the speaker in a specific application on seminar announcements, but not the best strategy to spot the seminar location or starting time. This has shown to be very effective for analysing documents with mixed genres, e.g. web pages containing both structured and unstructured material, quite a common situation in web documents [8].

Amilcare can work in three modes: training mode, test mode and production mode. The **training mode** is used to induce rules, so to learn how to perform IE in a specific application scenario. Input in training mode is: (1)a scenario (e.g. an ontology in the SW); (2) a training corpus annotated with the information to be extracted. Output of the training phase is a set of rules able to reproduce annotation on texts of the same type. The **testing mode** is used to test the induced rules on an unseen tagged corpus, so to understand how well it performs for a specific application. When running in test mode Amilcare first of all removes all the annotations from the corpus, then re-annotates the corpus using the induced rules. Finally the results are automatically compared with the original annotations and the results are presented to the user. Output of the test phase is: (1) the corpus reannotated by the system; (2) a set of accuracy statistics on the test corpus: recall, precision and details on the mistakes the system does. Amilcare uses an internal scorer, but it is also compatible with some standard scorers such as the MUC scorer [13]. During testing it is possible to decide to retrain the learner with different system parameters in order to tune its accuracy (e.g. to obtain more recall and/or more precision). Tuning takes a fraction of time with respect to training. The **production mode** is used when an application is released. Amilcare annotates the provided documents. If a user is available to revise its results, the learner uses the user corrections to retrain. The training/test/production modes can actually be interleaved so to produce an active learning based annotation. In active learning [2] user annotation and system annotation are interleaved in order to minimize the amount of user annotation. As we will see in the following this greatly reduces the burden of document annotation.

Amilcare's default architecture includes the connection with Annie, Gate's shallow IE system [11] which performs tokenization, part of speech tagging, gazetteer lookup and named entity recognition. Any other preprocessor can be connected via the API. The preprocessor is also the only language-dependent module, the rest of the system being language independent (experiments where performed in English and Italian).

Condition	Additional Knowledge				Action
Word	Lemma	LexCat	Case	SemCat	Tag
the	the	det	low		
seminar	seminar	noun	low		
at	at	prep	low		
4		digit	low		<time>
pm		noun	low	timeid	
will	will	verb	low		

Figure 2: A tagging rule

2.1 *The learning algorithm*

$(LP)^2$ induces two types of symbolic rules in two steps: (1) rules that insert annotations in the texts; (2) rules that correct mistakes and imprecision in the annotations provided by (1). Rules are learnt by generalising over a set of examples marked via XML tags in a training corpus. A **tagging rule** is composed of a left hand side, containing a pattern of conditions on a connected sequence of words, and a right hand side that is an action inserting an XML tag in the texts. Each rule inserts a single tag, e.g. </speaker>. As positive examples the rule induction algorithm uses XML annotations in a training corpus. The rest of the corpus is considered a pool of negative examples. For each positive example the algorithm: (1) builds an initial rule, (2) generalizes the rule and (3) keeps the k best generalizations of the initial rule. In particular $(LP)^2$'s main loop starts by selecting a tag in the training corpus and extracts from the text a window of *w* words to the left and *w* words to the right. Each piece of information stored in the *2*w* word window is transformed into a condition in the initial rule pattern, e.g. if the third word is "seminar", a condition word3="seminar" is created. Each initial rule is then generalised (see subsections 2.1.1) and the k best generalisations are kept: retained rules become part of the best rules pool. When a rule enters such pool, all the instances covered by the rule are removed from the positive examples pool, i.e. they will no longer be used for rule induction ($(LP)^2$ is a sequential covering algorithm). Rule induction continues by selecting new instances and learning rules until the pool of positive examples is empty. Some tagging rules (contextual rules) use tags inserted by other rules. For example some rules will be used to close annotations, i.e. they will use the presence of a <speaker> to insert a missing </speaker>. In conclusion the tagging rule set is composed of both the best rule pool and the contextual rules. Tagging rules when applied on the corpus may report some imprecision in slot filler boundary detection. A typical mistake is for example `"at <time> 4 </time> pm"`, where `"pm"` should have been part of the time expression. $(LP)^2$ induces rules for shifting wrongly positioned tags to the correct position. It learns from the mistakes made in tagging the training corpus. Correction rules are identical to tagging rules, but (1) their patterns match also the tags inserted by the tagging rules and (2) their actions shift misplaced tags rather than adding new ones. The induction algorithm used for the best tagging rules is also used for shift rules: initial instance identification, generalisation, test and selection. Shift rules are accepted only if they report an acceptable error rate.

In the testing phase, information is extracted from the test corpus in four steps: initial tagging, contextual tagging, correction and validation. The best rule pool is initially used to

Condition					Action
Word	Lemma	LexCat	Case	SemCat	Tag
	at				
		digit			<time>
				timeid	

Figure 3: A generalised tagging rule

tag the texts. Then contextual rules are applied in a loop until no new tags are inserted, i.e. some contextual rules can match also tags inserted by other contextual rules. Then correction rules correct imprecision. Finally each tag inserted by the algorithm is validated. In many cases there is no meaning in producing a start tag (e.g. <speaker>) without its corresponding closing tag (</speaker>) and vice versa, therefore uncoupled tags are removed.

2.1.1 Rule Generalization

The initial rule pattern matches conditions on word strings as found in a window around each instance. This type of rules is the typical type of rules wrapper induction systems produce. We have previously shown [6] that these types of rules are suitable for highly structured texts, but quite ineffective on free texts, because of data sparseness implied by the high flexibility of natural language forms. It is therefore important to generalise over the plain word surface of the training example. The initial rule pattern is integrated with additional conditions on the results of the linguistic preprocessor. This means that conditions are set not only on the strings (word="companies"), but also on its lemma ("company"), its lexical category ("noun"), case information ("lowercase"), a list of user defined classes from a user-defined dictionary or a gazetteer and annotations by a named entity recogniser. Figure 2 summarizes the new form of the initial rule. The initial rule effectiveness is compared against a set of more general rules obtained through a general to specific beam search that starts modelling the annotation instance with the most general rule (the empty rule matching everything in the corpus) and specialises it by greedily adding constraints. Constraints are added by incrementing the length of the rule pattern, i.e. by adding conditions on terms (matching strings or part of the knowledge provided by the linguistic preprocessor). The specialization process stops when the generated rules have reached a satisfying accuracy and coverage and any further specialization does not improve precision. In this way the rules that incorporate different levels of linguistic knowledge (from deep linguistic to word matching) are put in direct competition and just the best combination of *k* rules survive. Figure 3 shows a possible generalization of the rule in figure 2. The choice of the level of linguistic knowledge is local to the specific instance we are trying to model (local constraints, e.g. the information is located in a table), but it also depends on the ability to generalize to cover other instances (global constraints, e.g. it is a noun followed by a capitalised word). For this reason the approach satisfies the requirement of coping with different types of texts including mixed types, because it is able to model different parts of texts in which different information is located using different (linguistic) strategies. Details of the algorithm can be found in [6].

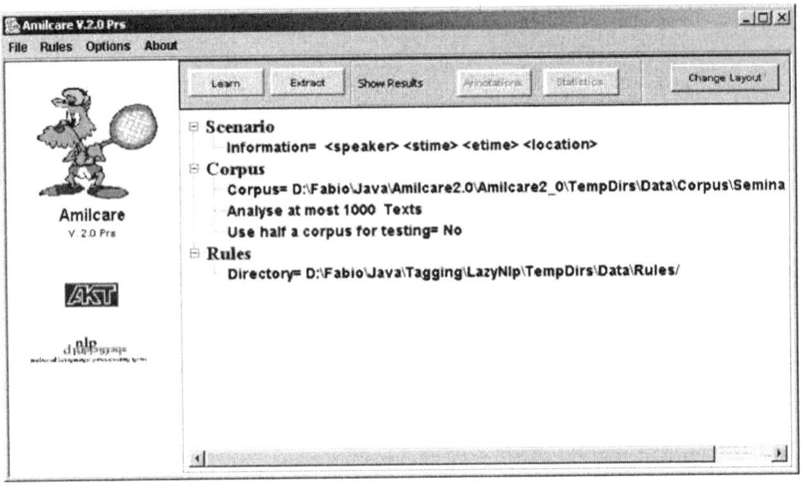

Figure 4: The interface for naive users

3 Different Views for Different Users

Amilcare provides different user types with different interaction methodologies so to exploit the knowledge of the user at hand to a maximum extent. In our experience in delivering adaptive IE systems we discovered that simplifying porting is not the main issue for the success of IE: it is necessary to enable different users with different capabilities to produce applications, whose complexity may be proportional to their knowledge of IE [8]. For this reason while Amilcare's naive users are just required to provide an annotated corpus and a list of tags (or ontology), IE experts can actually contribute to the IE grammars development. In this section we discuss the interaction methodology for three different user types: naive users, Amilcare experts and IE experts. Section 4.1 will actually discuss how Amilcare can be inserted in an existing annotation environment.

3.1 The Naive User's View

A naive (from the IE point of view) user will have knowledge of the domain, understand the texts, know where to extract information and will be able to provide XML tagged texts. XML tagged texts can be provided with a range of tools, from Alembic [12], to Melita [7], to MnM [27] or Ontomat [18]. Such tools provide intuitive interfaces that allow to annotate, ignoring the complexity of XML syntax. Amilcare can be trained on an annotated training corpus by using the interface shown in figure 4. The user is required to declare:

- the ontology used: this is a flat list of tags for many users (and in the example);
- the corpus to train on;
- the number of texts to be analysed within the corpus;
- the directory where the induced rules will be stored.

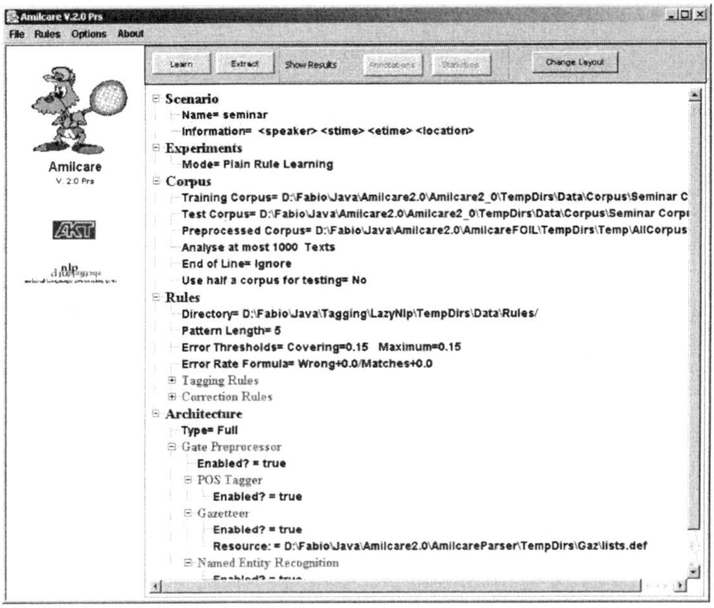

Figure 5: The Interface for the expert developer allowing deep control over the system

Then Amilcare is ready for learning. Simply pressing the "Learn Rules" button starts the process. When learning is over, it is possible (and generally advisable) to test the system effectiveness on a set of unseen annotated texts before delivering the application. In the same interface, just indicate the test corpus and click "Apply Rules". It is then possible to inspect the IE effectiveness on the test corpus in two ways: (1) "Show Results" allows to visually inspect the texts as annotated by the system, see Figure 6; (2) "Show Statistics" shows the effectiveness of the extraction process expressed using the usual IE metrics: number of original user annotations (Possible), number of annotation actually produced by the system (Actual), number of correct/wrong system annotations, number of missed annotations, number of partially correct annotations (i.e. overlapping with the user annotation, but not precise). Finally precision, recall and f-measure are provided. It is also possible to inspect the list of all the correct, wrong, partial and missed matches in lists that compare each system annotation with the corresponding user annotation. If the results are satisfying, the application can be delivered. If it is not, the most obvious action is to increase the size of the training corpus. Defining an application in this way is quite simple and any user able to annotate texts is able also to define an IE application with a very limited ad hoc training. It is also generally possible to obtain good applications in this way.

3.2 *The Amilcare Expert View*

An intermediate user figure between the IE expert and the completely naive user is the Amilcare expert, i.e. a user not able to delve into the complexity of IE (e.g. developing rules), but able to optimise Amilcare's results with respect to the application needs, for example by

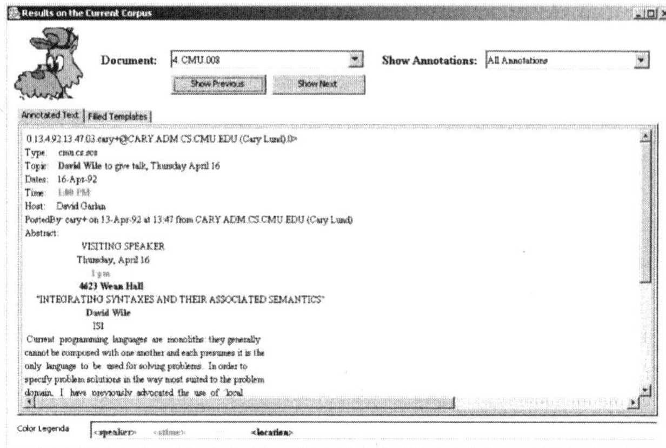

Figure 6: Results presentation of system's annotation for a text

better controlling the experimental process. In this case it is possible to influence a number of system parameters by tuning some knobs (see Figure 5). For example it is possible to adjust: (1) the precision recall balance; (2) the rule pattern length (the longer the rule pattern, the better the effectiveness but the longer the training time); (3) the minimum rule selection conditions (error threshold and minimum number of matches), influencing therefore the global accuracy. The effect of changing values of such parameters can be learned by performing a number of trials. No IE knowledge is necessary, just detailed knowledge of the system behaviour and knowledge of how to perform experiments is required. The quality of the application produced by the Amilcare expert is generally better than the one produced by the naive user as it is better optimised. Note that the transition from naive to Amilcare expert can be done gradually by learning how to turn some knobs or to better organise the experiment, leaving the rest of the parameters untouched. For this reason it is possible to satisfy a range of users rather than just two types. The Amilcare's expert is the more likely user type expected in real world applications.

3.3 The IE Expert's View

Experience has shown that IE experts, when available, suffer if they are not enabled to contribute to the application development in an active way [8]. For this reason Amilcare provides a number of tools for IE experts. It provides two modes for application development: system driven and user driven. In system-driven development users provide Amilcare with a training corpus to train on. Then users can inspect the induced rules and revise them (see Figure 7). It is possible to inspect all the developed rules and their (1) coverage on the corpus: correct matches (places where the rule provides the same annotation the user provided) and wrong matches (spurious annotations or misplaced annotations) are shown; (2) error rate (approximately wrong matches divided by number of matches); (3) total number of matches on the corpus. It is then possible to modify, delete or copy rules. The rule editor (Figure 8), supports editing by providing menus of possible fillers for different conditions, information on matches (correct and wrong) of the rule under development, etc. The other possibility is to develop

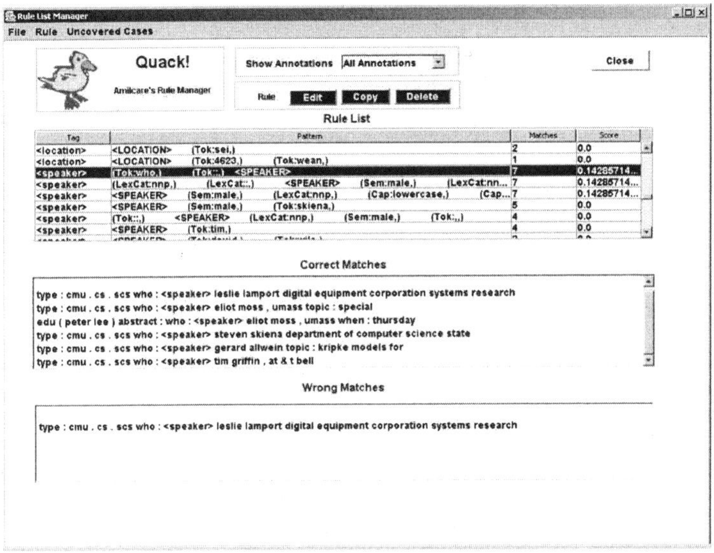

Figure 7: The Rule Manager enables the IE expert to inspect the grammar rules and their coverage

rules in a user-driven fashion. It is possible (1) to use the above mentioned strategy and editor and develop rules starting from scratch, then asking Amilcare to integrate/revise the manually developed rules by learning from the annotated corpus, (2) to use the Jape development environment included in Gate [11] to develop rules and then ask Amilcare to eventually integrate the rules. The Jape's and Amilcare rules are not compatible, but in this case Amilcare's rules will be applied afterwards and will correct/integrate the Jape rules results. The quality of the application developed by IE experts can be very high. The simple rule correction can considerably increase accuracy and reduce the need for a representative annotated corpus.

4 Amilcare as Support to Annotation

Amilcare can be used as active support to annotation for the SW. Different strategies can be used for integrating Amilcare with an Annotation Tool (AT). What we have seen so far is a batch mode, where Amilcare is controlled as a separate process via its own interface: it receives an annotated corpus in input and induces a set of rules, or it receives a corpus in input and returns a set of annotations (for rule testing/application). This is the most straightforward integration methodology. A more sophisticated integration can be obtained via the API, which allows full control on the system. It is possible to organise a batch interaction mode where users just interact with the AT, not with the IE system. To some extent the user could even ignore the presence of Amilcare behind the scenes. This is better organisation because the AT provides more suitable use(r)-specific interaction methodologies, being designed with a specific application in mind. Here the user annotates a batch of documents and the IE tool is trained on the whole batch. Then annotation is started on another batch and the IE system passes annotations to the interface which in turn proposes them to the annotating users. This is how Amilcare was integrated in MnM [27] and ONTOMAT [17]. In this section we will

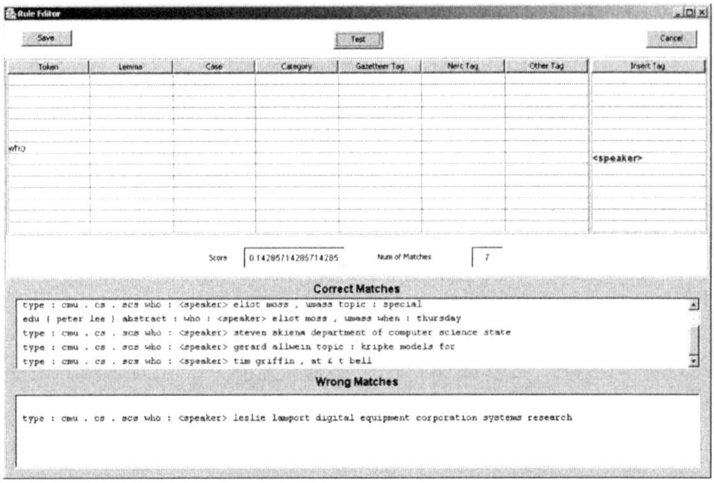

Figure 8: The Rule Editor allows to modify rules. It provides menus of possible fi llers for the different fi elds, information on matches (correct and wrong) of the rule under development

present a more sophisticated strategy as it was implemented in Melita [7]. It allows to better exploit the potentialities of the IE technology.

4.1 Towards Sophisticated IE-based Annotation

The goal of the interaction between AT and IE system is both maximizing effectiveness of the annotation process and minimizing the burden of annotating/correcting on the user's sides. In the ideal initial scenario a user environment with a manual AT is already existent. The goal is to silently insert the IE-based support to annotation without asking the user to change his/her way of working. There are two main features of the interaction between users, AT and IE System (IES) that are considered: timeliness and intrusiveness. The first shows the ability to react to user annotation: how timely is the system to learn from user annotations. The latter represents the level to which the system bothers the user, because for example it requires CPU time (and therefore stops the user annotation activity) or because it suggests wrong annotations. The annotation process is split into two main phases from the IES point of view: (1) training and (2) active annotation with revision. In user terms the first corresponds to unassisted annotation, while the latter mainly requires correction of annotations proposed by the AT (upon suggestion from the IES). During *training*, users annotate texts without any contribution from the IES which is mainly using the user annotations to train its learner. We can define two subphases: (a) bootstrapping and (b) training with verification. During bootstrapping the only IES task is to learn from user annotations. This sub-phase ends when the system has induced a minimum set of rules. During the second sub-phase, the user continues with the unassisted annotation, but the IES behaviour changes, as it uses its rules to silently compete with the user in annotating the documents. The IES automatically compares its annotations with those inserted by the user and calculates its accuracy. Missing annotations or mistakes are used to retrain the learner. The training phase ends when the IES accuracy reaches the user preferred level of accuracy (as declared by a user profile [7]). It is therefore possible to move to the next phase: active annotation. The active annotation with revision phase is heavily based on the IES suggestions and the user's main task is correcting and integrating suggested annotations (i.e. removing and adding annotations). Human actions are inputted back to the IES for retraining. This is the phase where the real system-user cooperation takes place: the system helps users in annotating; users feed back mistakes to help the system perform better. In user terms this is where the added value of the IES becomes apparent, because it heavily reduces the amount of annotation to insert manually. This supervision task is much more convenient from both cognition and actions. Correcting annotations is simpler than annotating bare texts, it is less time consuming and it is also likely to be less error prone.

The design of the interaction model aims to limit intrusiveness of the IES in a number of ways. First of all the IES does not require any specific AT or any specific adaptation by the user. It integrates in the usual user environment and provides suggestions through the AT in a way that is both familiar and intuitive to users. Secondly intrusiveness as a side effect of proactivity is coped with, especially during active annotation with revision, when the IES can bother users with unreliable annotations. The requirement here is to enable users to tune the IES behaviour so that the level of suggestions is appropriate. Notice that the acceptable level of intrusiveness is subjective: some users might like to receive suggestions largely regardless from their correctness, while others do not want to be bothered unless suggestions are absolutely reliable. Amilcare's internal "knob" tuning methods (e.g. to balance precision and recall) are too complex for most users, as they are designed for experts. In Melita the AT bridges the qualitative vision of users (e.g. a request to be more/less active or accurate) with the specific IES settings (e.g. change error thresholds), as also suggested in [10]. This is important because as mentioned the AT is designed for specific user classes and therefore able to elicit tuning requirements with the correct terminology for the specific context. Finally the IES training requires CPU time and this can slow down or even stop the user activity. For this reason most of the current systems use a batch mode of training so to limit training to specific moments (e.g. coffee time). In Melita background learning provides timely support without intrusiveness. The IES works in the background with two parallel and asynchronous processes. While the user annotates document n+1 the system learns the annotations inserted in document n (i.e. the last annotated). At the same time (i.e. as a separate process) the IES applies the rules induced in the previous learning sessions (i.e. from document 1 to document n-1) in order to annotate document n+1 (either for suggesting annotations during active annotation or in order to silently test its accuracy during unassisted learning). The advantage is that there is no idle time for users, as the manual annotation of a document generally requires a great deal more time than training on a single text and in any case the background learning can be performed by a low priority process. Timeliness is not fully obtained with the above interaction methodology: the IES annotation capability always refers to rules learned by using the entire annotated corpus but the last document. This means that the IES is not able to help when two similar documents are annotated in sequence. From the user point of view such a situation is equivalent to train on batches of two texts. In this respect the collaboration between the system and the user fails in being effective. We believe that timeliness is a matter of perception from the user side, not an absolute feature; therefore the only important matter is that users perceive it. When the order of document annotation is unimportant, it is possible to organize annotation so to avoid presenting similar documents in sequence (and hence hiding the small lack of timeliness). Melita uses a simple measure of similarity among texts: it runs Amilcare on the unannotated corpus; inserted annotations mean similarity of texts with respect to the part of the corpus annotated so far, no inserted annotation means actual difference. Such information is used to make timeliness more effective: a completely uncovered document is always followed by a fairly covered document. In this way difference between successive documents is very likely and therefore the probability that similar documents are presented within the batch of two (i.e. the system's blindness window) is very low. Incidentally this strategy also tackles another major problem in annotation, i.e. user boredom, which can make user productivity and effectiveness fall proportional to time. Presenting users with radically different documents avoids the boredom that comes from coping with very similar documents in sequence.

5 Evaluating IE's contribution

We performed a number of experiments for demonstrating how fast the IES can converge to an active annotation status and to quantify its contribution to the annotation task, i.e. its ability to suggest correctly. We selected the CMU seminar announcements corpus, where 483 emails are manually annotated with speaker, starting time, ending time and location of seminars, [14]. Such corpus was already used for evaluating a number of adaptive algorithms, [14, 2, 16, 15, 4]. In our experiment the annotation in the corpus was used to simulate human annotation. We have evaluated the potential contribution of the IE system at regular intervals during corpus tagging, i.e. after the annotation of 5, 10, 20, 25, 30, 50, 62, 75, 100 and 150 documents (each subset fully including the previous one). Each time we tested the annotation accuracy on the following 200 texts in the corpus (so when training on 25 texts, the test was performed also on the following 25 texts that will be used for training on 50). The ability to suggest on the test corpus was measured in terms of precision and recall. Recall represents here an approximation of the probability that the user receives a suggestion in tagging a new document. Precision represents the probability that such suggestion is correct. The maximum gain comes in annotating stime and etime. This is not surprising as they present quite regular fillers. After training on only 20 texts, the system is potentially able to propose 368 stimes (out of 491), 303 are correct, 18 partially correct, 47 wrong, leading to Precision=84 Recall=61 (see Table 5). With 30 texts the recognition reaches P=91, R=78, with 50 P=92, R=80. The situation is very similar for etime, while it is more complex for speaker and location, where recall grows slowly: after 75 texts the system reaches P=96, R=60 on location and P=90, R=50 on speaker. This is due to the fact that locations and speakers are much more difficult to learn than time expressions because they are much less regular. We performed the same type of analysis on other corpora such as the Austin TX Jobs announcement corpus [2] and found similar results. Our experiments show that the contribution of the IES can be quite high. Reliable annotation can be obtained with limited training, especially when adopting high precision IES configurations. In the case of the CMU corpus, our experiments show that it is possible to move from bootstrapping to active annotation after annotating some dozens of texts. This shows that the IES contribution heavily reduces the burden of manual annotation and that such reduction is particularly relevant and immediate in case of quite regular information (e.g., time expressions). In user terms this means that it is possible to focus the activity on annotating more complex pieces of information (e.g. speaker), avoiding to be bothered with repetitive ones (such as stime). With some more training cases the IES is also able to contribute in annotating more complex cases.

Tag	Amount of Texts needed for Training	Precision	Recall
etime	20	96	72
stime	30	91	78
location	30	82	61
speaker	25	91	35

Table 1: Support to annotation after training on some dozens of texts

6 Conclusion and Future Work

In this paper we have presented Amilcare, an adaptive IE system that is specifically designed to provide annotation for the SW. We believe that Amilcare is particularly well suited for the use in the SW because it enable even naive users to rapidly develop an IE-based support to annotation for specific SW services. This meets the requirements stated in the introduction for the use in a very dynamic SW scenario in which a great number of small ontological components and services are continuously developed and therefore the need for new (or improved) services to support annotation is constant. This will enable SW actors to develop (or extend/change) their existing services without requiring the constant presence of IE experts. We have also shown that the IE contribution to annotation can be quite high even with a limited number of training cases, relieving users from the burden of most of the annotation (even that used to actually train the IES!) since the very beginning. We believe that these results will help diffusing the use of IE for the SW: to date Amilcare has been released to a number of both academic and commercial institutions as support to either IE or annotation and it has been integrated in both ONTOMAT and MnM.

Two main issues are left for future work: the actual support to annotation (IE effectiveness) and the actual Amilcare's expressiveness. It is well known that IE systems reach 100% accuracy only in very simple cases. For this reason we definitely need to provide semi-automatic annotation services in which users producing SW documents are responsible to revise the IE suggestions. If the goal is to provide support for annotation for naive SW users (e.g. pet shop owners in [19]), imprecision could be missed in the revision process, greatly undermining the quality of annotation. At the present there is no solution other than continuing working on IE models to improve effectiveness. On the other hand the only alternative solution to IE is manual annotation: we believe that revising annotation is far easier than annotating from scratch, so the benefit of using IE is still there. Moreover the IE suggestions can be used to implicitly suggest users with a kind of standardisation of annotations (i.e. it is equivalent to another user suggesting); this is a proven way for helping in human annotation accuracy, used in many scientific exercises.

The second issue concerns Amilcare's expressiveness. There is no doubt that Amilcare is much more limited than full IE systems such as [20, 1]. For example it is able to spot information, but not to relate it (e.g. solving coreferences). This is because the goal was to provide a system very easy to use and port in the first instance. This can be a limitation in some applications [17]. We are currently working on a new version of Amilcare performing full IE. The main problem is not implementing a full IE system, but in making it usable by naive users: Amilcare is already inserted in Annie, therefore a methodology for a FASTUS-like approach [1] to IE is potentially available. Our goal is to enable also naive users to develop full IE applications and this implies further studies on and new models of user-system interactions.

Acknowledgements

This work was carried out within the AKT project (http://www.aktors.org), sponsored by the UK Engineering and Physical Sciences Research Council (grant GR/N15764/01). AKT involves the Universities of Aberdeen, Edinburgh, Sheffield, Southampton and the Open University. Its objectives are to develop advanced technologies for knowledge management. Melita was designed together with Alexiei Dingli, Daniela Petrelli and Yorick Wilks and was implemented by Alexiei. Thanks to Enrico Motta, Mattia Lanzoni, John Domingue (Open University), Steffen Staab, Siegfried Handschuh and Guylaine Guimfacq (University of Karlsruhe) for a number of useful discussions during the integration of Amilcare into MnM and Ontomat.

References

[1] APPELT, D., HOBBS, J., BEAR, J., ISRAEL, D., AND TYSON", M. 'FASTUS: A fi nite-state processor for information extraction from real-world text". *"Proceedings of the Thirteenth International Joint Conference on Artificial Intelligence (IJCAI-93)"* ("1993'), "1172–1178".

[2] CALIFF, M., AND MOONEY, R. Relational learning of pattern-match rules for information extraction. *Working Papers of the ACL-97 Workshop in Natural Language Learning* (1997), 9–15.

[3] CARDIE, C. Empirical methods in information extraction. *AI Journal 18*, 4 (1997), 65–79.

[4] CIRAVEGNA, F. Adaptive information extraction from text by rule induction and generalisation. In *Proceedings of 17th International Joint Conference on Artificial Intelligence (IJCAI)* (2001). Seattle.

[5] CIRAVEGNA, F. Challenges in information extraction from text for knowledge management. *IEEE Intelligent Systems and Their Applications 27* (2001), 97–111. November.

[6] CIRAVEGNA, F. $(LP)^2$, an adaptive algorithm for information extraction from web-related texts. In *Proceedings of the IJCAI-2001 Workshop on Adaptive Text Extraction and Mining held in conjunction with the 17th International Joint Conference on Artificial Intelligence* (2001). Seattle, http://www.smi.ucd.ie/ATEM2001/.

[7] CIRAVEGNA, F., DINGLI, A., PETRELLI, D., AND WILKS, Y. User-system cooperation in document annotation based on information extraction. In *Proceedings of the 13th International Conference on Knowledge Engineering and Knowledge Management, EKAW02* (2002), Springer Verlag.

[8] CIRAVEGNA, F., AND LAVELLI, A. Learningpinocchio: Adaptive information extraction for real world applications. In *Proceedings of 3rd Romand Workshop* (July 2001). Frascati, Italy.

[9] CIRAVEGNA, F., LAVELLI, A., AND SATTA, G. Bringing information extraction out of the labs: the pinocchio environment. In *Proceedings of the 14th European Conference on Artificial Intelligence* (2000), IOS Press. Berlin.

[10] CIRAVEGNA, F., AND PETRELLI, D. User involvement in adaptive information extraction: Position paper. In *Proceedings of the IJCAI-2001 Workshop on Adaptive Text Extraction and Mining held in conjunction with the 17th International Joint Conference on Artificial Intelligence* (2001). Seattle, http://www.smi.ucd.ie/ATEM2001/.

[11] CUNNINGHAM, H., MAYNARD, D., TABLAN, V., URSU, C., AND BONTCHEVA, K. "developing language processing components with GATE", 2002. www.gate.ac.uk.

[12] DAY, D., ABERDEEN, J., HIRSCHMAN, L., KOZIEROK, R., ROBINSON, P., AND VILAIN, M. Mixed-initiative development of language processing systems. In *Proceedings of the Fifth Conference on Applied Natural Language Processing* (1997).

[13] DOUTHAT, A. The message understanding conference scoring software user's manual. In *Proceedings of the 7th Message Understanding Conference* (1998). *www.itl.nist.gov/iaui/894.02/related$_p$rojects/muc/*.

[14] FREITAG, D. Multistrategy learning for information extraction. *Proceedings of ICML-98* (1998).

[15] FREITAG, D., AND KUSHMERICK, N. Boosted wrapper induction. In *ECAI2000 Workshop on Machine Learning for Information Extraction* (2000), R. Basili, F. Ciravegna, and R. Gaizauskas, Eds. www.dcs.shef.ac.uk/ fabio/ecai-workshop.html.

[16] FREITAG, D., AND MCCALLUM, A. Information extraction with hmms and shrinkage. In *AAAI-99 Workshop on Machine Learning for Information Extraction* (1999).

[17] HANDSCHUH, S., STAAB, S., AND CIRAVEGNA, F. S-CREAM - Semi-automatic CREAtion of Metadata. In *Proceedings of the 13th International Conference on Knowledge Engineering and Knowledge Management, EKAW02* (2002), Springer Verlag.

[18] HANDSCHUH, S., STAAB, S., AND MAEDCHE, A. CREAM — Creating relational metadata with a component-based, ontology driven framework. In *In Proceedings of K-Cap 2001* (Victoria, BC, Canada, October 2001).

[19] HENDLER, J. Agents and the semantic web. *IEEE Intelligent Systems Journal 16*, 2 (2001), 30–37.

[20] HUMPHREYS, K., GAIZAUSKAS, R., AZZAM, S., HUYCK, C., MITCHELL, B., CUNNINGHAM, H., AND WILKS, Y. Description of the university of sheffi eld lasie-ii system as used for MUC-7. In *Proceedings of the 7th Message Understanding Conference* (1998). *www.itl.nist.gov/iaui/894.02/related$_p$rojects/muc/*.

[21] KOGUT, P., AND HOLMES, W. Applying information extraction to generate daml annotations from web pages. In *Proceedings of the K-CAP 2001 Workshop Knowledge Markup & Semantic Annotation* (2001). Victoria B.C., Canada.

[22] KUSHMERICK, N., WELD, D., AND DOORENBOS, R. Wrapper induction for information extraction. In *Proceedings of the International Joint Conference on Artificial Intelligence (IJCAI), 1997.* (1997).

[23] MILLER, S., CRYSTAL, M., FOX, H., RAMSHAW, L., SCHWARTZ, R., STONE, R., AND WEISCHEDEL, R. Bbn: Description of the sift system as used for MUC7. In *Proceedings of the 7th Message Understanding Conference* (1998). *www.itl.nist.gov/iaui/894.02/related$_p$rojects/muc/*.

[24] MUC7. *Proceedings of the 7th Message Understanding Conference (MUC7).* Nist, 1998. *www.itl.nist.gov/iaui/894.02/related$_p$rojects/muc/*.

[25] MUSLEA, I., MINTON, S., AND KNOBLOCK, C. Wrapper induction for semistructured web-based information sources. In *Proceedings of the Conference on Automated Learning and Discovery (CONALD), 1998.* (1998).

[26] SODERLAND, S. Learning information extraction rules for semi-structured and free text. *Machine Learning 34*, 1 (1999), 233–272.

[27] VARGAS-VERA, M., MOTTA, E., DOMINGUE, J., LANZONI, M., STUTT, A., AND CIRAVEGNA, F. MnM: Ontology driven semi-automatic or automatic support for semantic markup. In *Proceedings of the 13th International Conference on Knowledge Engineering and Knowledge Management, EKAW02* (2002), Springer Verlag.

Annotation for the Semantic Web
S. Handschuh and S. Staab (Eds.)
IOS Press, 2003

Content-based Indexing and Searching of Multimedia Documents

Thierry Declerck † Jan Kuper ‡ Horacio Saggion Ł Anna Samiotou § and Peter Wittenburg ¶
DFKI GmbH, Language Technology Department †
Stuhlsatzenhausweg 3, D-66123 Saarbruecken, Germany
Department of Computer Science, University of Twente ‡
PO Box 217, 7500 AE Enschede, The Netherlands
Department of Computer Science, University Sheffield Ł
Regent Court, 211 Portobello St., Sheffield S1 4DP, UK
ESTeam AB §
Sikelianou 8-10, 146 71 Athens, Greece
Max Planck Institute for Psycholinguistics ¶
Wundtlaan 1, PB 310, 6500 AH Nijmegen, The Netherlands

Abstract. This chapter describes the role *natural language processing* (NLP) can play for multimedia applications. As an example of such an application, we present an approach dealing with the automatic conceptual indexing of multimedia documents which can then be searched by semantic categories instead of key words. This work has been investigated and developed in the EU funded project MUMIS. A novelty of the approach is to exploit multiple sources of information relating to video content (for example the rich range of textual and transcribed sources covering soccer games).

1 Introduction

This chapter describes the role *natural language processing* (NLP) can play in the automatic conceptual indexing of multimedia documents which can then be searched by semantic categories instead of key words. This topic was a key issue in the MUMIS project[1]. A novelty of the approach developed in MUMIS is to exploit multiple sources of information relating to video content (for example the rich range of textual and transcribed sources covering soccer games).

In the first part of the paper (section 2) we will propose a general discussion on the role that can be played by NLP for multimedia application. This overview is widely based on [2] and [3]. In the rest of of the paper we will exemplify the general topic with the detailed presentation of the MUMIS project that is concerned with the topic of multimedia indexing and searching, where we will also reserve a large part to the description of methods in use in IE. The presentation of this project is an extension and update of [11].

[1]MUMIS is a project within the Information Society Program (IST) of the European Union, section Human Language Technology (HLT). See for more information http://parlevink.cs.utwente.nl/projects/mumis/.

2 The Role of NLP for Multimedia Applications

[2] and [3] give an overview of the role that can be played by NLP in multimodal and multimedia systems. We summarize here the central points of those studies.

2.1 Multimodal and multimedia systems

The terms *multimedia* and *multimodal* are often source of confusion. [2] adopts the definitions as proposed in [23], which establishes a distinction between the terms *medium*, *mode* and *code*. The term *mode* (or *modality*) refers to the type of perception concerned, being for example visual, auditory or olfactory perception. The term *medium* refers to the carrier of (CD-ROM, paper etc.), to the devices (microphone, screen, loudspeakers etc.), as well to the distinct types of information (texts, audio or video sequences). The term *code* refers to the particular means of encoding information (sign languages or pictorial languages). One can speak of a multimedia system if this allows to *generate* and/or to *analyse* multimedia/multimodal information or provide some *access* to archives of multiple media. In existing applications, often the process of analysis applies only to multimodal data, whereas generation is concerned with the production of multimedia information.

2.2 Integration of modalities

We speak in the case of analysis of a process of *integration of modalities*, since all the available modalities need to be merged at a more abstract level in order to take the maximal advantage of every modality involved in the application. Certain representation formalisms, as they have been defined in the context of advanced NLP (see for example [22]), can play a central role in this process of fusion. So the well-defined technique of *unification* of typed feature structures, combined with a chart parser, is used in a system described in [18]. Using this formalism allows to build a semantic representation that is common to all modalities involved in the application, unifying all the particular semantic contributions on the base of their representation in typed feature structures

2.3 Media Coordination

In the case of the *generation* of multimedia material including natural language, for the purpose of *multimedia presentation*, one can speak of a process of *media coordination*: it is not enough to merge various media in order to obtain a coherent presentation of the distinct media involved. The information contained in the various media has to be very carefully put into relation if one wants to obtain real complementarities of media in the final presentation of the global information. And since systems for *natural language generation* have been always confronted with this problem of selecting and organising various contributions for the generation of an utterance, they can provide for a very valuable model for the coordination of media in the context of the generation of multimedia presentations. A lot of systems for natural language generation are therefore said to be *plan-based*.

Essentially two concepts from the field of automatic natural language generation are playing a role in systems for multimedia presentation: the concept of *schema* (see [24]) and the concept of *operator* (see [28]). The first concept describes a set of standard patterns of natural language discourse by means of predicates that indicate relationships between some parts of the presentation. The second concept deals more specially with the particular contributions of the distinct parts of the presentation and allows local revisions during the process of generation of the presentation.

2.4 Natural Language access to multimedia

Multimedia repositories of moving images, texts, and speech are becoming increasingly available. This together with the needs for 'video-on-deman' systems require fine-grain indexing and retrieval mechanisms allowing users access to specific segments of the repositories containing specific types of information.

It turns out that natural language can play a multiple role. It is first easier to access information contained in the multimedia archive using queries addressed to (transcript of) audio sequences or to the subtitles (if available) associated to the videos as to analyse the pictures themselves. It is further more appealing to access visual data by means of natural language, since the latter supports more flexible and efficient queries as the query based on image features. And ultimately natural language offers a good means for condensing visual information. The selected list of projects concerned with video indexing we give below is stressing this fact: at some point always some language data will be considered to support retrieval of images or videos.

In order to support this kind of natural language access, video material was usually manually annotated with 'metadata' such as people involved in the production of the visual record, places, dates, and keywords that capture the essential content of what is depicted. Still, there are a few problems with human annotation. First, the cost and time involved in the production of "surrogates" of the programme is extremely high; second, humans are rather subjective when assigning descriptions to visual records; and third, the level of annotation required to satisfy user's need can hardly be achieved with the use of mere keywords.

2.5 NLP techniques for indexing multimedia material

Many research projects have explored the use of parallel linguistic descriptions of the images (either still or moving) for automatic tasks such as indexing [56], classifying [58], or understanding [59] of visual records, instead of using only content-based (or visually-based) methods in use [54]. This is partly also due to the fact that NLP technologies are more mature for extracting meaning as the technologies in use in the field of image. Content-based indexing and retrieval of visual records is based on features such as colour, texture, and shape. Yet visual understanding is not well advanced and is very difficult even in closed domains. For example, visual analysis of the video of a football match can lead to the identification of interesting "content" like a shooting scene (i.e., the ball moving towards the goal) [60], but this image analysis approach will hardly ever detect who is the main actor involved in that scene (i.e., the shooter).

For accessing visual information with the help of natural language, certain systems make use of a shallow analysis of linguistic data associated with pictures, like the transcripts of audio comments or subtitles. In most of the case this is already enough in order to provide for a first classification and indexation of the visual data (see for example [20], [46] or [47]). Other systems use more sophisticated linguistic analysis, like *information extraction* (IE): the detection of *named entities* and of standard linguistic patterns can help the multimedia retrieval systems to filter out non-relevant sequences (for example the introduction of speakers in news broadcasting). An example of such systems is given in the "Broadcast News Navigator" developed at MITRE (see [26]) . The MUMIS projet, described in details below, is going even further, since full IE systems are analysing a set of so-called "collateral" (parallel) documents and produce unified conceptual annotations, including metadata information that is used for indexing the video material and supports thus concept-based queries on a multimedia archive. A similar approach is described in [37], where the domain of application is classical dance. In this work only a small set of textual documents is considered, in a monolingual setting.

3 Related approaches and projects

MUMIS differs in many significant ways from technologies developed in former or running projects. Most closely related to the thematic focus of MUMIS are the HLT projects Pop-Eye ([47], [20]) and OLIVE ([46], [19]). Pop-Eye used subtitles to index video streams and offered time-stamped texts to satisfy a user query, on request displaying a storyboard or video fragment corresponding to the text hit. OLIVE used automatic speech recognition to generate transcriptions of the sound tracks of news reports, which were then indexed and used in ways similar to the Pop-Eye project; both projects used fuzzy matching *information retrieval* (IR) algorithms to search and retrieve text, offering limited multilingual access to texts. Instead of using IR methods to index and search the transcriptions, MUMIS generates formal annotations building on and abstracting from a whole set of available documents, and merges information annotations from different media sources. The fusion result is then used to direct retrieval, through interface techniques such as pop-up menus, keyword lists, and so on. Search takes the user direct to the storyboard and video clippings.

The Informedia project at Carnegie-Mellon-University [42] has a similar conceptual baseline to MUMIS. The innovative contribution of MUMIS is that it uses a variety of multilingual information sources and fuses them on the basis of formal domain-specific annotations. Where Informedia primarily focuses on special applications, MUMIS aims at the advancement and integratibility of *human language technology* (HLT) enhanced modules to enable information filtering beyond the textual domain. Therefore, MUMIS can be seen as complementary to Informedia with extensions typical for the multilingual European context.

The THISL project [49] is about spoken document retrieval, i.e., automatic speech recognition is used to auto-transcribe news reports and then information retrieval is carried out on this information. One main focus of THISL is to improve speech recognition. Compared to MUMIS it lacks the strong language processing aspects, the fusion of multilingual sources, and the multimedia delivery.

Columbia University was running a project [53] to use textual annotations of video streams to indicate moments of interest, in order to limit the scope of the video processing task, which requires extreme CPU capacities. So the focus is on finding strategies to limit video processing. The University of Massachusetts (Amherst) is also running projects about video indexing [50], but these focus on the combination of text and images. Associated text is used to facilitate indexing of video content. The aspect of generating formal annotations from textual documents is not part of those projects.

Much work has been done on video and image processing (Virage [42], the EUROMEDIA project [40], Surfimage [48], the ISIS project [43], IBM's Media Miner, projects funded under the NSF Stimulate program [45], and many others). This technology in general can indicate, for example, scene changes using very low-level cues and to extract key frames at those instances to form a storyboard for easy video access. The project ASSAVID (see [5] and [6]) is giving an excellent example of such a technology for the sport domain, and is giving fruitfull hints on the still unsolved issue of precisely adjusting time-coded events extracted from textual documents and the places in the video streaming, as detecting on the base of the analysis of picture features. The use of MPEG-7 ([9], [1] and [36]) as a standard for multimedia annotation, including textual annotation, can probaly help a lot in providing future solutions to this issue.

Some institutions are running projects to detect subtitles in the video scene and create a textual annotation. This task is very difficult, given a sequence of real scenes with moving backgrounds and so on. Even more ambitious tasks such as finding real patterns in real movies (tracing the course of the ball in a soccer match, for example) have still some way to go.

4 MUMIS: a Multimedia Indexing and Searching Environment

MUMIS is proposing an integrated solution to the problem of multimedia indexing and search. The solution consists of using information extracted from different sources (structured, semi-structured, free, etc.), modalities (text, speech), and languages (English, German, Dutch) all describing the same event to carry out data-base population, indexing, and search.

MUMIS makes an intensive use of linguistic and semantic based annotations (see also the chapter on linguistic annotation for the web in this volume), coupled with domain-specific information, in order to generate formal annotations of events that can serve as index for videos querying. MUMIS applies IE technologies on multilingual and multimedia information from multiple sources. The novelty of the approach is not only the use of these 'heterogeneous' sources of information but also the combination or cross-source fusion of the information obtained from each source. Single-document, single-language information extraction is carried out by independent systems that share a semantic model and multi-lingual lexicon of the domain. The result of all information extraction systems is merged by a process of alignment and rule-based reasoning that also uses the semantic model.

For this purpose the project makes use of data from different media (textual documents, radio and television broadcasts) in different languages (Dutch, English and German) to build a specialized set of lexicons and an ontology for the selected domain (soccer). It also digitizes non-text data and applies speech recognition techniques to extract text for the purpose of annotation.

Audio material is being analysed by Phicos [61], an HMM-based recognition system, in order to obtain transcriptions of the football commentaries (spontaneous speech). It uses acoustic models, word-based language models (unigram and bigram) and a lexicon. For Dutch, English, and German different recognition systems have been developed. i.e. different phone sets, lexicons, and language models are used. Transcriptions for 14 German, 3 Dutch, and 8 English matches have been produced. [39] gives more details on the *automatic speech recognition* (ASR) and the transcription work done in the context of MUMIS.

The core linguistic processing for the annotation of the multimedia material consists of advanced information extraction techniques for identifying, collecting and normalizing significant text elements (such as the names of players in a team, goals scored, time points or

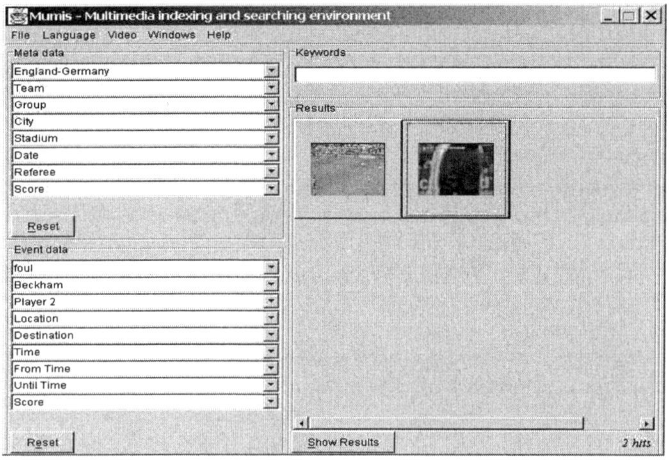

Figure 1: MUMIS User Interface. Thumbnails proposed for the query 'Show me the fouls commited by Beckham"

sequences etc.) which are critical for the appropriate annotation of the multimedia material in the case of soccer. One system per language has been used or developed.

Each system delivers a XML aoutput, which serves as the input of a *merging component*, whose necessity in the project is due to the fact that MUMIS is accessing and processing multiple sources from distinct media in distinct languages. The merging tool is combining the semantically related annotations generated from those different data sources, and detect inconsistencies and/or redundancies within the combined annotations. The merged annotations are then stored in a database, where they will be combined with relevant metadata that are also automatically extracted from the textual documents.

Keyframes extraction from MPEG movies around a set of pre-defined time marks - result of the information extraction component - is being carried out to populate the database. JPEG keyframes images are extracted that serve for quick inspection in the user interface. The software used for off-line keyframe extraction is Spikes: it takes a movie file, a list of times stamps, and the size of the keyframe and produces a list of keyframes.

The on-line part of MUMIS consists of a state of the art user interface allowing the user to query the multimedia database (e.g., "The fouls committed by Beckham"). The user is first presented with selected video key-frames as thumbnails that can be played obtaining the corresponding video and audio fragments. Figure 1 shows the results obtained when selecting the fouls committed by Beckham in the England-Germany match.[2]

4.1 Formal Annotations for the Soccer Domain

Soccer has been chosen as the domain to test and apply the algorithms to be developed. There are a number of reasons for this choice: availability of people willing to help in analyzing user

[2]A web version of the demonstrator is under construction at the time of the redaction of this chapter.

requirements, existence of many information sources in several and possibly large economic and public interest.

The principles and methods derived from this domain can be applied to other as well. This has been shown already in the context of text-based information extraction, for which methodologies for a fast adaptation to new domains have been developed ([29], [30] and [10]). And generally speaking the use of IE for automatic annotation of multimedia document has the advantage of providing, besides the results of the (shallow) syntactic processing, accurate semantic (or content/conceptual) information (and thus potential annotation) for specific pre-defined domains, since a mapping from the linguistically analyzed relevant text parts can be mapped onto an unambiguous conceptual description. Thus in a sense it can be assumed that IE is supporting the word sense disambiguation task (see the chapter on linguistic annotation for the web in this volume).

It is also commonly assumed (see among others [8]) that IE occupies an intermediate place between *information retrieval* (with few linguistic knowledge involved) and *text understanding* (involving the full deep linguistic analysis and being still not realized for the time being.). IE being robust but offering only a partial (but mostly accurate) syntactic and content analysis, it can be said that this language technology is actually filling the gap between available low-level annotated/indexed documents and corpora and the desirable full content annotation of those documents and corpora. This is the reason why MUMIS has chosen this technology for providing automatic annotation (at distinct linguistic and domain-specific levels) of multimedia material, allowing thus to add queryable "content information" to this material. And if MUMIS was not explicitly designed for supporting knowledge management tasks, it nevertheless suggests that the meaningful organization of domain-specific multimedia material proposed by the project can be adapted to the organization of the distributed information of an enterprise and thus support the sharing and access to companies expertise and know-how.

4.2 The Multimedia Material in MUMIS

The MUMIS project is about automatic indexing of videos of soccer matches with formal annotations and querying that information to get immediate access to interesting video fragments. For this purpose the project chose the European Football Championships 2000 in Belgium and the Netherlands as its main database. A major project goal is to merge the formal annotations extracted from textual and audio material (including the audio part of videos) on the EURO 2000 in three languages: English, German, Dutch. The material MUMIS has to process can be classified in the following way:

1. Reports from Newspapers (reports about specific games, general reports) which is classified as free texts (FrT)
2. Tickers, close captions, Action-Databases which are classified as semi-formal texts (SFT)
3. Formal descriptions about specific games which are classified as formal texts (FoT)
4. Audio material recorded from radio and TV broadcasts
5. Video material recorded from TV broadcasts

1. to 4. is being used for automatically generating formal annotations in order to index 5. MUMIS is investigating the precise contribution of each source of information for the overall goal of the creation of merged formal annotations on events and other relevant information. Examples of German FrT and SFT are given in figures 2 and 3.

England - Deutschland 1:0 (0:0)

England: Seaman (2,5) - G. Neville (3,5), Keown (3), Campbell (2), P. Neville (4,5) -
Ince (3,5), Wise (5) - Beckham (4), Scholes (3) - Shearer (3), Owen (5) -
Trainer: Keegan
Deutschland: Kahn (2) - Matthaeus (3) - Babbel (3,5), Nowotny (2,5) - Deisler (3),
Hamann (2,5), Jeremies (3,5), Ziege (3,5) - Scholl (5) - Jancker (4), Kirsten (5) -
Trainer: Ribbeck
Eingewechselt: 61. Gerrard fuer Owen,
72. Barmby fuer Scholes - 70. Rink fuer Kirsten,
72. Ballack fuer Deisler, 78. Bode fuer Jeremies
Tore: 1:0 Shearer (53., Kopfball, Vorarbeit Beckham)
Schiedsrichter: Collina, Pierluigi (Viareggio), Note 2 -
bis auf eine falsche Abseits-Entscheidung souveraen und sicher
Zuschauer: 30000 (ausverkauft)
Gelbe Karten: Beckham - Babbel, Jeremies

Figure 2: Example of a so-called formal text, where one can see that only 5 distinct time points can be extracted, concerning the player subsitutions ('Eingewechselt') and one goal ('Tore').

Gruppe A: England - Deutschland 1:0 (0:0)

7. Ein Freistoss von Christian Ziege aus 25 Metern geht ueber das Tor.
12. Ziege flankt per Freistoss in den Strafraum und Jeremies versucht es per Kofball,
verfehlt den Kasten jedoch deutlich.
16. Scholes flankt gefaehrlich von der Torauslinie in den Fuenfmeterraum,
doch Ziege hat aufgepasst und kann klaeren.
...
53. Beckham flankt per Freistoss an der deutschen Abwehr vorbei auf den Kopf von Alan Shearer,
der voellig freistehend zum 1:0 fuer die Englaender verwandelt.
...

Figure 3: Example of a so-called semi-formal text, where one can see that here more time points are available, and that those can be complementary to the time points to be extracted from formal texts.

Since the information contained in formal texts can be considered as a database of true facts, they play an important role within MUMIS. But nevertheless they contain only little information about a game: the goals, the substitutions and some other few events (penalties, yellow and red cards). So there are only few time points available for indexing videos. Semi-formal texts (SFT), like live tickers on the web, are offering much more time points sequences, related with a higher diversity of events (goals scenes, fouls etc,) and seem to offer the best textual source for our purposes. Nevertheless the quality of the texts of online tickers is often quite poor. Free texts, like newspapers articles, have a high quality but the extraction of time points and their associated events in text is more difficult. Those texts also offer more background information that might be interesting for the real fans.

4.3 Processing Steps in MUMIS

4.3.1 Media Pre-Processing

Media material has been delivered in various formats (AudioDAT, AudioCassettes, Hi-8 video cassettes, DV video cassettes etc) and qualities. All audio signals (also those which are part of the video recordings) are digitized and stored in an audio archive. Audio digitization is done with 20 kHz sample frequency, the format generated is according to the de-facto "wav" standard. For digitization any available tool can be used such as SoundForge.

Video information (including the audio component) of selected games have been digitized into MPEG1 streams first. Later it will be encoded in MPEG2 streams. While the quality of MPEG1 is certainly not satisfying to the end-user, its bandwidth and CPU requirements are moderate for current computer and network technology. The mean bit rate for MPEG1 streams is about 1.5 Mbps. Current state-of-the-art computers can render MPEG1 streams in real time and many network connections (Intranet and even Internet) can support MPEG1. MPEG2 is specified for about 3 to 5 Mbps. Currently the top-end personal computers can render MPEG2, but MPEG2 is not yet supported for the most relevant player APIs such as JavaMediaFramework or Quicktime. When this support is given the MUMIS project will also offer MPEG2 quality.

For all separate audio recordings as for example from radio stations it has to be checked whether the time base is synchronous to that one of the corresponding video recordings. In case of larger deviations a time base correction factor has to be estimated and stored for later use. Given that the annotations cannot be created with too high accuracy a certain time base deviation will be accepted. For part of the audio signals manual transcriptions have to be generated to train the speech recognizers. These transcripts will be delivered in XML-structured files.

Since keyframes will be needed in the user interface, the MUMIS project will develop software that easily can generate such keyframes around a set of pre-defined time marks. Time marks will be the result of information extraction processes, since the corresponding formal annotations is referring to to specific moments in time. The software to be written has to extract the set of time marks from the XML-structured formal annotation file and extract a set of keyframes from the MPEG streams around those time marks. A set of keyframes will be extracted around the indicated moments in time, since the estimated times will not be exact and since the video scenes at such decisive moments are changing rapidly. There is a chance to miss the interesting scene by using keyframes and just see for example spectators. Taking a number of keyframes increases the chance to grab meaningful frames.

4.3.2 Multilingual Automatic Speech Recognition

Domain specific language models have been trained. The training can be bootstrapped from written reports of soccer matches, but substantial amounts of transcribed recordings of commentaries on matches are also required. Novel techniques have been investigated to interpolate the base line language models of the Automatic Speech Recognition (ASR) systems and the domain specific models. Moreover, techniques must be developed to adapt the vocabularies and the language models to reflect the specific conditions of a match (e.g., the names players have to be added to the vocabulary, with the proper bias in the language model). In addition, the acoustic models have been adapted to cope with the background noise present in most recordings.

Automatic speech recognition of the sound tracks of television and (especially) radio programmes can make use of closed caption subtitle texts and information extracted from formal texts to help in finding interesting sequences and automatically transcribing them. Further, the domain lexicons is helping with keyword and topic spotting. Around such text islands ASR is used to transcribe the spoken soundtrack. The ASR system has been enriched with lexica containing more keywords, to increase the number of sequence types that can be identified and automatically transcribed. Prelimieary results and problems have been document in [39]. Due to the extreme background noise present in the audio files, the results of ASR can not be expected to be very good. But transcripts are giving a very valuable: the time of the utterance is given in the encoding.

An example of a (manually improved) transcription from English TV comment is given below. We can not go in details here, but one can see that transcription of audio materials can be quite challeging for NLP, since a lot of utterances are causing problems, like the values of the word feature *w* show: “Sh”, “eh”.

```
<tau ref="407" s="EngDldE2" tb="4724.396" te="4728.254" tt="eq" tq="man">
    <tw ref="407.1"   tb="4724.396" te="4727.373" ...   w="I"/>
    <tw ref="407.2"   tb="4724.396" te="4727.373" ...   w="don't"/>
    <tw ref="407.3"   tb="4724.396" te="4727.373" ...   w="know"/>
    <tw ref="407.4"   tb="4724.396" te="4727.373" ...   w="if"/>
    <tw ref="407.5"   tb="4724.396" te="4727.373" ...   w="it"/>
    <tw ref="407.6"   tb="4724.396" te="4727.373" ...   w="was"/>
    <tw ref="407.7"   tb="4724.396" te="4727.373" ...   w="Jeremies"/>
    <tw ref="407.8"   tb="4724.396" te="4727.373" ...   w="or"/>
    <tw ref="407.9"   tb="4724.396" te="4727.373" ...   w="Sh"/>
    <tw ref="407.10"  tb="4724.396" te="4727.373" ...   w="eh"/>
    <tw ref="407.11"  tb="4727.373" te="4728.254" ...   w="Scholes"/>
    <tw ref="407.12"  tb="4727.373" te="4728.254" ...   w="one"/>
    <tw ref="407.13"  tb="4727.373" te="4728.254" ...   w="of"/>
    <tw ref="407.14"  tb="4727.373" te="4728.254" ...   w="the"/>
    </tau>
    ....
```

4.3.3 Domain Modelling

Any domain-specific NLP applications need a model of the domain under consideration. This allow to process the documents with the help of generic NLP tools (see also here the chapter on linguistic annotation for the web in this volume), which can thus be used for every type of applications. The results of the NL analysis can be mapped onto a domain-specific organization of knowledge and produce a corresponding set of annotations, which can be very helpful, for example, for knowledge management applications.

Domain Ontology: An analysis of the domain and a user study led the project to propose 31 types of event for a football match (kick-off, substitution, goal, red card, etc.) that need to be identified in the sources in order to produce a semantic index. The elements to be extracted that are associated with these events are: players, teams, scores, and locations on the field. Time codes need to be extracted from the sources as well. All events and their participants have been organized in an ontology that has more than 300 concepts related as a 'is-a' hierarchy. This ontology is giving the base for the reasoning component of the prototype. The link between the concept and the three languages consists of a flexible XML format which maps concepts into lexical entries, as show below.

Multilingual Domain Lexicon Building: All the collected textual data for the soccer domain are used for building the multilingual domain lexicons. This data can be in XML, HTML, plain text format, etc. A number of automatic processes are used for the lexicon building, first on a monolingual and secondly on a multilingual level. Manual browsing and editing is taking place, mainly in order to provide the semantic links to the terms, but also for the fine-tuning of the lexicon according to the domain knowledge.

Domain lexicons are built for three languages, namely English, German and Dutch. The lexicons are delivered in a fully structured, XML-compliant, TMX-format (Translation Memory eXchange format, see [62] An example of the MUMIS lexicon generated so far:

```
<lex-element id="3.9" concept="Corner">
   <term-lang lang="DE" type="main">Ecke</term-lang>
   <term-lang lang="EN" type="main">corner</term-lang>
   <term-lang lang="NL" type="main">hoekschop</term-lang>
   <definition>A corner kick is awarded when the whole ball has:
   Crossed the whole goal linein the air oron the ground, was last
   touched by a defender and  goal was not scored</definition>
   <term-lang lang="DE" type="synonym">Eckball</term-lang>
</lex-element>
```

This lexicon is being revisited to conform to more formal representation languages (as discussed in the chapter on linguistic annotation in this volume).

4.3.4 Generation of Formal Annotations

The formal annotations are generated by the IE technology and are reflecting the typical output of IE systems, i.e.instantiated domain-specific templates or event tables. The slots to be filled by the systems are basically entities (player, teams etc.), relations (player_of, opponents etc.) and events (goal, substitution etc.), which are all derived from the current version of the domain ontology and can be queried for in the online component of the *MUMIS* system. All the templates associated with an event are including a time slot to be filled if the corresponding information is available in a least one of the sources consulted during the IE procedure. This time information is necessary for the indexing of the video material.

The IE systems are applying to distinct sources (FoT, FrT etc.) but they are not concerned with achieving consistency in the IE result on distinct sources about the same event (game): this is the task of the merging tools, described below.

Since the distinct textual sources are differently structured, from "formal" to "free" texts, the IE systems involved have adopted a modular approach: regular expressions for the detection of Named Entities in the case of formal texts, full chunk parsing for the free texts. On the base of the factual information extracted from the formal texts, the IE systems are also building dynamic databases on certain entities (like name and age of the players, the clubs they are normally playing for, etc.) or certain metadata (final score), which can be used at the next level of processing. Examples of annotations generated from formal and semi-formal texts are given in figure 4

4.3.5 Merging

Merging here is the process of checking whether various linguistic annotations from different sources can refer to the same entity or event. The merging component combines in fact the

<DOM=SOCCER TYPE=SUBSTITUTION TIME=61:00 SYN=NP
PLAYER_OUT=Owen PLAYER_IN=Gerrard>

<DOM=SOCCER TYPE=GOAL GOAL_TYPE=Kopfball SYN=NP TIME=53:00
SCORE=1:0 PLAYER=Shearer PREPARATION=Beckham>

Figure 4: Two examples of time-marks and their associated events (substitution and goal) automatically extracted from the formal text above.

7. Ein Freistoss von Christian Ziege aus 25 Metern geht ueber das Tor.
(7. A 25-meter free-kick by Christian Ziege goes over the goal.)

<EVENTS>
1-event_TYPE="Free-kick" 1-event DIST="Meter-from (25)" 1-event L PLAYER="Ziege"
1-event_EVENT_CLASS="goal_scene_fail" 1-event ART="Goal" 1-event TIME="7:00"
</EVENTS>

<META> DOM_NAME="SOCCER"</META>

<PLAYER>
<PLAYER_NAME>Ziege</PLAYER_NAME>
<PLAYER_NOTE>#(3,5)</PLAYER_NOTE>
<PLAYER_POS>#4 ##3</PLAYER_POS>
<PLAYER_NUMBER>##17</PLAYER_NUMBER>
<PLAYER_OLD>##28</PLAYER_OLD>
<PLAYER_CLUB>##FC Middlesbrough</PLAYER_CLUB>
<PLAYER_NO_PLAYS>##52</PLAYER_NO_PLAYS>
</PLAYER>

Figure 5: Example of the extraction of event with its associated relations entities and relations, taken from the same game. The information about the player is dymamically included from the processing ot the formal texts. In this case from the merging from 2 different formal texts, marked with # and ## respectively.

annotated partial information as extracted from various sources, such that more complete (and consistent) and less redundant annotations for the indexing of video can be obtained. The merging component makes use of inferential mechanisms for supporting the fusion of information. The use of general representation languages supporting all kind of operations on (typed) features as well as multiple inheritance (see the chapter on linguistic annotation in this volume for a description of such formalisms), combined with inference mechanisms, supports a better sequential organization of some events in larger scenarios. It allows also the induction of some events that are not explicitly mentioned in the sources under consideration (or which the IE systems might not have detected).

An example of merging of annotations extracted from 2 different formal texts on one game is given in figure 5, where merged information about a player (*Ziege*) has been dynamically integrated into the procesing of semi-formal texts. New information about a player availble in the semi-formal texts can be backward added into the merged annotations. This makes merging also quite interesting for the automatic and dynamic updating of information encoded in databases.

4.3.6 User Interface Building

The user first interacts with a web-portal to start a MUMIS query session. An applet is being down-line loaded in case of showing the sc MUMIS demonstration. This applet mainly offers a query interface. The user then enters a query that either refers to metadata, formal annotations, or both. The on-line system searchs for all formal annotations that meet the criteria of the query. In doing so it will find the appropriate meta-information and/or moments in some media recording. In case of meta-information it simply offers the information in scrollable text widgets. This is done done in a structured way such that different type of information can easily be detected by the user. In the case that scenes of games are the result of queries about formal annotations the user interface first presents selected video keyframes as thumbnails with a direct indication of the corresponding metadata. The user can then ask for more metadata about the corresponding game or for more media data. The actual sate of the demonstrator is show in figure 1 above.

5 Standards for Multimedia Content

MUMIS is looking for a compliance with existing standards in the context of the processing of multimedia content on the computer and so will adhere to standards such as MPEG4, which defines how different media objects will be decoded and integrated at the receiving station, and the emerging standard MPEG7, which is about defining standards for annotations which can be seen as multimedia objects. Further, MUMIS will also maintain awareness of international discussions and developments in the area of multimedia streaming (RTP, RTSP, JMF...), and are following the discussions within the W3C consortium and the EBU that are also about standardizing descriptions of media content.

6 Role of MUMIS for the Annotation of Multimedia Content

To conclude on the project, we would like to list the points where we think MUMIS is contributing, directly or indirectly, to the extraction and to the access of multimedia content. MUMIS:

1. Uses multimedia (MM) and multilingual information sources;
2. Carries out multimedia indexing by applying information extraction to a well-delineated domain and using already existing information as constraints;
3. Uses and extends advanced language technology to automatically create formal annotations for MM content;
4. Merges information from many sources to improve the quality of the annotation database;
5. Applies advanced IE to the output of ASR and the combination of this with already existing knowledge;
6. Defines a complex information annotation structure, which is stored in a standard document type definition (DTD);
7. Integrates new methods into a query interface that is guided by domain knowledge (ontology and multilingual lexicons).

In this sense MUMIS is contributing in defining semantic structures of multimedia contents, at the level proposed by domain-specific IE analysis. The full machinery of IE, combined with ASR (and in the future with Image Analysis, so for example with the results of the ASSAVID project) can be used for multimedia contents development and so efficiently support cross-media (and cross-lingual) information retrieval and effective navigation within multimedia information interfaces. There seems thus that this technology can play a highly relevant role for the purposes of knowledge detection and management. This is probably specially valid for the merging component, which is eliminating redundancies in the annotations generated from sets of documents and establishing complex reference resolutions, thus simplifying the access to content (and knowledge) distributed over multiple documents and media, which are also increasingly available on the Web.

7 Conclusions

We have seen that NLP methods and techniques can be extended in order to be useful also for multimedia. Unification grammars can be helpful for the organisation and analysis of multimodal and multimedia data. The plan-based organisation of the content to be delivered in automatic natural language generation can be applied to the selection and structure of content in the context of the automatic generation of multimedia presentation. And the use of IR analysis techniques can support a complex but flexible access to digital multimedia archives. But NLP has also to open itself to new forms of communication made possible through the developments in multimedia and multimodal applications. NLP no longer can confine itself to the analysis or the generation of textual documents, but has to go for a level of analysis such that its results can be used for the organisation of a multimedia and multimodal complex around natural language. Only in this sense, one can really speak of human language technology (HLT), taking into account various communication means in the creation, distribution and access of content and knowledge over the Web.

8 Acknowledgements

This research been supported by EC grant IST-1999-10651 for the MUMIS project.

References

[1] Adani N., Bugatti A., Leonardi R., and Migliorati P. Semantic description of multimedia documents: the Mpeg-7 approach. In Proceedings of the Conference on Content-Based Multimedia Indexing, CBMI-2001, Brescia, 2001.

[2] André E. Natural Language in Multimedia/Multimodal Systems. In Mitkov R. (ed.), Handbook of Computational Linguistics, Oxford, 2000.

[3] André E. The Generation of Multimedia Presentations. In Handbook of Natural Language Processing, Marcel Dekker, 2000.

[4] Appelt D.E. An Introduction to Information Extraction. In AI Communications (vol. 12), 1999.

[5] Assfalg J., Bertini M., Colombo C., and Del Bimbo A. Semantic annotations of sports videos. In Proceedings of the Conference on Content-Based Multimedia Indexing, CBMI-2001, Brescia, 2001

[6] Bertine M. and del Bimbo A. Multimedia content extraction from video streams. In Proceedings of the Conference on Content-Based Multimedia Indexing, CBMI-2001, Brescia, 2001.

[7] Brugman H., Bontcheva K., Wittenburg P. and Cunningham H. Integrating Multimedia and Textual Software Architectures for Language Technology. Technical report MPI-TG-99-1, MPI for Psycholinguistics, Nijmegen, Netherlands, 1999.

[8] Cunningham H. Information Extraction: A user Guide, Research Report CS-99-07, Department of Computer Science, University of Sheffi eld, May 1999.

[9] Day N. MPEG-7 Applications: Multimedia Search and Retrieval. In Proceedings of the First International Workshop on Multimedia Annotation, MMA-2001, 2001.

[10] Declerck T. and Neumann G. Using a parameterisable and domain-adaptive information extraction system for annotating large-scale corpora? Proceedings of the Workshop Information Extraction meets Corpus Linguistics, LREC-2000, 2000.

[11] Declerck T., Wittenburg P., Cunningham H. The Automatic Generation of Formal Annotations in a Multimedia Indexing and Searching Environment. Proceedings of the Workshop on Human Language Technology and Knowledge Management, ACL-2001, 2001.

[12] Declerck T. A set of tools for integrating linguistic and non-linguistic information. Proceedings of SAAKM 2002, ECAI 2002, Lyon.

[13] Djoerd H., de Jong F., Netter K. (Eds). 14th Twente Workshop on Language Technology, Language Technology in Multimedia Information Retrieval, TWLT 14, Enschede, Universiteit Twente, 1998.

[14] Grishman R., Sundheim B. Message Understanding Conference – 6: A Brief History. In Proceedings of the 16th International Conference on Computational Linguistics, COLING-96, 1996.

[15] Heflin J., Hendler J., and Luke S. SHOE: A Knowledge Representation Language for Internet Applications. Technical Report CS-TR-4078. Department of Computer Science, University of Maryland, 1999.

[16] Hellwig P. NATURAL LANGUAGE PARSERS A 'Course in Cooking. COLING-ACL '98– Pre-Conference Tutorial. 1998.

[17] Humphreys K., Gaizauskas R., Azzam S., Huyck C., Mitchell B., Cunningham H., Wilks Y. Description of the LaSIE-II System as used for MUC-7, in Seventh Message Understanding Conference (MUC-7), http://www.muc.saic.com/, SAIC Information Extraction. 1998.

[18] Johnston M. Unifi cation-based Multimodal Parsing, In Proceedings of the 17th International Conference on Computational Linguistics, COLING-98, 1998.

[19] de Jong F., Netter K. Olive: Speech-Based Video Retrieval. In Hiemstra D., de Jong F., Netter K. (Eds), Language Technology in Multimedia Information Retrieval (Proceedings of the 14th Twente Workshop on Language Technology, TWLT 14), Enschede, Universiteit Twente, 1998.

[20] de Jong F., Gauvin J., Hiemstra D., Netter K. Language-Based Multimedia Information Retrieval. In Proceedings of the 6th Conference on Recherche d'Information Assistee par Ordinateur, RIAO-2000, 2000.

[21] de Jong F. and Westerveld T. MUMIS: Multimedia Indexing and Searching. Proceedings of the Content-Based Multimedia Indexing Workshop (CBMI2001), 2001.

[22] Krieger H.-U., Schaefer U. TDL – a type description language for constraint-based grammars. In Proceedings of the 15th International Conference on Computational Linguistics, COLING-94, 1994.

[23] Maybury M. Multimedia Interaction for the New Millenium. In Proceedings of Eurospeech 99, 1999.

[24] McKeown K. Text generation, Cambridge University Press, 1985.

[25] McNaugh J. (Ed), Information Extraction meets Corpus Linguistics. LREC-2000, 2000.

[26] Merlino A., Morey D., Maybury M. Broadcast News Navigation using Story Segments. ACM International Multimedia Conference, 1997.

[27] Miller, G.A. WordNet: A Lexical Database for English. Communications of the ACM 11. 1995.

[28] Moore J., Paris C. Planning Text for Advisory Dialogues. In Proceedings of the 27th ACL, Vancouver, 1989.

[29] Sixth Message Understanding Conference (MUC-6), Morgan Kaufmann, 1995.

[30] Seventh Message Understanding Conference (MUC-7), http://www.muc.saic.com/, SAIC Information Extraction, 1998.

[31] Naphade Milid R. and T.S. Huang. Recognizing high-level concepts for video indexing. In Proceedings of the Conference on Content-Based Multimedia Indexing, CBMI-2001, Brescia, 2001.

[32] Neumann G., Backofen R., Baur J., Becker M., Braun C. An Information Extraction Core System for Real World German Text Processing. In Proceedings of the 5th Conference on Applied Natural Language Processing, ANLP-97, 1997.

[33] Piskorski J., Neumann G.. An Intelligent Text Extraction and Navigation System. In Proceedings of the 6th Conference on Recherche d'Information Assistee par Ordinateur, RIAO-2000, 2000.

[34] Saggion H. , Cunningham H., Bontcheva K., Maynard D, Ursu C. Hamza O. and Wilks Y. Access to Multimedia Information through Multisource and Multilanguage Information Extraction. 7th Workshop on Applications of Natural Language to Information Systems (NLDB 2002), 2002.

[35] Saggion H., Cunningham H., Maynard D., Bontcheva K., Hamza, O., Ursu, C. and Wilks, Y. Extracting Information for Information Indexing of Multimedia Material. Proceedings of 3rd Language Resources and Evaluation Conference (LREC'2002), 2002.

[36] Salembier P. An overview of Mpeg-7 multimedia description schemes and of future visual information challenges for content-based indexing. In Proceedings of the Conference on Content-Based Multimedia Indexing, CBMI-2001, Brescia, 2001.

[37] Salway A., Talking Pictures: Indexing and Representing Video with Collateral Texts. In Hiemstra D., de Jong F., Netter K. (Eds), Language Technology in Multimedia Information Retrieval (Proceedings of the 14th Twente Workshop on Language Technology, TWLT 14), Enschede, Universiteit Twente, 1998.

[38] Staab S., Maedche A., Handschuh S. An Annotation Framework for the Semantic Web. In The First International Workshop on Multimedia Annotation, Tokyo, Japan, 2001.

[39] Wester M., Kessens J.M. and Strik H. Goal-directed ASR in a Multimedia Indexing and Searching Environment (MUMIS). Proceedings of the 7th International Conference on Spoken Language Processsing (ICLSP2002), 2002.

[40] EUR: http://www.foyer.de/euromedia/

[41] GDA: http://www.csl.sony.co.jp/person/nagao/gda/

[42] INF: http://www.informedia.cs.cmu.edu/

[43] ISI: http://www.wins.uva.nl/research/isis/isisNS.html

[44] ISLE: http://www.ilc.pi.cnr.it/EAGLES/ISLE_Home_Page.htm

[45] NSF: http://www.nsf.gov./od/lpa/news/press/pr9714.htm

[46] OLI: http://twentyone.tpd.tno.nl/olive

[47] POP: http://twentyone.tpd.tno.nl/popeye

[48] SUR: http://www-rocq.inria.fr/ nastar/MM98/node1.html

[49] THI: http://www.dcs.shef.ac.uk/research/groups/spandh/projects/thisl

[50] UMA: http://ciir.cs.umass.edu/research/

[51] UNL:http://www.ias.unu.edu/research_prog/science_technology/universalnetwork_languge.html

[52] VIR: http://www.virage.com/

[53] COL: http://www.cs.columbia.edu/ hjing/sumDemo

[54] Veltkamp R. and Tanase M. Content-based Image Retrieval Systems: a survey. Technical report UU-CS-2000-34, Utrecht University, 2000.

[55] Chang S.F., Chen, W., Meng H.J., Sundaram H. and Zhong D. A Fully Automated Content-based Video Search Engine Supporting Spatio Temporal Queries. IEEE Transactions on Circuits and Systems for Video Technology, 1998.

[56] Netter K. Pop-Eye and OLIVE. Human Language as the Medium for Cross-lingual Multimedia Information Retrieval. Technical report, Language Technology Lab. DFKI GmbH, 1998.

[57] Hampapur A. Semantic video indexing: approach and issues. In SIGMOD-Record, 1998.

[58] Sable C. and Hatzivassiloglou V. Text-based approaches for the categorization of images. Proceedings of ECDL, 1999.

[59] Srihari R.K. Automatic Indexing and Content-Based Retrieval of Captioned Images, Computer 28/9, 1995.

[60] Gong Y., Sin L.T., Chuan C.H., Zhang H. and Sakauchi M. Automatic Parsing of TV Soccer Programs. Proceedings of the International Conference on Multimedia Computing and Systems (IEEE), 1995.

[61] Steinbiss V., Ney H., Haeb-Umbach R., Tran B.-H., Essen U., Kneser R., Oerder M., Meier H.-G., Aubert X., Dugast C. and Geller D. The Philips Research System for Large-Vocabulary Continuous-Speech Recognition. In Proc. of Eurospeech '93, 1993.

[62] http://www.lisa.org/tmx/tmx.htm.

Graphics

Annotation for the Semantic Web
S. Handschuh and S. Staab (Eds.)
IOS Press, 2003

Supporting Semantic Image Annotation and Search

J. Wielemaker, A. Th. Schreiber and B. J. Wielinga
University of Amsterdam, Social Science Informatics
Roetersstraat 15, NL 1018 WB Amsterdam, The Netherlands
E-mail: {jan,schreiber,wielinga}@swi.psy.uva.nl

Abstract. In this article we discuss an application scenario for semantic annotation and search in a collection of art images. This application shows that background knowledge in the form of ontologies can be used to support indexing and search in image collections. The underlying ontologies are represented in RDF Schema and are based on existing data standards and knowledge corpora, such as the VRA Core Categories 3.0, the Art and Architecture Thesaurus and WordNet. This work is intended to provide a "proof of concept" for indexing and search in a semantic web.

1 Introduction

In this article we are exploring the possibilities of using background knowledge for indexing and querying an image collection. Many of such collections currently exist and users are increasingly faced with problems of finding a suitable (set of) image(s) for a particular purpose. Each collection usually has its own (semi-)structured indexing scheme that typically supports a keyword-type search. However, finding the right image is often still problematic.

In this work we investigate an alternative approach. We explore the question whether ontologies can support the indexing and querying process in any significant way. This work should be seen as a "proof of concept". A the moment, the use of explicit background knowledge is often-mentioned as a way out of the search problems such as currently arise on the Internet and in multimedia databases. This new research area is part of the "semantic web" [1]. Emerging web standards such as RDF [4] are providing a syntactic format for explicating background knowledge of information resources. However, the added value of such semantic annotations still has to be proven. Within the scope of this work we have not done any detailed evaluation studies of the approach presented. Our sole aim is to see whether we can find sufficient evidence that this is a plausible approach worth further investigation.

2 Approach

Fig. 1 shows the general architecture we used within this study. All ontologies were represented in RDFS Schema [2]. The resulting RDF Schema files are read into the tool with help of the SWI-Prolog RDF parser [14, 6]. The annotation tool subsequently generates an user interface for annotation and search based on the RDF Schema specification. The tool supports loading images and image collections, creating annotations, storing annotations in a RDF file, and two types of image search facilities.

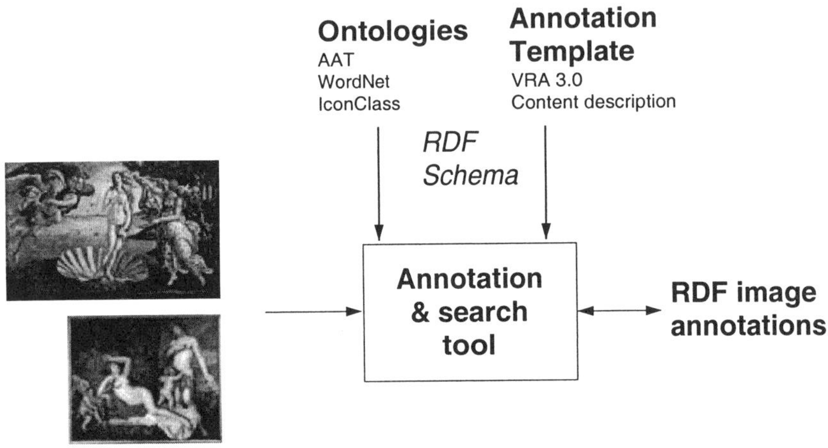

Figure 1: Overview of the approach in this study. The RDF Schema specifications of the ontologies and of the annotation template are parsed by the RDF/RDFS parser into the tool. The tool generates an annotation and search interface from these specifications. This interface is used to annotate and query images. The annotations are stored in an RDF file.

The architecture shown in Fig. 1 is in the same spirit as the one described by Lafon and Bos [3]. The main difference lies in the fact that we place more emphasis on the nature of the ontologies. In the rest of this paper the architecture depicted in Fig. 1 is described in more detail. The background knowledge is discussed in Sec. 3. The annotation and query aspects of the tool are discussed in, Sec. 4 in the form of an application scenario. Sec. 5 discusses the experiences gained.

This work is a sequel to earlier work on semantic annotation and search of a collection of photographs of apes [8]. As the sample domain for the present work we used 200 images of paintings.

3 Background Knowledge

3.1 Ontologies

For this study we used three thesauri, which are relevant for the art-image domain:

1. The Art and Architecture Thesaurus (AAT) [7] is a large thesaurus containing some 120,000 terms relevant for the art domain.

2. WordNet [5] is a large lexical database. WordNet concepts (i.e. "synsets") are typically used to describe the content of the image, e.g. "woman sitting on bed"

3. ICONCLASS [11, 10] is a iconographic classification system, providing a hierarchally organized set of concepts for describing the content of visual resources.

AAT, WordNet and ICONCLASS were translated into the RDF Schema notation. In a prior publication [15] one can find a discussion on issues arising when representing AAT in RDF Schema.

These sources share a significant number of terms. This could be used to design a new ontology by *merging* them. In the context of the Semantic Web however, it is important to *re-use* existing work rather than modifying it. Therefore we have added equivalence relations between terms appearing in multiple ontologies that refer to the same entity in the world. For example, the ICONCLASS concept **king** is linked to the AAT concept **kings (people)**, making all ICONCLASS subterms of **king** valid subterms of AAT **kings (people)** and visa-versa.

3.2 Annotation template

For annotation purposes the tool provides the user with an annotation template derived from the VRA 3.0 Core Categories [12]. The VRA template provides a specialization of the Dublin Core set of metadata elements, tailored to the needs of art images. The VRA Core Categories follow the "dumb-down" principle (i.e., a tool can interpret the VRA data elements as Dublin Core data elements).

The 17 VRA data elements (i.e. properties of an art image) were for visualization purposes grouped into three sets:

1. *Production-related descriptors* such as creator ("maker"), style/period, technique and, culture
2. *Physical descriptors* such as measurements and color
3. *Administrative descriptors* such as collection ID, rights and current location

In Fig. 2 one can see a tab with the set of production-related descriptors. The other VRA descriptors can be found on two other tabs.

In addition, we needed to provide ways for describing the subject matter of the painting. VRA provides a subject element, but we were interested in providing more structured content descriptions. For this purpose we used a simple "sentence structure" which was developed for a previous experiment [8]:

```
<agent> <action> <object> <setting>
```

Each content-description sentence should contain at least one agent or object. Agents and objects may have attributes ("modifiers"), such as color, cardinality and position. The "setting" can be described with relative time (e.g., '"sunset") and relative place (e.g., "a forest"). In addition, the scene as a whole can be characterized. The application scenario in the next section gives an example of the use of this template. Multiple sentences can be used to describe a single scene.

3.2.1 Linking the annotation template to the ontologies

Where possible, a slot in the annotation template is bound to one or more subtrees of the ontologies. For example, the VRA slot style/period is bound to two subtrees in AAT containing the appropriate style and period concepts (see also Fig. 3. Four VRA data elements are currently linked to parts of AAT: technique, style/period, culture and material. Most parts of the subject-matter description are also linked to subtrees of the ontologies. Here, heavy use is made of WordNet and ICONCLASS. The latter is in particular useful for describing scenes as a whole.

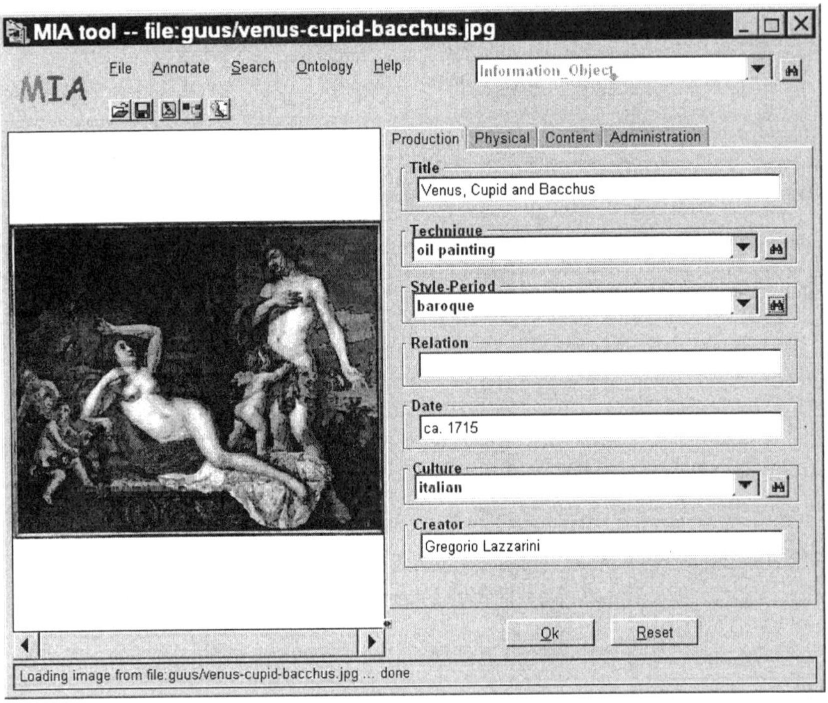

Figure 2: Snapshot of a semantic annotation and search tool for art images. The figure shows a fragment of the annotation window showing one one tab with VRA data elements for describing the image, here the production-related descriptors). The slots associated with a magnifier button are linked to one or more subparts of the underlying ontologies, which provide the concepts for this part of the annotation

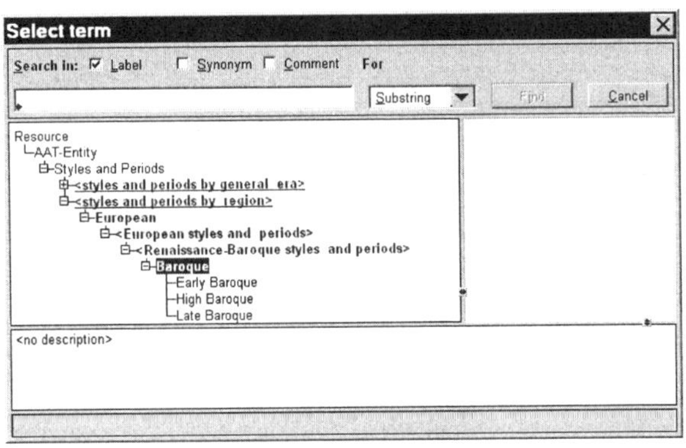

Figure 3: Browser window for values of style/period. The concept **baroque** has been selected as a value for this slot. The top-level concepts of the AAT subtrees from which we can select a value for style/period are shown with an underlined bold font (i.e., <**styles and periods by general era**> and <**styles and periods by region**>). The browser shows that there are three more specific concepts that could have been used (e.g. high baroque)

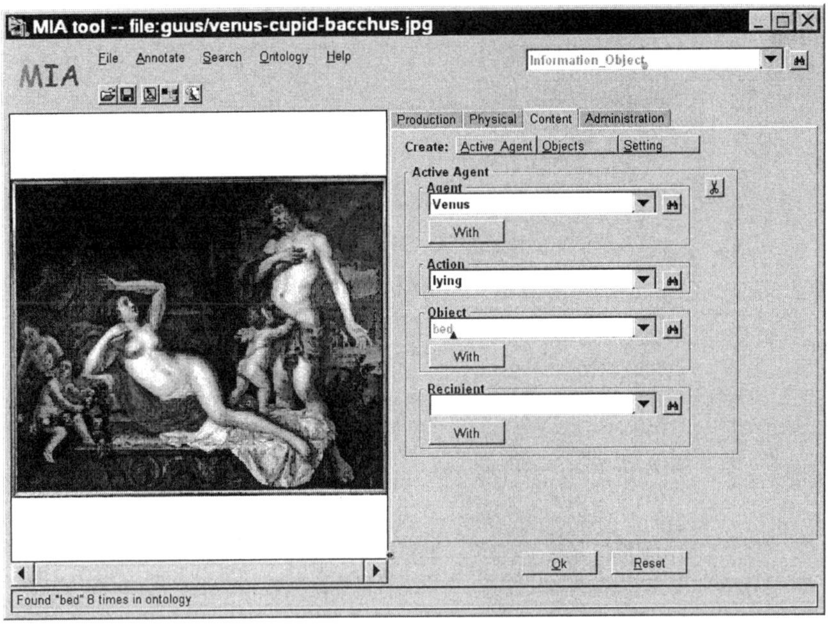

Figure 4: Description of the subject matter. Here, the content is described with the sentence "Venus (agent) lying (action) bed (object)". Multiple content descriptions can be entered for an image

4 An Application Scenario

4.1 Annotating an image

Fig. 2 shows a screen shot of the annotation interface. In this scenario the user is annotating an image representing a baroque Italian painting, depicting a mythological scene featuring Venus, Cupid and Bacchus. The figure shows the tab for production-related data elements. The three elements with a magnifier icon are linked to subtrees in the ontologies, in this case AAT. For example, if we would click on the magnifier for style/period the window shown in Fig. 3 would pop up, showing the place in the hierarchy of the concept **baroque**. We see that it is a concept from AAT. The top-level concepts of the AAT subtrees from which we can select a value for style/period are shown with an underlined bold font (i.e., <**styles and periods by general era**> and <**styles and periods by region**>). The ontology makes it esier for poeple to select the correct concept. For example, seeing that **baroque** contains three specializations the user might want to use one of these terms, e.g. **high baroque**.

The user interface provides some support for finding the right concept. For example, the user can type in a few characters of a term and then invoke a completion mechanism (by typing a space). This will provide a popup list of concepts matching the input string. In the browser window, more advanced concept search options can be selected, including substrings and use of synonyms.

The domain knowledge can be extended to cover more slots. For example, the creator slot could take values from the Getty thesaurus ULAN (Union List of Artist Names) [9].

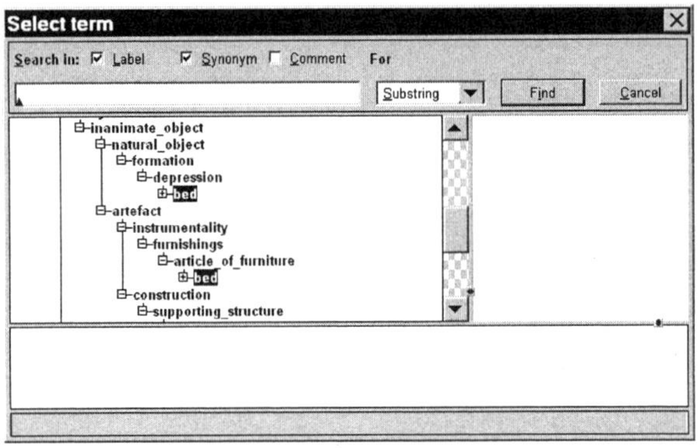

Figure 5: Disambiguating the term "bed". This window shows two of the concepts associated with `bed`. From the placement of the terms in the respective hierarchies, it is usually immediately clear to the indexer which meaning of the term is the intended one.

For annotation purposes the ontologies serve two purposes. Firstly, the user is immediately provided with the right context for finding an adequate index term. This ensures quicker and more precise indexing. Also, the hierarchical presentation helps to disambiguate terms. An example of this is shown in Fig. 4. Here, the user is describing the subject matter of the painting. Suppose she wants to say that "Venus is lying on a bed". The template on the right-hand side implements the content template as described in Sec. 3.2, in this case:

```
Agent:   Venus
Action:  lying
Object:  bed
```

When the user types in the term "bed" as the object in a content-description template, the tool will indicate that this an ambiguous term. In the user interface the term itself gets a green color to indicate this and the status bar near the bottom shows the number of hits in the ontologies. If one clicks on the magnifier button, the tool will provide the user with a choice of concepts in AAT and WordNet that are associated with this term (piece of furniture, land depression, etc.). Fig. 5 shows two of the concepts associated with "bed". From the placement of the terms in the respective hierarchies, it is usually immediately clear to the indexer which meaning of the term is the intended one.

Term disambiguation is a frequent occurrence in this type of application. For example, the term "Venus" may be associated with the Roman deity or with the planet.[1]

4.2 Searching for an image

The tool provides two types of semantic search. With the first search option the user can search for concepts at a random place in the image annotation. Fig. 6 shows an example of this. Suppose the user wants to search for images associated with the concept **Aphrodite**.

[1]In the "Venus lying bed" example, this disambiguation of "Venus" is not required, because the planet is not considered a legal value for an "agent" (this is debatable, by the way). However, general search for "Venus" (see the next subsection) will require disambiguation

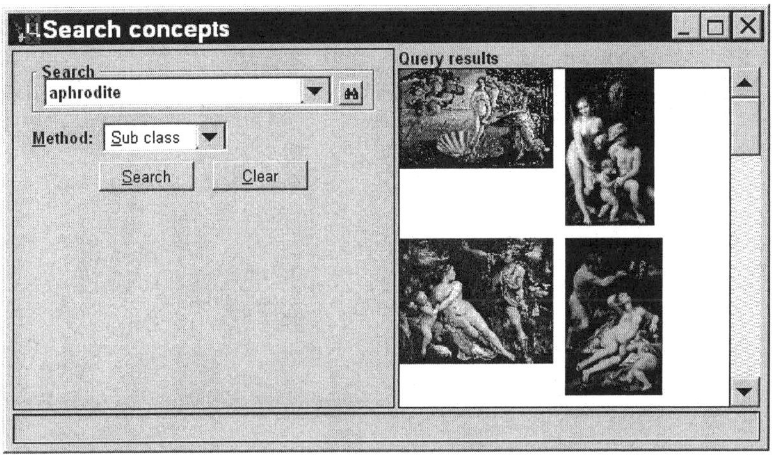

Figure 6: Example of concept search. The query "Aphrodite" will retrieve all images for which we can derive a semantic match with the concept **Aphrodite**. This includes all images annotated with the concept **Venus** (as a Roman deity). Only a small fragment of the search results is depicted

Because the ontologies contain an equivalence relation between Venus (as a Roman deity, not the planet nor the tennis player) and Aphrodite, the search tool is able to retrieve images for which there is no syntactic match. For example, if we would look at the annotation of the first hit in the right-hand part of Fig. 6, we would find "Venus" in the title ("Birth of Venus" by Botticelli) and in the subject-matter description (**Venus (a Roman deity) standing seashell**). The word "Venus" in the title can only be used for syntactic marches (we do not have an ontology for titles), but the concept in the content description can be used for semantic matches, thus satisfying the "Aphrodite" query.

General concept search retrieves images which match the query in some part of the annotation. The second search option allows the user to exploit the annotation template for search proposes. An example of this is shown in Fig. 7. Here, the user is searching for images in which the slot culture matches **Netherlandish**. This query retrieve all images with a semantic match for this slot. This includes images of **Dutch** and **Flemish** paintings, as these are subconcepts of **Netherlandish**.

5 Discussion

This article gives some indication on how a semantic web for images might work. Semantic annotation allows us to make use of concept search instead of pure syntactic search. It paves also the way for more advanced search strategies. For example, users may be specializing or generalizing a query with the help of the concept hierarchy when too many or too few hits are found.

In a previous study on a collection of ape photographs [8] we did some qualitative analysis on the added value with respect to keyword search. The provisional conclusion was that for some queries (e.g., "ape") keyword search does reasonably well, but for other sightly different queries (e.g., "great ape") the results are suddenly poor. This is exactly where semantic

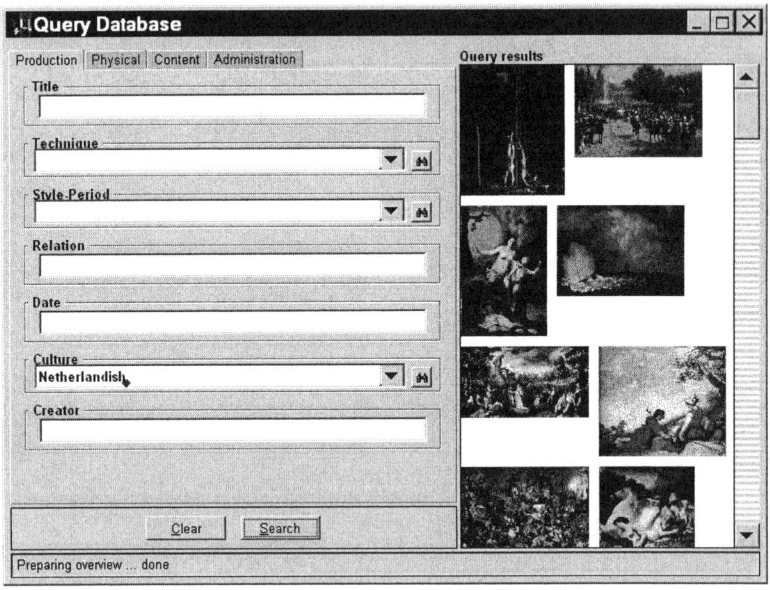

Figure 7: Search using the annotation template. The query "Netherlandish" for the slot culture retrieve all images with a semantic match for this slot. This includes images of **Dutch** and **Flemish** paintings, as these are subconcepts of **Netherlandish**

annotation could help.

Although our approach relies to some extent on manual annotation (as we did in this study), it should be possible to generate partial semantic annotations from existing annotations (which vary from free text to structured database entries). This would speed up the annotation process considerably. We are currently starting a follow-up study with a collection of 4,000 images of paintings for which we want to extract data such as title, creator, year and location from the existing annotation.

Our experiences with RDF Schema were generally positive. We made heavy use of the metamodelling facilities of RDF Schema (which allows one to treat classes as instances of other classes) for defining and manipulating the metamodels of the different thesauri. In our experience this feature is in particular needed in vases where one has to work with existing representations of large ontologies. This is a typical feature for a semantic web: you have to work with existing ontologies to get anywhere (we're not going to rebuild AAT), even if one disagrees with some of the design principles of the ontology.

For our purposes RDF Schema has some limitations in expressivity. We especially needed a notion of property cardinality and of equivalence between resources (classes, instances, properties). For this reason we plan to move at some near point in the future to OWL, the Web Ontology Language currently under development at W3C [13].

A major challenge from a knowledge-engineering perspective is to provide principled methods for adding ontology "glue". The equivalence relations mentioned in Sec. 3.1 are one example of this. In many cases existing ontologies can be augmented with additional background knowledge. For example, if we know the creator is André Derain (an artist in

ULAN), we could suggest that the style of the painting is "Fauve" (a style in AAT). But for this to work, we need to add knowledge linking ULAN and AAT. In this area much more work needs to be done to see what is feasible and what is not,

Acknowledgments This work was supported by the ICES-KIS project "Multimedia Information Analysis" funded by the Dutch government. We gratefully acknowledge the work of Maurice de Mare on the annotation of the images.

References

[1] T. Berners-Lee. *Weaving the Web*. Orion Business, London, 1999.

[2] D. Brickley and R. V. Guha. Resource description framework (RDF) schema specification 1.0. Candidate recommendation, W3C Consortium, 27 March 2000. See: http://www.w3.org.

[3] Y. Lafon and B. Bos. Describing and retrieving photographs using RDF and HTTP. Note, W3C Consortium, 28 September 2000. URL: http://www.w3.org/TR/2000/NOTE-photo-rdf-20000928.

[4] O. Lassila and R. R. Swick. Resource description framework (RDF) model and specification. Recommendation, W3C Consortium, 22 February 1999. URL: http://www.w4.org/TR/1999/REC-rdf-syntax-19990222.

[5] G. Miller. WordNet: A lexical database for english. *Comm. ACM*, 38(11), November 1995.

[6] Bijan Parsia. Rdf applications with prolog. URL: http://www.xml.com/pub/a/2001/07/25/prologrdf.html, 2001.

[7] T. Peterson. *Introduction to the Art and Architecture Thesaurus*. Oxford University Press, 1994. See also: http://www.getty.edu/research/tools/vocabulary/aat/.

[8] A. Th. Schreiber, B. Dubbeldam, J. Wielemaker, and B. J. Wielinga. Ontology-based photo annotation. *IEEE Intelligent Systems*, 16(3):66–74, May/June 2001.

[9] ULAN: Union List of Artist Names. The Getty Foundation. URL: http://www.getty.edu/research/tools/vocabulary/ulan/, 2000.

[10] J. van den Berg. Subject retrieval in pictorial information systems. In *Electronic Filing, Registration, and Communication of Visual Historical Data. Abstracts for Round Table no 34 of the 18th International Congress of Historical Sciences. Copenhagen*, pages 21–28, 1995. URL: http://www.iconclass.nl.

[11] H. van der Waal. ICONCLASS: An inconographic classification system. Technical report, Royal Dutch Academy of Sciences (KNAW), 1985.

[12] Visual Resources Association Standards Committee. VRA Core Categories, Version 3.0. Technical report, Visual Resources Association, July 2000. URL: http://www.vraweb.org/vracore3.htm.

[13] W3C Web Ontology Working Group. URL: http://www.w3.org/2001/sw/WebOnt/.

[14] J. Wielemaker. *SWI-Prolog RDF Parser*. SWI, University of Amsterdam, 2000. URL: http://www.swi-prolog.org/packages/rdf2pl.html.

[15] B. J. Wielinga, A. Th. Schreiber, J. Wielemaker, and J. A. C. Sandberg. From thesaurus to ontology. In Y. Gil, M. Musen, and J. Shavlik, editors, *Proceedings 1st International Conference on Knowledge Capture, Victoria, Canada*, pages 194–201, New York, 21-23 October 2001. ACM Press.

Annotation for the Semantic Web
S. Handschuh and S. Staab (Eds.)
IOS Press, 2003

Image Semantics without Annotations

Simone Santini
ssantini@ncmir.ucsd.edu
University of California, San Diego

Abstract. All searches in a database are semantic in nature: a user searches something based on a certain meaning that the results will share. This model, derived from traditional databases has been extended to image databases, but insufficient attention has been paid to the characteristics of signification in images and to the technical challenges and opportunities that they generate.

This paper presents an analysis of the relation between images and their meaning and argues that in image databases the process of signification is no longer unique, but it divides in at least three largely independently modalities. Each one of these modalities will require a different definition of the term "query" and, consequently, a different approach to query specification and processing, as well as to image representation.

keywords: image databases, image semantics, query modalities, query processing.

1 Introduction

Any statement to the extent that search by content in multimedia databases (specifically: images) is a complex and, as of today, unresolved problem would receive such a plebiscitary support that it could be considered a truism. Such apparently innocuous claim, however, hides some very problematic assumptions and, in a way, contains the seeds of its own undoing.

Search activities aim at accessing images based on their *meaning*, a meaning that (in the commonly accepted model) can be sufficiently formalized—at least to the point of making a technology of retrieval possible—without any reference to the cultural and structural context of the query and of the image creation process.

This assumption, which ultimately entails a reductionist approach to data retrieval, derives from a similar—and even stronger—foundation of traditional (symbolic) databases. I maintain that a fair share of the problems that plague content based image retrieval (and, by extension, content based video retrieval) come from the careless extension of these foundational presuppositions.

These presuppositions are, in my view, severely underestimating the essential process of interpretation as a creator of image semantics. The idea of semantic annotation arises naturally from such presuppositions for, if there is a semantic content of images independent of query-time interpretation, annotation is just a translation of such content in a more manageable form.

In the opening sections of this paper, I want to make the case that the situation is, in reality, more complicated. The analysis (carried out in greater detail in [13]) will reveal three modalities of queries, with different semantic underpinnings, called *closed world*, *linguistic*, and *emergent*[1]. While semantic annotation, in the standard sense of the word, is appropriate for the close world modality, it is not appropriate for the other two, for which alternative approaches will be proposed in the rest of the paper.

Before beginning, though, I think an example can convey better than any analysis the troublesome relation between images and their meaning (the example is from Mexican photographer Pedro Mayer, and is reported in [12]). In response to the question "would not a photograph of a pencil on a table always be just that, a photograph of a pencil on a table?" he replied:

> [Researcers in Peru had] the idea of using cameras to discover the codes being used by these people. They would ask a simple question and then elicit from the children [...] a response with a picture made with very simple cameras.
>
> They wanted to know what these children thought of "exploitation" [...]
>
> One child came back with a picture of a nail on a naked wall. At first the instructors thought that the child had misunderstood the idea of the experiment. But upon further investigation they found out that these children were living in an extremely poor town, several miles outside of Lima, and in order to make a little bit of money they walked every day all those many miles into town to shine shoes. And so that they did not have to carry back and forth the heavy load of the shoe boxes they rented a nail on the wall at someone's place in town. And the man that rented the nail charged them for this half of what they earned for the whole day.
>
> As you can see, sometimes a nail on the wall means much more than a nail on the wall. Or for a Cuban child the picture of a pencil on a table might have implications dealing with the blockade, as they had no pencils for a long time.

Simple images can have enormously complex meanings and implications which depend not only on *how* and *by whom* they were produced, but also on *why* are they being searched.

2 Image Semantics

The question of the relation between the image-sign and its object can be stated very simply and directly: are images icons, indices, or symbols? I can't present a complete analysis of the question here, but the following brief notes will suffice.

Iconicity refers to a relation whereby a sign is related to its object (that is, it *signifies* the object) through similarity. So, a picture of Winston Churchill would signify by virtue of its similarity with the actual face of Winston Churchill. But, as Eco [6] points out, the relation of similarity, per se, is too generic to support signification. Unless similarity is qualified, it is always possible to find a way in which any thing is similar to any other, and signification would dissolve into an hermetic feast of allegories and metaphors, in which everything is a sign for everything else.

Similarity is not sufficient for creating a sign relation, but it can provide the material for the creation of an *iconic ground*, on which a sign relation may or may not rest. The criteria by which similarities come to constitute iconic grounds, and iconic grounds come to constitute

[1] In [13], I called this the *user* modality. I have since realized that such term was a misnomer, and have come to believe that the term *emergent* might better convey the nature of such modality of signification.

sign relations are cultural, and it is only after the sign relation is established by this cultural activity that iconicity can be used as a taxonomical device to separate the sign relations that rest on iconic grounds from the others (what Sonesson [18] calls *secondary iconicity*): the creation of the sign relation itself can't be based on similarity.

Consider the picture of a red Ferrari, a piece of cardboard, a red apple, and a red Ferrari. The picture and the cardboard are similar because made of the same material but, culturally, this similarity does not create an iconic ground. A color similarity like that between the picture and the apple is sufficient to create an iconic ground (the same similarity leads to the sign relation between red and blood) but, in this case, the iconic ground does not generate a sign relation (the picture of the Ferrari does not "stand" for the apple). Finally, the iconic ground generates a sign relation between the picture and the red Ferrari. Note that images database techniques allow one to make the distinction between similarity and iconic ground (only certain visual features are considered for the determination of similarity), but consider *all* iconic grounds as sign relations.

Indexicality is the relation which a sign and its object enter when there is a direct physical relation between the two, as in the relation between smoke and fire, in which the former is a sign of the latter by virtue of a physical causality between them. This kind of relation would appear to exist between a photograph and its subject since, at one time, the film was impressed through a causal chain of events originating in (or, at least, going through) the subject. The two relations, however, are not the same: for one thing, the photographic sign does not imply a spatial and temporal contiguity with the subject[2]; moreover, to say that there is a purely mechanical connection between the object and its photograph ignores or, at least, underestimates the role of the photographer as an interpreter of reality. This role is evident in staged photographs: a picture created to signify a happy couple doesn't lose its meaning just because the two people depicted might not—in real life—know each other: the photograph is not a depiction of reality (nor is it meant to be), but a message from the photographer to the viewer.

But even with documentary photograph—in which the subjects are what they appear to be—one should always consider the presence of the photographer, who filters the possible subjects, frames them, and uses the paraphernalia of the photographic craft (some of which are symbolic, as I will argue shortly) to express a message. The most obvious examples are found in explicit attempts to deceive, as in the famous photographs of Lenin talking to the workers from which Stalin had the figure of Trotsky removed, but they are present every time in which a photographers chooses a particular subject at the exclusion of others in the vicinity, a particular angle, light, and so on.

Finally, certain aspects of photographic and filmic signification are symbolic (that is, depending on an arbitrary cultural convention–arbitrary being the key term here), as is evident in certain aspects of the film language, like the convention that a "dissolve" marks the passage of a relatively long period of time, while a "cut" maintains the temporal continuity of the scene. Symbols are often used in genres like cartoons (characters that start running at high speed leave a cloud behind; when they fall from a rock the whole frame shakes, and so on), but they are present in all genres—including documentary—with conventions like the highest

[2]That is, photographs persist in the absence of the subject, and this persistent is essential for their status as signs.

dramaticity of heavily contrasted pictures, or the placement of the subject at the center of the frame[3].

Pictures, taken in isolation, have no assertive value, but rely on some external context to predicate their content. Note that this is true not only for pictures, but also for sentences taken in isolation, and even for records in highly formalized databases. The sentence "Martin Luther was born in Mexico" is not a lie unless it is placed in a context in which it is supposed to convey a true fact about the birth place of Martin Luther. In a book of English grammar, in which the sentence has the sole purpose of explaining the use of the locution "to be born," it would be entirely appropriate. A sentence is as incomplete as a picture, but with a crucial difference: the contextual indicators of the assertive function of a sentence can be expressed in the same sign system in which the sentence is expressed (i.e. language), while this is not possible in the case of a picture.

Signification in a highly formalized and restricted environment, such as a relational database, also proceeds along conceptually similar lines. Assume that a relational table like the following is given:

Berkowitz	BRKSML56D03D403H	90000
Connors	CNNRBR67M15F301A	80000
Fitzpatrick	FTZLBR45E52B203K	95000

These records are not predicates, since they lack a context to interpret them. In a database this context is formalized in the *schema*. Supplying the schema:

Name	Fiscal Code	Salary (USD)

the table becomes a series of predicates like "Fitzpatrick earns 95000 US Dollars per year, and her fiscal code is FTZLBR45E52B203K." The interpretation of a record is not exhausted in the schema, which represents only a series of pointers into a semantic field that it does not define completely. Further interpretative rules are required which can be either explicit (like the normative rules that govern the Italian fiscal code, from which one can deduce that Fitzpatrick is a woman, born on May 12, 1945) or implicit (like the social customs for naming babies, from which one can deduce that, in all likelihood, the contents of the "Name" column are family names). The schema also leaves ambiguities that can only be solved by an ad-hoc normative outside of the database. For instance, the salary of the people identified by an Italian fiscal code is given in US dollars; but in the US, salaries are customarily given as a gross—i.e. before taxes—figure, while in Italy they are customarily given as a net—i.e. after taxes—figure. So, is Connors making $80,000 per year net or gross? The difference can be important, especially to Connors.

The schema is a function that maps the values of the records to positions in a semantic field. Whether or not this operation is sufficient to fully circumscribe the meaning of an entry depends in part on the definition of the semantic field: the more restricted and disambiguated (i.e. formalized) the field is, the more can a schema provide an autonomous reading of the record, without having to resort to extra-schematic means. A foundational assumption of

[3]Photographers, of course, can and do break these conventions, but this doesn't diminish their strength: breaking a convention, e.g. placing a subject on the side of a frame, takes its meaning from the fact that a convention exists and it is, in a particular case, broken. In other words: placing the subject on the side of a picture in a culture in which the convention dictates that the subject should be in the center doesn't have the same meaning as placing the subject on the side in the absence of conventions.

symbolic databases and formalized semantics systems is that this restriction can always be determined a priori, so that the schema can represent a full characterization of the meaning of records. In the previous case, for instance, whether the salary is a gross or net figure is an a priori characteristic of the semantic field: all possible alternative interpretative paths are restricted by a similar a priori formalization, and it is assumed that a finite set of rules, united to the usual conventions of the application domain will be sufficient to determine the meaning of the records.

If the records in the relational database of the example are replaced with images (or with some suitable set of features that describes the contents of an image), the question arises naturally of what kind of artifact will play the rôle of the schema.

I submit that, in general, pictures acquire meaning only in the presence of a *textual* discourse (in a rather general acceptation of the term that I will consider shortly). The picture of a young man, driving a sports car in the streets of Paris with a beautiful woman at his side can only have a meaning within a social discourse in which non-utilitarian cars are a sign of wealth, Paris is a romantic city, and sexually desirable women (and, in other circumstances, men) are objectified into a connotation of success. Without this surrounding discourse, the picture would have no meaning[4].

3 Modalities of Signification

From the considerations in the previous section, it appears that pictures are not predicates but entities which are predicated by some form of accompanying text. Calling *eidoneme* the unit of signification in images[5], the problem can be posed in the following terms: *what is the nature of the textual component of an eidoneme?* In particular, should it be restricted to a piece of text normatively associated to the image (e.g. a caption) or, if not, what forms of linguistic discourse should it include?

Identifying the textual discourse with pieces of text attached to individual images is unreasonably constraining. To notice but one exception, techniques based solely on image content work reasonably well in certain domains, as in trademark identification [5] or medical applications [9], because in these domains, the social discourse is sufficiently fixed to provide the necessary interpretant for the image data without the need of explicit text. On the other end of the spectrum, the predication part of the eidoneme is not necessarily explicit, but can be constituted by a shared social text or, more or less explicitly, by the user's interaction with the images. These qualifications generate three possible modalities of signification and, consequently, of search.

Linguistic Modality. An image database operates in a linguistic modality if—and to the extent in which—the images are connected to a library of text that is capable, by itself, to express meanings. It should be noted that not only doesn't this definition require that there be a univocal correspondence between a particular image and the text that describes its content, but goes a long way towards prohibiting it. Simple linguistic devices like labels or brief

---

[4] An alternative but, I believe, not incompatible way of stating the same property is that a picture has no denotation that is, no useful literal meaning (except for the trivial syntactic meaning of the pixel values)—if the woman in the Paris picture were replaced with a perfectly disguised cardboard cutout, the denotation of the picture would change, but not any of its meanings, which are purely connotative and culturally supported.

[5] From the Greek *ειδον*–to see, in a construction parallel to *grapheme*.

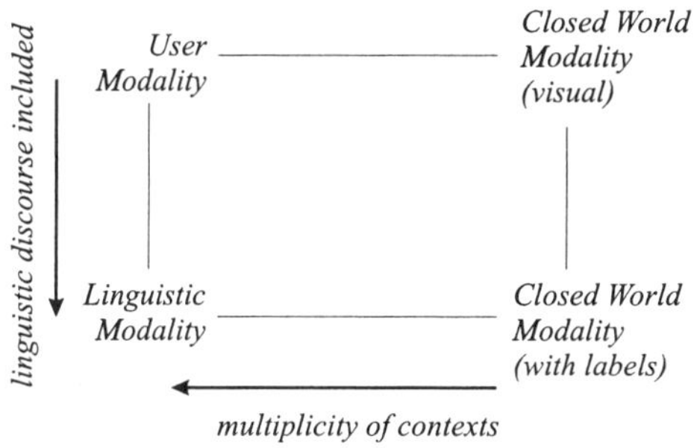

Figure 1

captions provide a symbolic description of the contents of an image within the confines of a given context: labels presuppose a context, but don't create it.

Closed World Modality. In the closed world modality, the context—and the semantic restrictions that come with it—is given by a set of habits and conventions that exist a priori (independently of the existence and the function of the database) and that are explicitly known and acknowledged by the user community of the database. An immediate consequence of this modality is that polysemy is reduced (although not completely eliminated): in a medical database, a spleen will have nothing to do with XIX century French poetry, and in a trademark database a dove will not be a symbol of peace. These considerations suggest that a database with a simple labeling or captioning scheme works in closed world modality: many a failure of labeling can be ascribed to attempts to use it in applications requiring a linguistic modality of signification.

Emergent Modality. In emergent modality the discourse that accompanies and predicates the images is created by the user or a community of users during the interaction with the information system. In this modality, the interaction with the database is structured as a conversation (which in general has many participants, either users or databases) or a narrative, which establish the boundaries and conventions of the context in which the group operates. An answer to a query is in this case a mere by-product of this context-determining conversation [15].

Context often includes concepts and practices specific of the general area in which the database is used. In this sense, the emergent modality blends with the closed world modality as the general area of interest becomes more restricted and formally defined so that one of the possible contexts becomes preponderant. On the other hand, the discourse of the application area can be (partially, at least) expressed in linguistic terms, which can be incorporated in the database, blending the emergent modality with the linguistic modality. The relation between the three modalities can be represented in a diagram like that of Fig. 1 This paper will present techniques for the determination of image semantics that operate in the linguistic and emergent modalities.

4 The world-wide-web as linguistic context

The world-wide web is a good example of how a database can operate in linguistic modality for a variety of reasons. First, images on the eb are not, in general, there by themselves, but are collected in web pages and web sites whose content is, partially at least, text. Second, the environment in which the images rest is structured in semantically meaningful ways, from the internal structure of the pages to the broader structure induced by the links between the pages. Furthermore, these structures are explicitly anchored to the syntax of the pages through the use of "tags," so that the relation between syntax and semantics is more direct than in general English test. Third, the presence of such structure influences the style of web text in a way that makes it easier to interpret. Informative portions of text tend to concentrate around significant syntactic structures [4], and the text itself is different from general English: Amitay [2] found that on the web, compared to "official" English, sentences are more fragmented and often fragments don't have a proper sentence structure. In general, delimiters are less frequently used in web pages: the word "the" makes up about 7% of regular written English, but only 3% of "web English."

These characteristics make the world-wide web an ideal test case for operating databases in linguistic modality. Given the premises of the model, it should be clear that the issue here is not to create a model of *images* that happen to be placed on the web but, rather, to create a model *of the web* in which the role of images can be adequately specified and connected to the other documents and to their structure.

4.1 A model of the web with images

In this section, it is my intention to define several models of the world wide web, progressively refining them in order to highlight the rôle of images in it and the relations between images and text documents.

At the most general level, the web is a graph $W = (D, E, \phi)$, where D is a set of *documents*, and E is the set of edges, and ϕ is a function that associates to every edge $e \in E$ an ordered pair of nodes: $\phi(e) = (d_1, d_2)$, with $d_1, d_2 \in D$, that is, $\phi : E \to D \times D$[6] In this case the link is said to go from document d_1 to document d_2. Given a document d, its *downstream neighborhood* is the set

$$\nu(d) = \{d' \in D : \exists e \in E : \phi(e) = (d, d')\} \tag{1}$$

while its *upstream neighborhood* is the set

$$\nu^*(d) = \{d' \in D : \exists e \in E : \phi(e) = (d', d)\} \tag{2}$$

The two functions $\nu, \nu^* : D \to 2^D$ are adjoint in the sense that

$$d_1 \in \nu(d_2) \Leftrightarrow d_2 \in \nu^*(d_1). \tag{3}$$

[6]In many cases a graph is defined simply as $W = (D, E)$, where D is the set of nodes (documents, in this case), $E \subset D \times D$ is the set of edges, each edge being an ordered pair of documents. This definition is equivalent to that in this paper for *simple graphs*, but can't be generalized to *multigraphs*, since two edges between the same pair of documents would be undistinguishable. Since on the web there can be multiple links between the same two documents, it is more appropriate to start from the multigrah model as a basis.

Edge type	Syntactic HTML Construct
document-to-document	<a href=".....">Link text</A>
document-to-image	<img src="...."/>
image-to-document	<a href="....."><img src="...."/></A>

Table 1: Syntactic definition of the different types of edges

The functions ν and ν^* can be extended to a set of nodes N as $\nu(N) = \bigcup_{d \in N} \nu(d)$ and $\nu^*(N) = \bigcup_{d \in N} \nu^*(d)$.

The *outdegree* of a node is the number of edges leaving that node, that is, $o(d) = |\{e \in E : \pi_1(\phi(e)) = d\}|$[7]. Similarly, the *indegree* of a node d is the number of edges entering the node, that is $i(d) = |\{e \in E : \pi_2(\phi(e)) = d\}|$. The concepts of indegree and outdegree can easily be generalized to sets of nodes.

Links are labeled, with labels drawn from a set Λ which can be finite or infinite. The labeling function $l : D \times D \rightarrow \Lambda \cup \{\perp\}$ ($\perp \notin \Lambda$) is defined as

$$l(e) = \begin{cases} \lambda \in \Lambda & \text{if } e \in E \\ \perp & \text{otherwise} \end{cases} \tag{4}$$

For the purposes of this chapter, it will be sufficient to consider the web as formed exclusively of text and images, ignoring other data types like video, audio, etc.

The distinction between text and images modifies the model in the sense that the graph is now a *colored* graph, with nodes of two types: *documents* and *images*. Consequently, edges are of different types: *document-to-document*, *document-to-image*, and *image-to-document* (I will assume that the graph contains no image-to-image edges, which seems to be largely the case for the web). These types of edges derive from well identified syntactic constructs in the html code that constitutes the web, as shown in Table 1.

Finally, one must consider the way in which images are modeled and in which they are associated to the text of the pages. Images are indexed using a fragment of the text of the page, near the IMG tag, relevant to them (the *anchor text* [14], the title of the page, and its keywords, while documents are indexed using the complete text of the page, regardless of the position of images. There are therefore two different circumstances in which a text-based index is extracted from a document: for the creation of a *document index*, associated to the whole document, and for the creation of an *image text index* for each image contained in the document. Each element in the index is a word, defined by a string, and has associated a weight. Defining it as a data type for inclusion in the database, each element in the index is a datum of type *word*, defined as:

$$\text{word} : (\text{text} : \mathit{string}, \text{w} : \mathbb{R}) \tag{5}$$

Documents and images are also data types in the database. Documents are characterized by an unique identifier and a set of words describing its contents:

$$\text{doc} : (\text{id} : \mathbb{N}, \text{wds} : \{\text{word}\}) \tag{6}$$

[7]Following the standard notation, for every pair (a, b), the two projections π_1 and π_2 are defined as $\pi_1(a, b) = a$ and $\pi_2(a, b) = b$.

Images are also represented by a data type including a unique identifier, a text index, and a visual feature. In this section I am interested only in the text index portion of the description, so I will leave the visual features unspecified by making images a parametrized data type. Any visual feature that allows the determination of a visual similarity between images can be used. See [17] for an overview of visual features commonly used in content based image retrieval. Images are a sub-type of document, since they also have an identifier and a set of words associated with them:

$$\mathrm{img}(\mu) = \mathrm{doc} + (\mathrm{vis} : \mu) \tag{7}$$

Labels also can contain different types of information, but in the database they are required to specify at least a *relevance measure* between the documents that they join, which is a real value between 0 and 1. So, as a data type, the set of label Λ is also parametrized by whatever additional information is added, and is defined as

$$\Lambda(\mu) = (\mathrm{r} : \mathbb{R}, \mathrm{x} : \mu) \tag{8}$$

Relevance can be assigned either automatically at insertion time, as I will consider later, or updated explicitly using specific database operations.

The following definition therefore applies:

Definition 1. *A web image database is a graph $W(\alpha, \mu) = (D(\alpha), E(W), \phi, l)$, where:*

- *D is a set of documents of type $D : \{d : doc|img\}$*
- *$E(W)$ is the set of edges of the graph.*
- *$\phi : L \to D \times D$ is the edge connection function*
- *$l : L \to \Lambda(\mu)$ is the labeling function, where $\Lambda(\mu)$ is the type of the labels.*

The data type of such a graph will be indicated as $\Gamma(\mathrm{doc}, \Lambda(\mu))$.

In the following, the operations for the manipulation of the database will be defined but, first, I will consider briefly the construction of the text index and the visual features for the representation of the image contents.

4.2 Construction of the text index

Following acquisition, the text collected in the pages and the image tags is analyzed to make it suitable for indexing. First, all uninformative words are removed. There are two classes of such words: the first is composed of very common words in the English language (such as "the," "which," and so on), while the second is composed of words widely used in web pages, such as "url," "http," "click," "buy," and so on. These words give no information about the content of a page, and are ignored.

Common words removal is followed by *stemming*, a procedure that reduces the size of the index by eliminating variations of the same words. A typical example of stemming in English is the removal of the final "s" from plurals, so that, for instance, "books" and "book" will be considered as the same term. The system presented here uses Porter's stemming algorithm[10]. The terms produced by stemming are used directly as an index.

Indexing terms that come from the different areas of the page (the anchor text, the collection of keywords and the title of the page) have different expected relevance for the characterization of the contents of the images. When the page is analyzed, the three different areas are summarized in three separate sets of terms, which then contribute differently to the final index through the use of different a priori *thematic weights*.

Weighting. In general, the anchor text is the most relevant for indexing, followed by the keywords and the title. I used the following three thematic weights: $\nu_a = 1.2/2$ for the anchor text, $\nu_k = \nu_t = 0.4/2$ for the keywords and the title.

Each term is also assigned a weight measuring its potential indexing quality, determined using probabilistic weighting [8]. Let T_μ be a term to which a weight needs to be assigned, df_μ the *term frequency* of T_μ (that is, the number of documents in which T_μ appears as a term), and $tf_{\mu k}$ the term frequency of T_μ for image I_k (that is, the number of times T_μ appears as a term in the index of image I_k.) The *basic term weight* for T_μ in image I_k, $\beta_k(T_\mu)$ is then given by

$$\beta_k(T_\mu) = tf_{\mu k} \log \frac{N_I - df_\mu}{df_\mu} \tag{9}$$

where N_I is the number of images in the database. This weight formula captures the two characteristics that make a term highly discriminative:

1. it appears in relatively few documents in the collection (low value of df_μ), and
2. it appears many times in the image in question (high value of $tf_{\mu k}$).

The weight of a term is then multiplied by the thematic weight corresponding to the section in which the term was found. If, in the index of image I_k, the term T_μ appears $t^a_{\mu k}$ times in the anchor text, $t^k_{\mu k}$ times among the keywords, and $t^t_{\mu k}$ times in the title, then the associated weight is

$$\alpha_{\mu,k} = \alpha(T_\mu, I_k) = (t^a_{\mu k}\nu_a + t^k_{\mu k}\nu_k + t^t_{\mu k}\nu_t) \log \frac{N - df_\mu}{df_\mu}. \tag{10}$$

5 Image-text integration

The database system presented so far contains two different representations for images: a textual representation based on the terms extracted from the page that links to the image, and a visual representation based on suitable image features. The most interesting aspect of these representations, however, comes from the possibility of interaction between the two.

In the visual engine, an image is represented as a vector of features, giving rise to the "visual" distance measure d_v. Let $\{I_k, k = 1, \ldots, N\}$ be the database of images, and $\{T_\mu, \mu = 1, \ldots, M\}$ be the database of terms. Also, let the weight of the μth term for the kth image be $\alpha_{\mu,k}$, computed as in (10). An image can then be represented in the "term space" as

$$I_k = \sum_{\mu=1}^{M} \alpha_{\mu,k} T_\mu. \tag{11}$$

Similarly, a term can be represented in the image space as

$$T_\mu = \sum_{k=1}^{N} \alpha_{\mu,k} I_k. \tag{12}$$

In this model, the similarity between terms, $\langle T_\mu, T_\lambda \rangle$, is given by

$$s_l(T_\mu, T_\lambda) = \langle T_\mu, T_\lambda \rangle = \sum_{k=1}^{N} \alpha_{\mu,k} \alpha_{\lambda,k}, \tag{13}$$

and the lexical similarity between images, $\langle I_k, I_h \rangle$ is given by

$$s_l(I_k, I_h) = \langle I_k, I_h \rangle = \sum_{\mu=1}^{M} \alpha_{\mu,k} \alpha_{\mu,h}. \tag{14}$$

Note that, if $A = \{\alpha_{\mu,k}\}$ is the matrix of the terms weights, then the similarity between I_k and I_h is the element (k, h) of the $N \times N$ matrix AA', while the similarity between terms T_μ and T_λ is the (μ, λ) element of the $M \times M$ matrix $A'A$.

The visual distance between images can be transformed in a visual similarity as $s_v(I_k, I_h; \theta)$ $g(d_v(I_k, I_h; \theta))$, where g is a positive function with $g' < 0$ and $g'' \geq 0$. The visual and lexical similarities can then be combined using a disjunction operator $\vee$. (This is a geometrical translation of the fact that two images are similar if they are visually similar *or* if they are associated to similar terms.) The result is the *total image similarity*:

$$s_t(I_h, I_k; \theta, A) = s_v(I_k, I_h; \theta) \vee (AA')_{hk}. \tag{15}$$

The operator $\vee$ can be drawn to a class of disjunction operators known as s-norms [7]. For example, the *Hamacher sum* is defined as

$$x \vee y = \frac{x + y - 2xy}{1 - xy} \tag{16}$$

Assume that the user (through means that I will present in the next section) has selected a subset of N images and has determined the similarity between them according to the current query.

The result is an $N \times N$ matrix Ψ such that the element ψ_{ij} is the desired similarity between the images I_i and I_j. The visual similarity measure s_v will be changed using suitable optimization techniques[16] so as to minimize the error

$$\min_\theta \sum_{hk} \left[s_v(I_k, I_h; \theta) - \psi_{kh} \right]^2. \tag{17}$$

In addition, through the change in the similarity between images, the configuration Ψ will also change the similarity between terms: the weight matrix A will have to change in such a way that $AA' = \Psi$. Once this is done, one can determine the new term similarity matrix $A'A$ and, from this, the new similarity between terms, so that the terms can be placed in the text window.

This results in a rather intractable quadratic problem, so an approximate solution is necessary. Instead of solving the quadratic problem, one can try to "move" the matrix a step in the right direction, that is, to find a matrix $\tilde{A}$ such that

$$\tilde{A}\tilde{A}' = (1-\gamma)AA' + \gamma\Phi \tag{18}$$

for some small constant γ. Since γ is small, the matrix $\tilde{A}$ will not be too different from A. In particular, one can write $\tilde{A} = A + E$, where $E = \{\epsilon_{ij}\}$ is composed of small elements. The previous equation can be expanded as

$$\tilde{A}\tilde{A}' - AA' = \gamma(\Psi - AA') \tag{19}$$

and

$$\tilde{A}\tilde{A}' = (A+E)(A+E)' = AA' + AE' + E'A + EE' \approx AA' + AE' + E'A \tag{20}$$

where the last approximation derives from the assumption that E is composed of small elements whose squares are negligible. The equation therefore becomes

$$AE' + EA' = \gamma(\Psi - AA'). \tag{21}$$

The right hand side is typically symmetric, since Ψ is, and therefore the left hand side is also symmetric, from which it follows that $EA' = AE'$, and the equation becomes

$$AE' = \gamma(\Psi - AA'). \tag{22}$$

This is a system of $N \times M$ linear equations in the unknown matrix E. The solution of this system will give a matrix E that represents the first "step" of the weight matrix A in the direction of the similarities Ψ. One can then define

$$A \leftarrow A + E \tag{23}$$

and repeat the whole process. At the end, the result will be a matrix A that will allow the calculation of the new term-to-term similarities as influenced by the similarity between the images associated to those terms.

The similarity matrix Ψ typicall comes from the user interface, as will be discussed in the next section, therefore in general there will be only a handful of non-zero entries, corresponding to a small group of images that the user has selected. Instead of solving the whole system (which is intractably large), it will then be sufficient to consider a reduced matrix A consisting of the images whose similarity has been re-defined in the matrix Ψ and the terms associated to those images or, if this still result in a very large system, only of the most influential terms for those images (i.e. the terms with the highest weights).

6 Interfaces for Emergent Semantics

One question from the previous section is still open, namely the source of the matrix Ψ that contains the "desired" image similarities. The matrix Ψ comes, as will be pointed out in this section, from an interface that works in *emergent modality* and, in this sense, represents the trait d'union between the linguistic modality and the user modality. The presence of this

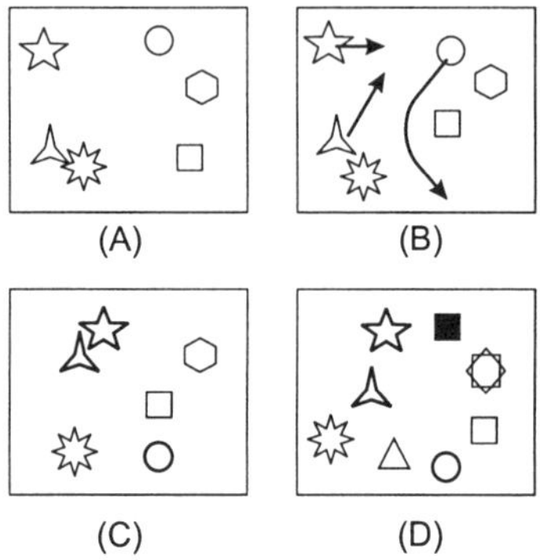

Figure 2: Schematic description of an interaction using a direct manipulation interface

connection should not come as a surprise, in light of figure 1. "Pure" linguistic modality requires a self-contained, self-coherent linguistic discourse, but this is seldom available: more often the available discourse is imperfectly specified and ambiguous to some extent.

In this case, the need to clarify the semantics of the text and to operate on the relation between text and images is left to the user. The "emergent semantics" interface that I briefly sketch in this section provides the possibility for doing so.

An user interaction using an exploratory interface is shown schematically in Fig. 2. In Fig. 2.A the database proposes a certain distribution of images (represented schematically as simple shapes) to the user. The distribution of the images reflects the current similarity interpretation of the database. For instance, the triangular star is considered very similar to the octagonal star, and the circle is considered similar to the hexagon. In Fig. 2.B the user moves some images around to reflect his own interpretation of the relevant similarities. The result is shown in Fig. 2.C. According to the user, the pentagonal and the triangular stars are are quite similar to each other, and the circle is quite different from both of them.

As a result of the user assessment, the database will create a new similarity measure, and re-order the images, yielding the configuration of Fig. 2.D. The pentagonal and the triangular stars are in this case considered quite similar (although they were moved from their intended position), and the circle quite different. Note that the result is not a simple rearrangement of the images in the interface. For practical reasons, an interface can't present more than a small fraction of the images in the database. Typically, we display the 100-300 images most relevant to the query. The reorganization consequent the user interaction involves the whole database. Some images will disappear from the display (the hexagon in Fig. 2.A), and some will appear (e.g. the black square in Fig. 2.D).

7 Database Query and Navigation

A web image and text database is a graph of type $\Gamma(\text{doc}, \Lambda)$ and the goal of an image and text query system is essentially to assist an user navigate this graph. In order to do this, the database must provide adequate data management operations. I will first introduce the abstract model of these graph operations, and then introduce the actual operators. For the graph structure management, the operators are largely based on those of the Aqua data model[19].

7.1 General overview

In addition to graphs, the model includes simple data types such as integers, floating point numbers, strings, and so on, sets, and functions. Functions are first class types, that is, they can be assigned values, be passed as parameters, and be returned by other functions. All expressions in the data algenra are composed of *terms*. A term is either

- a variable, constant, or function symbol. The type of a function taking arguments of type T_1 and producing results of type T_2 will be represented as $T_1 \rightarrow T_2$;
- a lambda abstraction
$$\lambda(x_1 : T_1, \ldots x_n : T_n).t : T \tag{24}$$
where $x_1, \ldots, x_n$ are variables, t is a term, and $T, T_1 \ldots, T_n$ are data types;
- an application
$$t_0(t_1 : T_1, \ldots, t_n : T_n) : T \tag{25}$$
where $t_1, \ldots, t_n$ are terms and t_0 is a function type.

As a shortcut, given a set of nodes N from a graph, the expression $GC(N)$ (GC for "Graph Completion") will indicate the graph obtained taking the nodes in N and all the edges joining them, with their associated labels.

A *visual similarity function* is a function $f : X \times X \rightarrow [0,1]$, where X is the data type of the visual features of the images. A *textual similarity function* is a function f : doc × doc → $[0, 1]$, which measures the text similarity between two documents. Any similarity measure s can be transformed at any moment in a distance function d by the composition $d = g \circ s$, where $g' < 0$ and $g'' \geq 0$ (see [13]).

A *similarity combination operator* is a function

$$\diamond : (X \times X \rightarrow [0,1]) \times (X \times X \rightarrow [0,1]) \rightarrow (X \times X \rightarrow [0,1]) \tag{26}$$

which transforms two similarity functions into another similarity function. For example, the pointwise multiplication "·" defined as $(f_1 \cdot f_2)(x,y) = f_1(x,y)f_2(x,y)$ is a combination. Informally, I will also use the same operator $\diamond$ to combine scores rather than scoring functions. In this case, the type of the operator is $\diamond : [0,1] \times [0,1] \rightarrow [0,1]$.

Given two documents d_1 and d_2, a *path* between them is a list of edges $e = [e_1, \ldots, e_q]$ such that $\pi_1(\phi(e_1)) = d_1$, $\pi_2(\phi(e_q)) = d_2$, and, for $i = 2, \ldots, q$, $\pi_1(\phi(e_i)) = \pi_2(\phi(e_{i-1}))$.

The *path similarity* along a path p from document d_1 to document d_2, given the score composition operator $\diamond$ is given by

$$\Sigma_\diamond(p) = (\cdots((l(p_1).r \diamond l(p_2).r) \diamond l(p_3).r) \cdots \diamond l(p_q).r) \tag{27}$$

Let $P(d_1, d_2)$ be the set of paths from d_1 to d_2. The relevance similarity between d_1 and d_2 is the minimum over this set of the path similarities between d_1 and d_2:

$$\Sigma(\diamond)(d_1, d_2) = \min_{p \in P(d_1, d_2)} \Sigma_\diamond(p) \tag{28}$$

The relevance transitive closure of a document, with relevance r is the graph

$$T(\diamond)(d, r) = GC(\{d' : \Sigma(\diamond)(d, d') \geq r) \tag{29}$$

The downstream and upstream neighborhood functions (1) and (2) can be generalized to the k-downstream and k-downstream neighborhoods as

$$\nu(d,k) = \begin{cases} \nu(d) & \text{if } k = 0 \\ \nu(\nu(d,k-1)) & \text{otherwise} \end{cases} \tag{30}$$

and similarly for $\nu^*(d,k)$.

7.2 Algebra Operators

This section introduces the operators that the database defines in order to work on the graphs.

Graph Creation The following operators create and modify the web graph.

$\mathbf{graph} : \Gamma(\mathbf{doc}, \Lambda)$; $\mathbf{graph}[\text{doc}, \Lambda]$ creates an empty graph with nodes of type "doc" and edge labels of type Λ.

$\mathbf{append} : \Gamma(\mathbf{doc}, \Lambda) \times \Gamma(\mathbf{doc}, \Lambda) \times \mathbf{doc} \times \mathbf{doc} \times \Lambda \rightarrow \Gamma(\mathbf{doc}, \Lambda)$; $\mathbf{append}(G, H, n_1, n_2, \lambda)$ with $n_1 \in \mathbf{nodes}(G)$ $n_2 \in \mathbf{nodes}(H)$ builds a graph whose node set is the union of the node sets of G and H, and whose node set is the union of the node sets of G and H with an additional edge from the node n_1 of G to the node n_2 of H. This edge has label λ.

$\mathbf{insert} : \Gamma(\mathbf{doc}, \Lambda) \times \mathbf{doc} \rightarrow: \Gamma(\mathbf{doc}, \Lambda)\times$; $\mathbf{insert}(G, n)$ inserts the node n into the graph without connecting it to other nodes.

$\mathbf{insert} : \Gamma(\mathbf{doc}, \Lambda) \times \mathbf{doc} \times \mathbf{doc} \times \lambda \rightarrow: \Gamma(\mathbf{doc}, \Lambda)\times$; $\mathbf{insert}(G, d_1, d_2, \lambda)$ inserts an edge with lael λ between the documents d_1 and d_2.

$\mathbf{delete} : \Gamma(\mathbf{doc}, \Lambda) \times \mathbf{doc} \rightarrow \Gamma(\mathbf{doc}, \Lambda)$; $\mathbf{delete}(G, n)$, with $n \in \mathbf{nodes}(G)$ removes from the graph G the node n and all the edges connected to it.

$\mathbf{delete} : \Gamma(\mathbf{doc}, \Lambda) \times E(G) \rightarrow \Gamma(\mathbf{doc}, \Lambda)$; $\mathbf{delete}(G, e)$ removes the edge e from the graph G.

$\mathbf{nodes} : \Gamma(\mathbf{doc}, \Lambda) \rightarrow set\{\mathbf{doc}\}$; $\mathbf{nodes}(G)$ returns the set of nodes of the graph G.

$\mathbf{edges} : \Gamma(\mathbf{doc}, \Lambda) \rightarrow set\{E(G)\}$; $\mathbf{edges}(G)$ returns the set of edges of the graph G.

$\mathbf{type} : \mathbf{doc} \rightarrow \{img, txt\}$; determines whether a document is a text or an image.

$\sigma : \Gamma(\mathbf{doc}, \Lambda) \times (\mathbf{doc} \rightarrow \{true, false\}) \rightarrow \Gamma(\mathbf{doc}, \Lambda)\}$; $\sigma(G, \lambda x.Px)$ returns the graph formed by all the nodes that satisfy the predicate P and all the edges connecting them.

$\mathbf{union} : \Gamma(\mathbf{doc}, \Lambda) \times \Gamma(\mathbf{doc}, \Lambda) \rightarrow \Gamma(\mathbf{doc}, \Lambda)$; $\mathbf{union}(G_1, G_2)$ (also expressed in infix form as $G_1 \cup G_2$) returns the union of the two graphs G_1 and G_2.

$\mathbf{intersection} : \Gamma(\mathbf{doc}, \Lambda) \times \Gamma(\mathbf{doc}, \Lambda) \rightarrow \Gamma(\mathbf{doc}, \Lambda)$; $\mathbf{intersection}(G_1, G_2)$ (also expressed in infix form as $G_1 \cap G_2$) returns the intersection of the two graphs G_1 and G_2.

$\nu : \mathbf{doc} \times \mathbb{N} \rightarrow \Gamma(\mathbf{doc}, \Lambda)$; k-downstream neighborhood introduced in the previous section.

$\nu^* : \mathbf{doc} \times \mathbb{N} \rightarrow \Gamma(\mathbf{doc}, \Lambda)$; k-upstream neighborhood introduced in the previous section.

$TC : (\mathbb{R} \times \mathbb{R} \rightarrow \mathbb{R}) \rightarrow \mathbf{doc} \times \mathbb{R} \rightarrow \Gamma(\mathbf{doc}, \Lambda)$; score transitive closure operator introduced in the previous section. Note that, in the definition, the operator is *curried*[20] that is, applying it to a score combination operator $\diamond$ one obtains a function $T(\diamond) : \text{doc} \times \mathbb{R} \rightarrow \Gamma(\text{doc}, \Lambda)$ that computes the score-transitive closure with respect to that operator.

7.3 Database Organization and Operators

An image database is formed by one or more relations, or *tables*, of the form $T(h : \mathbb{N}, p_1 : T_1, \ldots, p_m : T_n, x_1 : X_1, \ldots, x_n : X_n)$, where h is a unique image handle, $T_1, \ldots, T_m$ are data types, the p_i's are names of fields, $X_1, \ldots, X_n$ are feature types, and x_i is the name of the ith field or *column* of the table.

The kth row of the table is indicated as $T[k]$, and it contains the handle some features relative to one of the images stored in the database. $T[k].h$ is the handle of the image, and $T[k].x_i$ is the value of the ith feature descriptor of the image. In addition to the explicit fields, each row of the table has a *score field* ς (of type $\mathbb{R}$) such that $T[k].\varsigma$ is the distance between the image in the kth row and the current query[8]. The value of the field ς is assigned by the scoring operator Σ introduced later on. If h_0 is a handle, the notation $T[h_0]$ will be used to indicate the row k for which $T[k].h = h_0$.

Given a feature type X, let $\mathfrak{D}(X)$ be the set of distance functions defined on X. All distance functions considered take values in the interval $[0, 1]$ and are *curried*, that is, they are of type $d : X \rightarrow X \rightarrow [0, 1]$. Given an element $x : X$, and $d \in \mathfrak{D}(X)$, the function $d(x) : X \rightarrow [0, 1]$ assigns to every element of X its distance from x. Such a function is called a *scoring function*, and the set of all scoring functions for a feature type X is indicated as $\mathfrak{S}(X)$. Each table T has associated a distance, indicated as $T.d$, such that, if the signature of T is $(\mathbb{N}, X_1, \ldots, X_n)$, then $T.d \in \mathfrak{D}(X_1 \times \cdots \times X_n)$. Each row of the table has associated a scoring function

$$T[k].d = T.d(T[k].x_1, \ldots, T[k].x_n) \in \mathfrak{S}(X_1 \times \cdots \times X_n) \tag{31}$$

that measures scores with respect to the image described by the row. Moreover, a library of distance combination operators is defined.

Given a scoring function s, and a table $T(\mathbb{N}, X_1, X_2, \ldots, X_n)$ the *scoring operator* $\Sigma_T(s)$ assigns a score to all the rows of T using the scoring function s. That is, $\Sigma_T(s)$ is a table with the same signature as T and

$$(\Sigma_T(s))[k].\varsigma = s(T[k].x_1, \ldots, T[k].x_n) \tag{32}$$

Given a table $T(\mathbb{N}, X_1, X_2, \ldots, X_n)$, the k lowest distances operator $\sigma_k^{\#}$ returns a table with the k rows of T with the lowest distance from teh query. The operators $\sigma_k^{\#}$ and Σ_T are generally used together: the operator $\sigma_k^{\#}(\Sigma_T(s))$ is called the k-nearest neighbors operator for the scoring function s.

The operator $\sigma_\rho^{<}$ returns all the rows of a table T with a distance less than ρ. The operator $\sigma_\rho^{<}(\Sigma_T(s))$ is called the range query operator for the scoring function s.

[8]The use of the term *score* implied in this definition is a bit anomalous. In normal discourse, a score is positively correlated with significance, so that significant images have high score. In this case, however, score is a distance, which means that significant images have low scores.

The operator σ_P is the usual predicate selection operator on a table T. In the databases that we consider here, P has either the form $h = h_0$, where $h_0 \in \mathbb{N}$ is a handle, or $h \in H$, where H is a set of handles. Note that the notation $T[h_0]$ introduced above is a shorthand for $\sigma_{h=h_0}(T)$ which, because of the unicity of the handles, always returns a table with a single row.

The projection operator $\pi_{c_1,\ldots,c_m} T$ creates a table containing all the rows of table T and only the columns $c_1, \ldots, c_m$.

Finally, the $\diamond$-join $\underset{\diamond}{\bowtie}$ is a join operator in which two tables T and Q are joined on their handle field to form a new table $W = T \underset{\diamond}{\bowtie} Q$. If $T = T(h : \mathbb{N}, x_1 : X_1, \ldots, x_n : X_n)$ and $Q = Q(h : \mathbb{N}, y_1 : Y_1, \ldots, y_n : Y_n)$, then

$$W = W(h : \mathbb{N}, x_1 : X_1, \ldots, x_n : X_n, y_1 : Y_1, \ldots, y_n : Y_n) \quad (33)$$

The row q such that $W[q].h = h_0$ is obtained by collecting the features of the rows $T[i]$ and $Q[j]$ such that $T[i].h = Q[j].h = h_0$. The table W has a distance function $W.d = T.d \diamond Q.d$ and, if the qth row of W was obtained by joining the ith row of T with the jth row of Q, it has score $W[q].\varsigma = T[i].\varsigma \diamond Q[j].\varsigma$ and $W[q].d = T[i].d \diamond Q[j].d$

7.4 Examples

The following examples illustrate the query process over a web image and text database. I will use a notation derived from ML[20] with the addition of a comprehension syntax [21, 3] to express the results of the query.

In this examples, I will make a rather informal use of similarity functions for visual features and for textual features. I will use the symbol s^v for visual similarity functions and the symbol s^t for textual similarity function. I will also assume that combination operators will be available as needed. How to manage these operators, and how to get them out of the database is a topic beyond the scope of this paper.

Example 1 Given a document d and an image i, find the image visually closest to i among those in the documents whose relevance for d is at least r.

query q1$(d, i, r) \Rightarrow$
let
  $Q = \mathrm{TC}(\diamond)(d, r)$
  $I = \sigma(\mathrm{nodes}(Q)), \lambda x.(\mathrm{type}(x) = img))$
  $s = s_v(i)$
in
$\sigma_k^{\#}(\Sigma(s, I))$
end

The first line builds, in Q, the graph of the documents whose relevance for the given one is at least r. This graph will contain, in general, both text documents and images. The following step breaks the structure of the graph, by taking only the nodes, and selects only those nodes that are of type "image." The third statement buids a scoring function given by a suitable similarity with the given image.

Finally, the query statement takes the k nearest neighbors to the given image taken among the images of the set I.

Example 2 Retrieve all the images from the pages pointing to document d that contain the word "mousetrap" with a weight of at least r

query $\mathrm{mtrap}(d, r) \Rightarrow$
let
$$U = \sigma(\mathrm{nodes}(\nu^*(d,1)), \lambda x.(type(x) == text))$$
$$P(d) = \mathrm{and}\{true|q \leftarrow d.wds, q.w > r, q.text = \text{“mousetrap''}\}$$
$$D = \{d|d \leftarrow U, P(d)\}$$
in
$\{i|type(i) = img, i \leftarrow \nu(d), d \leftarrow D\}$ end

The first step builds the set of documents that link to d, and extracts the set of nodes of type "text." Note that the images themselves might contain the word "mousetrap," but the query explicitly requests all the images from the pages pointing to document d so one must start by considering the full text of the pages, that is, the documents of type "text."

The second text defines a function that returns "true" if a document contains the word "mousetrap" with a weight of at least r. This is done using the comprehension syntax on the "and" monoid, whose details are beyond the scope of this paper[1].

The third step uses again the comprehension syntax to build the set of documents that satisfy the predicate P. Finally, the query statement extracts all the images from these documents. Note that in the web model used in this paper, images are linked to documents that is, to go from a document to an image therein contained, one must traverse a link. This is the reason why the statement contains the function $\nu(d)$.

Example 3 Find all images that either more similar than q to image i, or that belong to documents whose relevance for the page containing i is at least r.

query $\mathrm{rel}(i, q, r) \Rightarrow$
let
$$I = \sigma_q^<(\Sigma(s_v(i))$$
$$P = \sigma(\mathrm{nodes}(\nu^*(i,1)), \lambda x.(type(x) == text))$$
$$J = \{d|d \leftarrow TC(\diamond)(d'), type(d) == text, d' \leftarrow P\}$$
in
$\{i|i \leftarrow \sigma(\nu(J,1), \lambda x.(type(x) == img)) \cup I\}$ end

7.5 Interface Projection Operator

The operators introduced in the previous sections served mainly to query the web graph in a way that incorporates images and text. This section and the following will introduce two operators that are used in conjunction to the emergent semantics interface, and that implement the trait d'union between user modality and language modality. The first one, presented in this section, is the Interface Projection Operator.

The result of a query of the type expressed in the previous section is typically a set of columns extracted from all the images that satisfy the query. These columns, quite often, will contain one or more feature types. In the example 1 above, for example, a more realistic expression for the last line would be

$$\pi_{\mathrm{name,histogram,wavelet}}(\sigma_k^{\#}(\Sigma(s, I))) \tag{34}$$

which returns a result composed of the name of an images their histograms, and their wavelet features. In the comprehension notation used in example 2, the same output would be specified as

$$\{(i.\text{name}, i.\text{histogram}, i.\text{wavelet}|\mathit{type}(i) = \mathit{img}, i \leftarrow \nu(d), d \leftarrow D\}. \qquad (35)$$

While the name of the images is an usable element per se (it can be displayed, or used to retrieve a thumbnail of the image, etc.), it is not clear how an interface should use the two feature types.

In an interface like those presented in the previous sections, the features are used to determine the placement of the images in the interface space: images are placed in the interface in such a way that their relative distances reflect the distance (in the feature space) between their feature representations. To do this, however, it is necessary to translate the feature representation of the images into two-dimensional positions in the display space[9]. The projection operator performs this task.

The operator takes a distance function from a (composite) feature space X to real numbers and produces a function that transforms a set of elements of X into a set of points in $\mathbb{R}^2$, that is, the operator is of type $\Pi : \mathfrak{D}(X) \rightarrow \{X\} \rightarrow \{\mathbb{R}^2\}$.

The query fragments above would then be written, for use with an emergent semantics interface as:

$$(\text{id} \times \Pi(s_h \diamond s_w))(\pi_{\text{name,histogram,wavelet}}(\sigma_k^{\#}(\Sigma(s, I)))) \qquad (36)$$

where $\langle f_1 \times f_2 \rangle(x, y)\ f_1(x) \times f_2(y)$ and

$$\{(i.\text{name}, \Pi(s_h \diamond s_w)(i.\text{histogram}, i.\text{wavelet})|\mathit{type}(i) = \mathit{img}, i \leftarrow \nu(d), d \leftarrow D\}. \qquad (37)$$

Given a set of images $\{x_i, i = 1, \ldots, P\}$, represented in a suitable feature space, the operator $\Pi(s)$, with $s \in \mathfrak{D}(X)$ operates as follows.

Imagine to attach a spring of length $E(x_i, x_j) = s(x_i, x_j)$ between images x_i and x_j. The spring is attached only if the distance between x_i and x_j in the feature space is less than a threshold τ. If the distance is greater than τ, the two images are left disconnected. That is, their distance in the display space is left unconstrained. The use of the threshold τ can be shown to create a more "structured" display space. The result of the operator Π is the solution of the following optimization problem

$$\{X_i, Y_i\} = \text{minarg} \sum_{x_i, x_j : E(x_i, x_j) < \tau} \left(((X_i - X_j)^2 + (Y_i - Y_j)^2)^{\frac{1}{2}} - E(x_i, x_j) \right)^2 \qquad (38)$$

Standard optimization techniques can be used to solve this problem [11].

7.6 Query Operator

The query operator solves the opposite problem than the projection operator: given a group of images in certain positions of the interface, it starts from a given distance function and modifies it to satisfy as well as possible the constraints of the interface.

[9]Interfaces can also represent images in a cube, in which case it would become necessary to translate the features into three-dimensional positions. The operators for two and three dimensions are conceptually the same, and I will only consider the two-dimensional one, although I will write the equations in a rather general format.

The type of this operator is $\coprod : \mathfrak{D}(X) \to \{(X, \mathbb{R}^2)\} \to \mathfrak{D}(X)$, and the operator application $\coprod(s)(A)$ returns a distance function obtained modifying the function s in such a way that the distance between the feature vectors X of the images returned in the set A match as well as possible the distances between the respective projections in $\mathbb{R}^2$. The set $A = \{(x : X, (p_x, p_y) : \mathbb{R}^2\}$ is returned by the interface. Note that, in practice, the interface will not return the feature vector X of the images it contains, but their identifier. I will use the operator $\coprod : \mathfrak{D} \to \{(\mathbb{N}, \mathbb{R}^2)\} \to \mathfrak{D}$, which takes the image positions on the interface and their identifiers as a short-hand for

$$\coprod(s)\left(\pi_X(\sigma_{\mathrm{id}\in X}(D))\right) \tag{39}$$

Queries involving the user interface are typically iterative. Example 1, for instance, can be transformed in a query suitable to be part of an iterative loop as:

query $\mathrm{q1}(d, i, r, A) \Rightarrow$
let
$Q = \mathrm{TC}(\diamond)(d, r)$
$I = \sigma(\mathrm{nodes}(Q)), \lambda x.(\mathrm{type}(x) = img))$
$s = \coprod(s_v(i))(A)$
in
$\{i.\mathrm{name}, \Pi(s)(i.\mathrm{X}) | i \leftarrow \sigma_k^{\#}(\Sigma(s, I))\}$
end

Note that the feature X that characterizes an image needs not be a visual feature, but it can contain terms that are used to characterize the image. In this case, the query operator will determine the lexical similarity (14) or the total similarity (15) using the methods illustrated in section 5.

The query operator, like the projection operator, solves an optimization problem, this time in the space $\mathfrak{D}(X)$ of the distance functions defined on the features X. If the distance function s in $\coprod(s)(A)$ belongs to a family of functions depending on a number of parameters ξ, then the problem is reduced to a standard (regularized) optimization problem in $\mathbb{R}^n$. Further details on this issue are available in [15].

8 Interaction Examples

The way in which the system exploits the correlation between images and text in order to identify the meanings that the user has in mind is probably best illustrated by a walk-through of the system interface. The main components of the system interfaces are two windows: an *image window* and a *text window*, an example of which is shown in Figures 3 and 4. The user typically starts the interaction by typing one or two keywords, and receives a *configuration* of images in the image window and a configuration of words in the text window. The spatial relations between images (and between words) in the interface reflects the relation between them in the feature space. So, if two images are placed next to each other, it means that, according to the similarity criterion that the system is using at the moment, the images are very similar to each other. The user interact with the system in three ways:

1. The user can select images and move them around the image window, placing them in positions that reflect his or her current idea of similarity between them. For instance, the

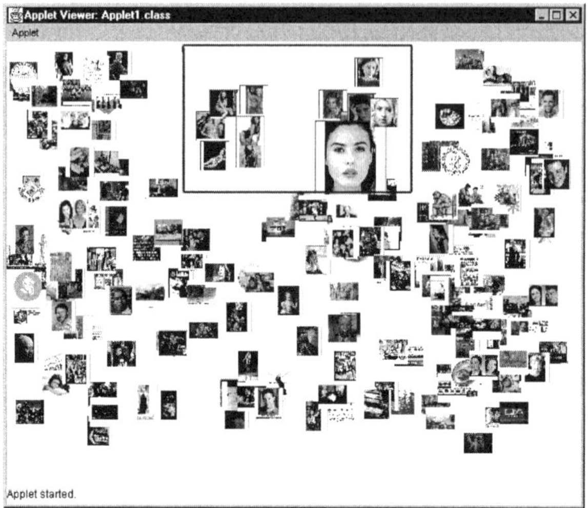

Figure 3: The image window in the system interface

images inside the rectangle in figure 3 have been selected[10] and placed in position. There are two groups of images: one contains faces of women, the other contains full body pictures of women. The user is interested in both these classes.

2. The user can select words, and move them around the text window, much like is done in the case of images. In the window of figure 4, the user has selected and placed words related to women.

3. The user can add new words to the text window and place them in relation with the words already there.

The system responds with a new configuration which better reflects the user's concept of similarity both in the image window and the words window[16]. Consider, for instance, a configuration in the words window. Figure 5 represents a hypothetical configuration in the word interface. In Figure 5 (A), the database presents a certain configuration of words. From this configuration it is evident that the word "tree" is considered ambiguous, since it could refer to a natural tree, or to the computer science data structure. In Figure 5 (B), the user selects a certain number of terms related to the "forest" tree, and groups them together, indicating that these terms should be considered similar. In Figure 5 (C), the interface responds by changing the configuration, bringing in more similar words, and eliminating some of the words related to the undesired meaning of the word. Similar changes take place at the same time in the image window.

[10]The rectangle in figure is not part of the interface, but it has been added to make the selection more visible. The interface uses a red rectangle around the images to mark the selected images which is barely visible in the color reproduction of the interface, and completely invisible in the black and white printed version.

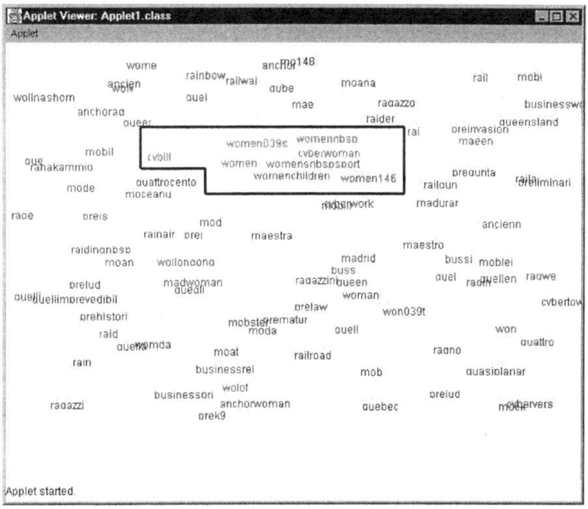

Figure 4: The text window in the system interface

9 Conclusions

This paper has discussed some issues in the definition of a database in which images derive their meaning both from their visual features and from the structure of the web in which they are immersed (linguistic query modality).

I have introduced a model of the web in which documents are of type image or of type text. Texts are characterized by word indices, while images are characterized both by word indices and by a visual feature. Text features are extracted using standard information retrieval techniques, while visual features are derived from a spectral decomposition of the region adjacency graph of the image.

The resulting web graph is stored in the database. The paper proposed a data algebra for querying and navigating this graph using visual similarity, textual similarity, and relations induced by links.

Also, the paper introduced the connection between the linguistic query modality and another modality, which I called *user*. In this interaction mode, the user manipulates directly the inter-image and inter-term similarities. I have introduced operators that can enrich the query system to include user modality queries and their interactions with the linguistic modality queries.

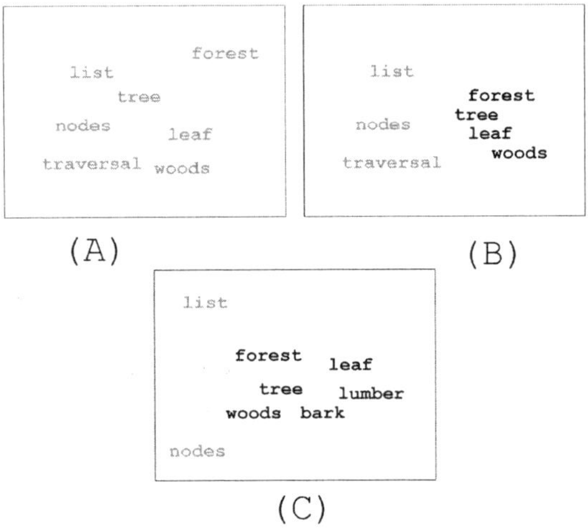

Figure 5: Example of interaction with the text window

References

[1] Antonio Martinez Alcantara and Bill Buckles. Supporting array types in monoid comprehensions.

[2] E. Amitay. Using common hypertext links to identify he best phrasal description of target web documents. In *Proceedings of the 21st ACM SIGIR Conference on Research and Development in Information Retrieval, Melbourne, Australia*, 1998.

[3] P. Buneman, L. Libkin, D. Suciu, V. Tannen, and Limsoon Wong. Comprehension syntax. *SIGMOD Record (ACM Special Interest Group on Management of Data)*, 23(1):87–96, 1994

[4] Suomen Chakrabarti, Byron Dom, Prabhakar Raghavan, Sridar Rajagopalan, David Gibson, and Jon Kleinberg. Automatic resource compilation by analyzing hyperlink structure and associated text. In *Proceedings of the Seventh International World Wide Web Conference, Brisbane, Australia*, 1998.

[5] J. P. Eakins, J. M. Boardman, and M. E. Graham. Similarity retrieval of trademark images. *IEEE Multimedia*, 5(2), 1998.

[6] Umberto Eco. *A Theory of Semiotics*. Indiana University Press, Bloomington, 1976.

[7] Ronald Fagin. Combining fuzzy information from multiple systems. In *Proceedings of the 15th ACM Symposium on Principles of Database Systems, Montreal*, pages 216–226. 1996.

[8] William B. Frakes and Ricardo Baeza-Yates, editors. *Information Retrieval, Data Structures and Algorithms*. Prentice Hall, Englewood Cliffs, 1992.

[9] Euripides Petrakis and Christos Faloutsos. Similarity searching in medical image databases. *IEEE Transactions on Knowledge and Data Engineering*, 9(3):435–447, 1997.

[10] M. F. Porter. An algorithm for suffix stripping. *Program*, 14(3):130–137, 1980.

[11] William H. Press, Brian P. Flannery, Saul A. Teulolsky, and William T. Vetterling. *Numerical Recipes, The Art of Scientific Computing*. Cambridge University Press, 1986.

[12] Fred Ritchin. *In Our Own Image*. Aperture, 1999.

[13] Simone Santini. *Exploratory Image Databases: Content Based Retrieval*. Academic Press, 2001.

[14] Simone Santini. A query paradigm to discover the relation between text and images. In *Proceedings of SPIE Vol. 4315, Storage and Retrieval for Media Databases*, 2001.

[15] Simone Santini, Amarnath Gupta, and Ramesh Jain. Emergent semantics through interaction in image databases. *IEEE Transactions on Knowledge and Data Engineering*, 2001.

[16] Simone Santini and Ramesh Jain. User interfaces for emergent semantics in image databases. In *Proceedings of the 8th IFIP Working Conference on Database Semantics (DS-8), Rotorua (New Zealand)*, January 1999.

[17] Arnold Smeulders, Marcel Worring, Simone Santini, Amarnath Gupta, and Ramesh Jain. Image databases at the end of the early years. *IEEE Transactions on Pattern Analysis and Machine Intelligence*, 23(1), January 2001.

[18] Göran Sonesson. Sémiotique visuelle et écologie sémiotique. *RSSI*, 14(1-2):31–48, 1994.

[19] Bharati Subramanian, Stanley Zdonik, Theodore Leung, and Scott Vandemberg. Ordered types in the aqua data model. Technical Report CS-93-10, Dept. of Computer Science, Brown University, 1993.

[20] Jeffrey Ullman. *Elements of ML Programming*. Prentice Hall, 1994.

[21] Philip L. Wadler. Comprehending monads. In *Proceedings of the 1990 ACM Conference on Lisp and Functional Programming, Nice, France*, 1990.

Annotation for the Semantic Web
S. Handschuh and S. Staab (Eds.)
IOS Press, 2003

MUSETTE: uses-based annotation for the Semantic Web

Pierre-Antoine Champin, Yannick Prié
{champin|yprie}@lisi.univ-lyon1.fr
Cognition and Experience Team - LIRIS
University Claude Bernard of Lyon
http://experience.univ-lyon1.fr/

Abstract. In Tim Berners-Lee's vision of the Semantic Web, software agents must be able to retrieve knowledge relevant to the end-user's task, despite the heterogeneity and scale issues which are inherent to the web. Annotating web resources is considered a promising way to achieve this vision. We argue in this chapter that every actual use of a resource may provide useful knowledge about that resource and therefore should annotate it.

We propose a framework for taking uses into account and annotating resources with their uses. This framework is the result of a generalization effort in our team after a number of projects focusing on modeling uses and experience. We believe that this framework is relevant to the Semantic Web where uses-based annotation may prove valuable.

1 Introduction

As the next step in the evolution of the World Wide Web, the Semantic Web must provide more "intelligent" services, taking into account the end-users' tasks and needs. This means that not only data must be made available (as is principally the case today), but also meta-data allowing a software agent to "learn" how to interpret the data: Document Type Definitions, XML-Schemas, RDF annotations, etc. In other words, *knowledge* rather than plain data must be handled. This also implies that social factors must be taken into account, such as privacy and trust.

Annotation can be defined as the process of attaching some additional information to a resource, in order to facilitate some task involving that resource. An emerging idea is that annotating resources on the Web may help to achieve the purpose of the Semantic Web. Firstly, because most existing resources are not designed to be "semantically" used by software agents. Secondly, even when they are, one may not have privilege to add such information to a given resource. Thirdly, and probably the most important, expressible knowledge for a given resource may not be suitable to every imaginable task. We even argue that it is impossible to enumerate every potential use of a resource.

On the other hand, every specific use of a resource may become a valuable source of knowledge about how that resource *can* be used. It seems therefore relevant to consider that using a resource *annotates* that resource. The MUSETTE framework is a general approach to provide a mechanism to achieve and handle this kind of annotation. We describe this framework in section 2, then give a simple example of its application in the next section. In section 4, we discuss the relevance of the approach by 're-reading' some applications through the newly introduced concepts. Finally we conclude.

2 The MUSETTE framework

In this section we present the MUSETTE (Modeling USEs and Tasks for Tracking Experience) framework, that we propose for representing the uses of a system and annotate the used resources accordingly.

2.1 Use model

To represent the uses of resources, one has to choose the context in which these uses are observed. The context can be very restricted (e.g. a single application) or very large (e.g. a set of interconnected computers), depending on what one wants to track exactly and of course on the available means to track uses. Once the boundaries of the observed system are chosen, one needs to choose which elements and behaviors of the system will be tracked, depending again on what is considered of interest and on what can effectively be observed[1] from the system. This is what we call the *use model*.

Use model:
The use model of a system is the set of observable *objects of interest*. Those can be either *entities* (including, but not limited to, resources in use) or *events* which can occur during the use of the system (including, but not limited to, operations performed by the user).

The use model also defines a set of *relations* with which the objects of interest can be linked together.

Note that this definition is a minimum requirement. The sets of objects of interest and relations may be more or less structured with orders or hierarchical relations, but we do not require it. This will be discussed later, in section 4.2.

2.2 Use trace

At a given moment, the state of the system can be described in terms of entities from the use model. During a given period of time, what happens can be described in terms of events from the use model. In MUSETTE, an actual use of the system is represented that way and called the *use trace*.

[1]Note that the notion of 'observability" is relative to the state of the art: shapes or characters may be considered 'observable" from a video stream, provided that one has the appropriate extraction software.

Use trace:
A use trace of a system is an alternate sequence of *states* and *transitions*. Each state is described with entities from the use model, while transitions are described with events from the use model. Entities and events in the use trace may be connected to each other with the relations defined in the use model.

Just as there is not only one possible use model for a system, there is not only one way of describing the system or the actions of the user: how often a state is captured (every given period of time, every click, every mouse move?), what entities it actually contains (only the ones displayed on the screen, every object in memory?) and how entities and events are actually connected, are all a matter of choice, depending on what is of interest and what is technically feasible.

2.3 Explained task signatures

Use traces are hard to handle *as is* (this is the kind of data usually processed with data-mining techniques in order to extract knowledge). It is then necessary to *explain* the use trace with the notion of task. Task models have been largely studied in the AI and cognitive science literature —see for example [4, 9]. However, our purpose here is slightly different: we do not intend to describe precisely the tasks and even less to prescribe them, but only to detect their occurrences in the use trace in order to explain it. It is clear however that the more precisely a task is modeled, the better the explanations.

Explained task signature:
An explained task signature is primarily composed the of a pattern of objects of interest from the use model, constrained by a number of relations (from the use model, or other external relations computable on the objects). That pattern, or *signature*, is defined so as to match occurrences of the corresponding task in the use traces. It is enriched by annotating objects of the pattern with *explanations* of their role in performing the task.

Again, MUSETTE does not commit to a particular kind of explanations. It can be notes in natural language, other objects of interest from the use model (e.g. for eliciting implicit objects), or even objects of interest from some other (more specific) use model[2].

2.4 Use cases

Provided a collection of explained task signatures, the somewhat continuous use traces can be cut into significant parts instantiating the signatures, thus corresponding to the occurrences of the tasks.

[2]Every use model can in fact be seen as describing a particular task in a more general use model. E.g. the use model of a word-processing application is a task explanation from the point of view of the productivity suite, which has a more general use model; the use model of a web-mail service is a task explanation from the point of view of the web browser.

Use case:
A use case is a part of the use trace matching a given explained task signature, enriched by the explanations provided with that signature.

Obviously, some objects of interest in the use trace may belong to several use cases, since the user's behavior may be complex, and several tasks may be performed concurrently. On the other hand, some parts of the use trace may not belong to any use case at all, since the collection of explained task signatures can not usually cover all the possible tasks of some (imaginative) users. Note however that some signatures can be quite general and then have a broad coverage, while having less informative explanations (like "Clicking on a link" for a web browser).

As we stated in the introduction, we consider that every use of a resource annotates that resource. From that point of view, a resource involved in a use trace would be annotated by every object of interest with which it is in relation, or in the same state/transition, or in a nearby state/transition, etc. Eventually, the whole use trace would indirectly annotate it.

Use cases allow precise contexts to be identified in which a limited set of objects of interest from the use trace is a *relevant* annotation of that resource (that relevance being attributed to the fact that those objects of interest were all involved in the same task). Such annotations can be used by Semantic Web agents to reason about the resource. The advantage of layering use cases on top of the use trace is that each agent can take into account only some explained task signatures (and hence the corresponding use cases). Furthermore, one is not limited to the explained task signatures provided initially: whenever new tasks are discovered (by extracting them from the raw use trace, by interviewing users, etc.) and modeled, new use cases can be identified in the use trace, providing new annotations suited to previously not handled tasks.

3 Applying MUSETTE, an example

In this section, we present a possible (though simplistic) application of the MUSETTE framework to an application which is assumed be well known to the reader: a web browser. The whole example is illustrated in Figure 1 and detailed below. It is worth noting that the design choices made for this example were aimed at making it pedagogical and concise, rather than really useful.

3.1 Use model

For the sake of simplicity, we limit our use model to four kinds of entities and four kinds of events. Entities are Web pages (*Page*), hyperlinks (*Link*), images (*Image*) and preference settings (*Pref*). Events are clicking on a link (*Click*), saving a page or an image (*Save*), bookmarking a page (*BkMrk*) and setting the preferred language (*Lang*).

The use model also provides relations between event types and entity types, in order to define which relations should occur in the use trace between the corresponding events and entities. In Figure 1 we only show such relations for one event type (*Click*), so that the figure remains readable.

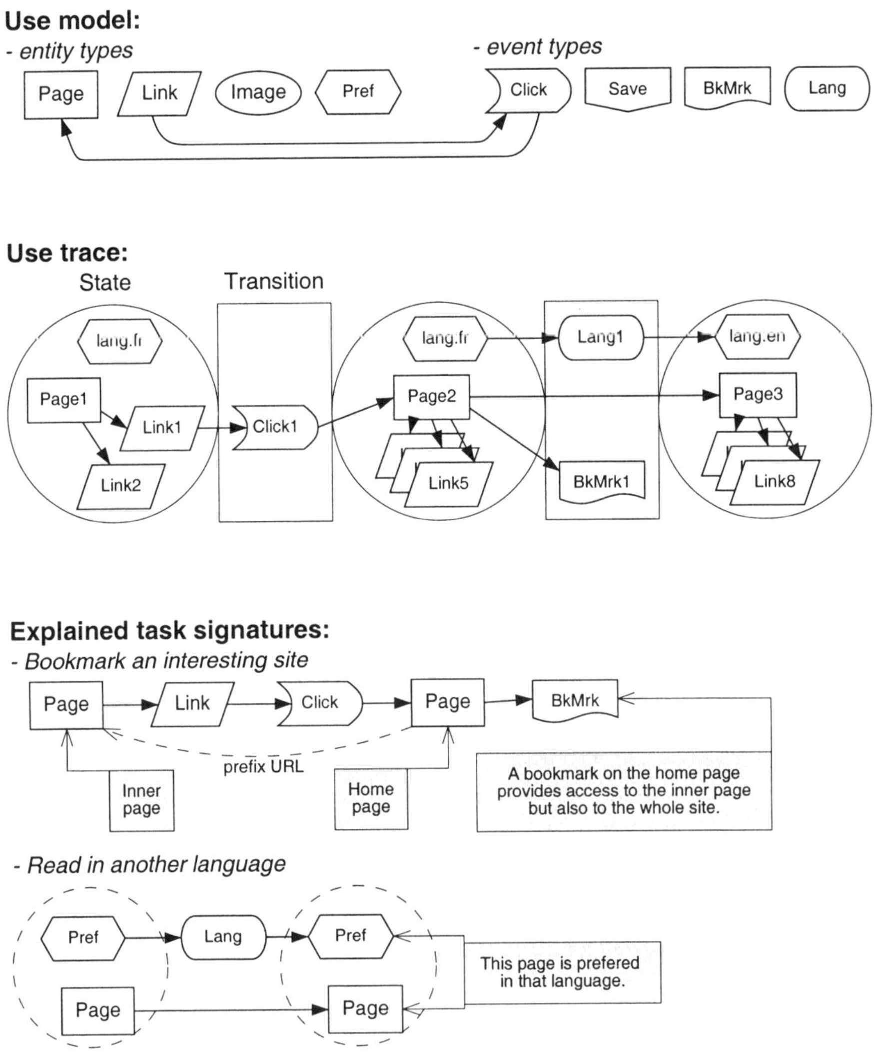

Figure 1: Applying MUSETTE to a web browser – a simple example

3.2 Use trace

Below the use model in Figure 1 stands a part of an example use trace. Each state is represented by a circle, enclosing the entities composing the state. Each transition is represented by a rectangle, enclosing the events composing the transition. The use trace could be interpreted as follow: the user is reading a web page (*Page1*) containing two links (*Link1*, *Link2*), and her preferred language is set to French (*lang:fr*). She then clicks on *Link1* (*Click1*), which brings her to a new page with many links (*Page2*), her preferred language not changed. She then chooses to bookmark *Page2* (*BkMrk1*) and to change her preferred language to English (*Lang1*). This event brings her to the English version of *Page2* (*Page3*).

3.3 Explained task signatures

We provide two explained task signatures for interpreting the use model of our example.

Bookmarking an interesting site

The rationale of this task is that, when an interesting page is found, the site or sub-site containing the page (i.e. the home page of the site) may be rather bookmarked than the page itself (which we call the *inner page*). Indeed, the home page generally provides an easy access to the inner page and may furthermore provide access to other related, therefore also interesting pages.

The occurrence of such a task can be easily detected in the use trace with the pattern given in Figure 1. A link is traversed from a page to an 'upper' page on the same site (i.e. a page with a shorter URL), then the latter is bookmarked. The constraint between the two pages is represented by the dotted arrow, while the explanations are represented by the gray rectangles.

Reading in another language

This task consists in changing the preferred language of the browser in order to read a translated version of the current page (when such a translated version is available). This is what is represented by the pattern in Figure 1, with the dotted circles meaning that the enclosed entities must belong to the same state. An explanation in a gray rectangle gives an interpretation of that task signature: the corresponding page is supposed to be preferred in the second language.

3.4 Use cases

The piece of use trace given in Figure 1 contains two use cases with regard to the small collection of explained task signatures provided (see Figure 2). The first one is an occurrence of *Bookmark an interesting site*, with *Page1*, *Link1*, *Click1*, *Page2*, *BkMrk1* as its matching objects of interest. The second is an occurrence of *Reading in another language*, matched by *lang:fr*, *Lang1*, *lang:en*, *Page2* and *Page3*.

In the context of being the home page of a site, *Page2* is annotated by *Page1*, as a page of particular interest in that site. On the other hand, in the context of being a French page, *Page2* is annotated by *Page3*, as a preferable translation.

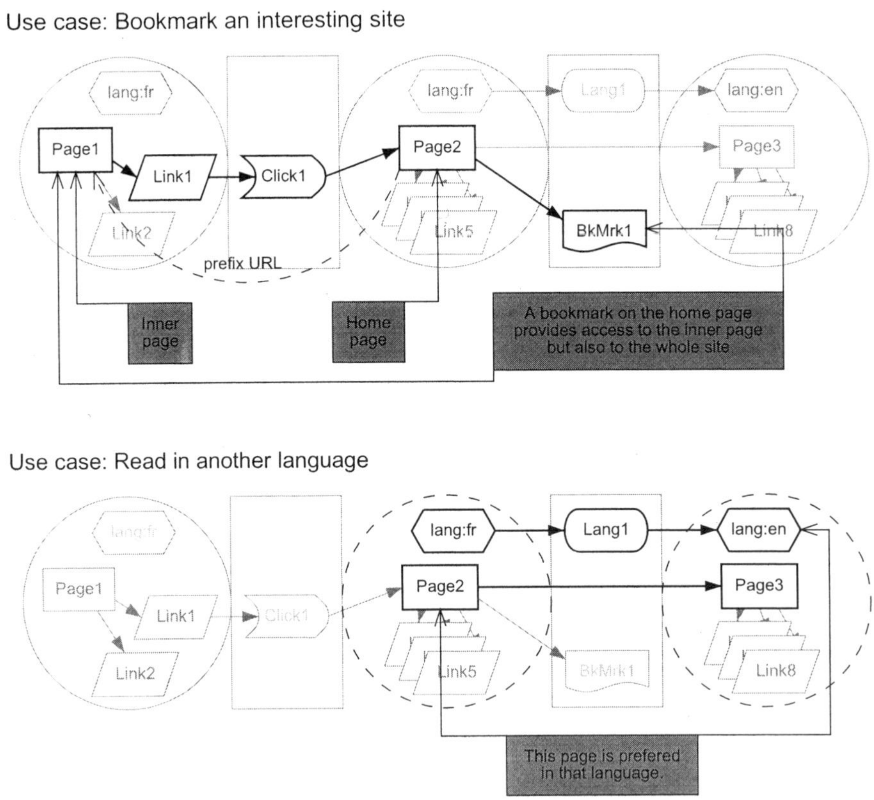

Figure 2: Two use cases in the simple browser example

4 Discussion

In this section, we discuss the relevance of the MUSETTE framework. First, we present a number of projects "explained" through the MUSETTE approach and the newly introduced concepts (use model, explained task signature, use case). Then we discuss how annotation by uses and other kinds of annotation can be combined and complement each other.

4.1 MUSETTE *applied*

The framework described here is the result of a generalization effort we made, after a number of projects in our team implying reuse of experience in various domains.

In the PADIM project [10], the system helps the operator of a supervision environment to customize this environment adequately to events in the supervised system. The use model is composed the interface components (*supervision objects*) and the states of the corresponding industrial devices. Since the domain knowledge is very complex, no precise task signature is provided, but use cases (*supervision episodes*) can however be delimited, according to the supervision object being focused at a given moment. We then consider *one* very general task signature, which could be called "Focus on supervision element". Those use cases are then proposed for reuse by the system in a similar context (last operation performed, state of the current supervision environment).

The case of the ARDECO project [3], in the domain of mechanical design, is quite similar. The domain knowledge is very complex and no precise task signature is given to the system. The use model, on the other hand, is well known and very structured (mechanical components, geometrical operators, constraints, etc.). The system is able to detect use cases (*design episodes*) according to recurrent behaviors of designers when changing task. Here again, design episodes from a similar context are proposed for reuse when the designer requires help.

In the distant learning environment PIXED [14], tasks are more described since learners express their goal by means of a *target notion*. The use model is composed of pedagogical activities (i.e. hyper-documents linked to a notion) and tests accessible to the learner. A use case is a path through several pedagogical activities and tests in order to learn the target notion. They can be characterized (explained) as a success or a failure depending on the result of the final test. The system can propose successful use cases to learners, with regard to their initial profile (the notions they are supposed to already know and their previous successful or failed activities).

In addition to consulting documents and passing tests, learners and teachers can also annotate pedagogical activities in order to improve them and provide hints to other learners. This shows that annotation with uses can integrate very well with other annotation systems, as will be discusses in section 4.2.

We also believe that MUSETTE can be used to explain other systems using (more or less explicitly) annotation by uses. One of the most famous is the search engine GOOGLE™. Linking one's page to a web resource is indeed a typical use of that resource, and the whole hypertext structure of the web can be seen as a use trace of that very simple use model. Ranking mechanisms, used by GOOGLE to improve their results, can be seen as the application of explained task signatures on top of such a use trace. The relevance of that use model and of the associated explained task signatures, has been largely demonstrated by the success of GOOGLE.

4.2 MUSETTE *and other kinds of annotation*

Formal vs. informal annotation

Many related works in the field of the Semantic Web rely on strictly formalized annotation of informal content. Hence, languages such as SHOE [13] or DAML-OIL [8, 5] provide means of describing ontologies, and projects like CREAM [12, 11] provide applications to annotate HTML pages in order to make their content available to software agents with inference capabilities. The MPEG-7 effort [16] aims at providing the same kind of languages and tools for multimedia content.

Although the advantages of using ontologies have been largely advocated in the Semantic Web community, it implies a certain cost-benefit trade-off. Building a reliable ontology is hard to achieve: ontologies rely on a common understanding of the domain which may be hard to get at the scale of the web (hence the scope of ontologies, limited to communities called *ontogroups* in the Ontobroker system [6]). Furthermore, ontologies and therefore ontological annotations, are suited to a particular task and we emphasized in the introduction the virtually infinite variety of tasks in which a resource can be used.

This explains the development of more flexible annotation systems like Annotea [2, 15], where annotations are basically free text, but can be tagged in XML and extended with the RDF-Schema mechanism. We are also working on an annotation system for audiovisual content, relying on an interconnected set of terms which is not necessarily related to a well formalized structure — project RECIS [7].

MUSETTE does not commit to a particular level of formalization for annotations. This actually only depends on the level of formalization of the use model and the explanations associated to task signatures. The example in section 3 does not provide a well structured use model and only textual explanations in the task signatures, but more elaborate ones could be used instead. The advantage would be that reasoning about the use trace be much more powerful. The drawback would be a greater effort to set the system up. Furthermore, not every domain or application is sufficiently well known to be strictly formalized.

However, some applications of MUSETTE could also apply a hybrid use model, some part of which being related to an ontology, and some other part being less formalized. The latter could then be ignored by inference engines, though usable by other reasoning mechanisms (such as case based reasoning [1]).

Annotations as part of the use model

As we already mentioned, annotating with uses is not the only way of annotating resources. Many applications offer tools to *manually* annotate a document or a part of a document, usually with metaphors such as a highlighting pen or a sticky note. Those kind of annotations are straightforwardly taken into account in MUSETTE as soon as they are part of the use model and furthermore if the annotation task is identified by a corresponding explained task signature.

Manual annotations are all the more valuable that they may provide support to tasks that are not well supported by the rest of the use model (by setting explicit relations between objects not initially meant to be linked). Thus, they may even allow us to discover new task signatures and get a better understanding of the use trace.

5 Conclusion

In this chapter, we first underlined the fact that every use of a resource may provide useful knowledge about that resource, be it only *how* that resource can be used. It appears relevant therefore to annotate resources with their uses. For that purpose, we presented MUSETTE (Modeling USEs and Tasks for Tracking Experience), a framework for annotating resources by their uses. The way resources are used is captured in use traces, which rely on a use model. Explained task signatures allow use cases to be identified in the trace. Those use cases represent *contextually relevant* annotations of the resources they involve, and can be processed by different kinds of reasoning mechanisms. This framework is flexible enough to allow highly formalized annotations with powerful inferences, or free form annotations to be used with other reasoning mechanisms (e.g. case based reasoning). It also allows newly discovered tasks to be taken into account by adding new explained task signatures and re-interpreting the use trace accordingly. We showed how this framework was applied in different kinds of applications and discussed its relevance for achieving the Semantic Web.

References

[1] Agnar Aamodt and Enric Plaza. Case-based reasoning: Foundational issues, methodological variations, and system approaches. *AICom*, 7(1):39–59, 1994.

[2] The Annotea project. `http://www.w3.org/2001/Annotea/`.

[3] Pierre-Antoine Champin and Patrick Bougé. Une représentation épisodique des connaissances pour l'assistance à la réutilisation en CAO. In Bruno Bachimont, editor, *13èmes journées francophones d'Ingénierie des Connaissances*, pages 175–183, Rouen, France, May 2002. In french.

[4] Balakrishnan Chandrasekaran, John R. Josephson, and V. Richard Benjamins. The Ontology of Tasks and Methods. In *Proceedings of the 11th Knowledge Acquisition Modeling and Management Workshop, KAW'98*, Banff, Canada, April 1998.

[5] The Darpa Agent Markup Language (DAML) project. `http://www.daml.org/`.

[6] Stefan Decker, Michael Erdmann, Dieter Fensel, and Rudi Studer. Ontobroker: Ontology based access to distributed and semi-structured information. In R. Meersman et al., editor, *Semantic Issues in Multimedia Systems. Proceedings of DS-8*, pages 351–369. Kluwer Academic Publisher, Boston, 1999.

[7] Elöd Egyed-Zsigmond, Alain Mille, Yannick Prié, and Jean-Marie Pinon. Trèfle : un modèle de traces d'utilisation. In *13èmes journées francophones d'Ingénierie des Connaissances*, Rouen, France, May 2002. In french.

[8] D. Fensel, I. Horrocks, F. Van Harmelen, S. Decker, M. Erdmann, and M. Klein. OIL in a Nutshell. In R. Dieng et al., editor, *Knowledge Acquisition, Modeling, and Management, Proceedings of the European Knowledge Acquisition Conference (EKAW-2000)*. Lecture Notes in Artifi cial Intelligence, LNAI, Springer-Verlag, October 2000.

[9] Dieter Fensel, Enrico Motta, V. Richard Benjamins, Stefan Decker, Mauro Gaspari, Rix Groenboom, William Grosso, Mark Musen, Enric Plaza, Guus Schreiber, Rudi Studer, and Bob Wielinga. The Unifi ed Problem-solving Method Development Language UPML. Delivrable, University of Karlsruhe, Institute AIFB, 1999.

[10] Béatrice Fuchs, Alain Mille, and Benoit Chiron. Using explanations to guide adaptation. In *Workshop on Adaptation in Case-Based Reasoning, 12th European Conference on Artificial Intelligence*, Budapest, Hungary, August 1996.

[11] Siegfried Handschuh and Steffen Staab. Annotation of the shallow and the deep Web. In this book, 2003.

[12] Siegfried Handschuh, Steffen Staab, and Alexander Maedche. *CREAting relational Metadata (CREAM) - a framework for semantic annotation*. Frontiers in artificial intelligence and applications. IOS press, Amsterdam (NL), 2002.

[13] Jeff Hefln, James Hendler, and Sean Luke. SHOE: A Knowledge Representation Language for Internet Applications. Technical report, Dept. of Computer Science, University of Maryland at College Park, 1999.

[14] Jean-Mathias Héraud. Pixed: towards the sharing and the re-use of experience to assist training. In *World Conference on Educational Multimedia, Hypermedia & Telecommunications*, Denver, USA, June 2002.

[15] Marja-Riitta Koivunen and Ralph R. Swick. Collaboration through Annotations in the Semantic Web. In this book, 2003.

[16] Mpeg-7 overview. `http://mpeg.telecomitalialab.com/standards/mpeg-7/mpeg-7.htm`.

Usage of Annotations

COHSE: Conceptual Open Hypermedia Service

Sean Bechhofer, Carole Goble
Department of Computer Science, University of Manchester, UK

Leslie Carr, Wendy Hall, Simon Kampa, Dave De Roure
Department of Electronics & Computer Science, University of Southampton, UK

Abstract. The COHSE (Conceptual **O**pen **H**ypermedia **Se**rvice) Project brought together an Open Hypermedia system with an Ontology Service in order to provide an architecture for the semantic web. Open Hypermedia provides an extensible framework within which to support *document linking* while Ontology Services provide *machine-processable* descriptions of content. Here we describe COHSE and what annotation means to COHSE.

1 Introduction

The Semantic Web (SW) vision, as articulated by Tim Berners-Lee [4], is of a Web in which resources are accessible not only to humans, but also to automated processes, e.g., automated "agents" roaming the web performing useful tasks such as improved search (in terms of precision) and resource discovery, information brokering and information filtering. The automation of tasks depends on elevating the status of the web from machine-readable to something we might call machine-understandable. The key idea is to have data on the web defined and linked in such a way that its meaning is explicitly interpretable by software processes rather than just being implicitly interpretable by humans.

To realise this vision, it is necessary to associate *metadata* (i.e., data describing content/functionality) with web resources. In particular, we may wish to annotate resources with *semantic* metadata that provides some indication of the content of a resource. This is a step along the way from simple textual annotations, as the intention within the SW context is that this information will be accessible not only to humans but also to software agents. In order to do this we require: languages which will support the representation of semantic metadata; mechanisms for the annotation of web resources; and applications which present and use this information.

Here we discuss COHSE [7], a system that brought together an open hypermedia system with ontological services in order to provide linking and presentation of documents based on their content.

2 The Semantic *Web*

The issues surrounding the implementation of the Semantic Web are the focus of much current research. The bulk of this work, however, focuses on particular issues such as the implementation and representation of metadata, for example the Resource Description Framework (RDF) and RDF Schema (RDF(S)) – see [16] for a discussion of the roles of these languages and of XML/XML Schema. Richer languages such as OIL and DAML+OIL [12] have also been developed and the W3C's Web Ontology Working Group [10] are moving towards a standardisation proposal for an Ontology Web Language (OWL).

Less attention has been paid to the issues surrounding the *delivery* of such information once it has been located and the presentation of results, specifically to humans rather than software agents. Tim Berners-Lee's vision of the Semantic Web [4] is that of a universe of network accessible information, specifically:

- a means of people-to-people communication through shared knowledge. The idea is that users can not only can browse, but can also create; and
- collaboration extending to computers. Machines become capable of analysing all the data on the Web – the content, links and transactions between people and computers. The Semantic Web should provide a space in which software agents can, through access to a vast amount of everything which is society, science and its problems, become tools to work with us.

In the recent enthusiasm to move the Web to one that has machine understandable semantics for automated processing we are in danger of forgetting that it has been successful as structure that humans can browse. In other words, the Semantic Web is still a *web*, a collection of linked nodes. Navigation of links is currently, and will remain for humans if not machines, a key mechanism for exploring the space. The Semantic Web is viewed by many as a knowledge base, a database or an indexed and searchable document collection; in the COHSE project we view it as a *hypertext*: a linked structure for browsing.

3 Ontological Hypermedia

An influential early categorisation of hypertext [17] noted that links were either *extensional* (explicitly authored and stored e.g. to implement an intended navigational ordering) or *intensional* (not explicitly stored as links but derived in some manner from the content). The study (which predates the Web) recommended an increase in the support for intensional linking, based on the requirements for managing the complex interconnectedness of a scholarly literature (particularly for biblical or literary studies).

Subsequent systems (e.g. Hyperbase [36], Hyper-G [1], Devise Hypermedia [22], Microcosm [14], WWW [5]) and standards (Dexter [23], HyTime [29], HTML [35], XLink [19]) which addressed the concept of linked documents focused on links which were authored and stored (either as part of, or separately from the documents). In fact, a significant amount of effort over the subsequent years has been directed in the standards committees at the thorny issues of how to model and express extensional links in a reasonably robust and universal fashion. Even the ability to "point at" or address the appropriate part of a document's content is complex and difficult to implement, let alone the ability to describe the semantics for a collection of pointers that form a link. A well-rehearsed problem with extensional links in the context of the Web is how to store and manipulate links as first-class objects, independently of documents, while maintaining referential integrity in an uncontrolled authoring environment [13].

Although intensional links avoid this problem, they depend on an understanding of the document content. If this is not achieved by the "author", then there must be some computational entity (be it a subroutine, DLL, Web Service or Intelligent Agent) capable of (i) recognising a potential link anchor and (ii) working out what to link it to. This recognition software can be a part of the system (and configured to "know" the appropriate requirements of the application) or independent of the system which must perform a retro-fit of the suggested links. In the Web, an example of the former case is a script on a company's Web server which links the names of that company's products to their Web pages. An example of the latter case is a general language service which annotates technical terms with explanatory notes; only those explanations relevant to the specific user should be maintained ([17] suggests a dictionary or part-of speech linker that would affect every word in the document).

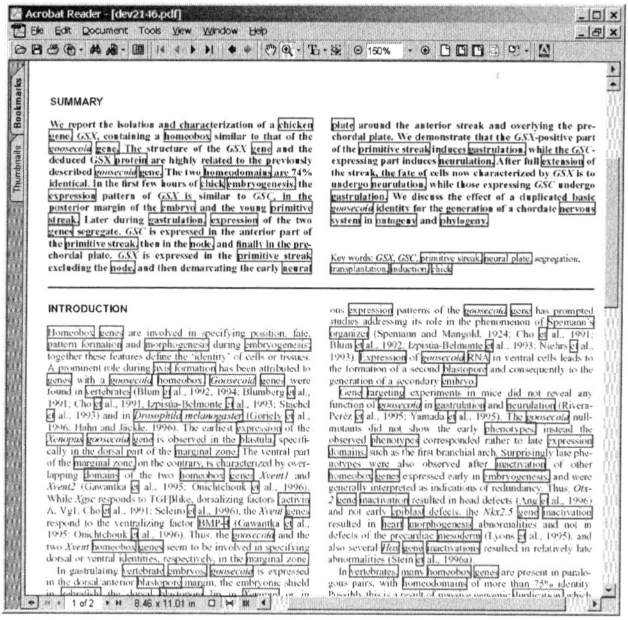

Figure 1: Example of Uncontrolled Links in DLS

The Microcosm system [14] (and its Web-based successor DLS [9]) implemented linking semantics which were a combination of extensional and intensional linking. An entry in a linkbase (extensional) declared that occurrences of a particular term may be linked to a particular destination but devolved the responsibility of recognising where the term occurred and under what circumstances the link should be activated to the runtime browsing environment (intensional). This split paradigm relied on both a skilled link author (to make appropriate generic links to lead into their documents and out to other resources) and on a skilled hypertext integrator (to partition the various links appropriately between modular sets of linkbases which can be automatically activated for the right users when they visit the right pages). Experience shows that failure in the authoring task results in a familiar paucity of links whereas failure in the system administrator's task results in users' being overwhelmed by inappropriate selections of links (see Figure 1). We refer to this second case as the "prolific but ignorant linker".

The problems of extensional linking are well-known and widely experienced: the significant authoring effort required to create and maintain links may not be forthcoming, even in an environment such as scientific research where longevity of access to publications is a key requirement [32]. An intensional approach to bibliographic linking [26] uses linking software adapted to understand the formats of bibliographies and to look up the results in a database of digital library holdings. In this case, for example colour can be used to indicate different classes of links. Even so, both the roles of authorship (writing the bibliography) and hypertext integration (collecting a suitable database of articles to act as link destinations) are still apparent.

In order to decrease the reliance on authoring effort in a linking environment, we need to employ more sophisticated content recognition software. We want to be able to recognise the kinds of things that are mentioned in the text, and understand the relationship between those things and other things which we may have links to, which may feature in glossaries, dictionaries or subject-specific portals. In addition to these so-called "generic" links (those based on words or terms occurring in the text), annotation data can also explicitly provide information that describes content – information that an agent can make use of during the linking process.

The promise of ontology-driven linking then, is the potential to use an agreed common collection of significant concepts, expressed as an agreed vocabulary in a given natural language, modelled together with agreed inter-relationships. In fact, the key objective is to reuse a model which has already been constructed for other knowledge management purposes. (In other words, to get improved linking functionality "for free".) Not only could the lexicons of the ontology identify the natural language terms which signify a significant concept, but the explicit relationships (and carefully quantified semantics) could help to overcome the problem of the 'prolific but ignorant linker' by providing an understanding of what can be linked, to dovetail in with the linking application's in-built knowledge of what kinds of things should be linked (subject key terms, foreign terms, named entities, general concepts) to achieve a particular goal (glossary explanation, tutorial support, related information). In tandem with explicit annotation data, this provides a rich framework for building linked structures.

4 Annotation

> **annotation** *noun.* A note by way of explanation or comment added to a text or diagram.
>
> *New Oxford Dictionary of English*

Annotation takes many forms. Marshall [34] writes that "[annotation] has been construed in many ways: as link making, as path building, as commentary, as marking in or around existing text, as a decentering of authority, as a record of reading and interpretation, or as community memory". There are a number of different annotation types that we can identify[1].

Textual Annotation is the process whereby notes or commentaries are added to resources. Annotations of this kind have been used for many years in communities such as

[1]Note that this is not an exhaustive classification.

biology. For example the SWISS-PROT database [37] contains protein sequence information along with annotations describing functions, structure, domains, sites and so on. Within a database like SWISS-PROT, the annotations are first-class citizens, and are, in effect, the data. Although some use is made of controlled vocabularies such as GO [38], the hand-crafted and hand-curated annotations are primarily aimed at human readers.

This is the kind of activity supported by Annotea [30, 40, 31]. Extensions to the basic schema allow the use of richer annotation types [11] (for example commentaries can be marked as replies or gathered into threaded discussions), but a principle characteristic of this approach is that it is primarily aimed at human readers (and authors).

Systems such as the Distributed Links Service (DLS) [9] or 3rd Voice [33], allow the addition of links to arbitrary documents (including those in control of a third party). With **Link Annotation**, the content of the annotation is given, not by some text, but by a link destination (and possibly associated behaviour). Again, link annotation can be seen to be an activity primarily targeted at human readers.

Finally, we can consider what might be called **Semantic Annotation**, where the content of the annotation consists of some rich semantic information. This idea of semantic annotation has been pursued in both the Ontobroker [15] and SHOE [25] projects and more recently in COHSE [7]. Semantic Annotation is targeted not only at human readers of resources, but also at software agents – this then brings with it the requirement that relationships are explicitly represented. The use of semantic information taken from well defined *ontologies* provides this explicit representation and will allow agents to make decisions based on those resource descriptions (for example the COHSE editorial component as described here).

Returning to Marshall [34], a number of different axes or dimensions are identified that reflect the forms of annotation. Included in these are a notion of *formal* vs. *informal*. Informal includes personal notes written in the margin while reading an article. Formal is deemed to be metadata following structural standards and assigned values using conventional naming authorities. The use of semantic annotation, drawing on conceptual models represented using well-defined knowledge representation languages can be seen to sit at the extreme end of the formal spectrum, perhaps even more so than Marshall's original intension of formality. Also of interest is the identification of *explicit* vs. *tacit* annotation. According to Marshall, many personal annotations are tacit – they are telegraphic and incomplete and rely on contextual information for their interpretation. For example, a bookmark, highlighted sentence or the annotation *"No!"* are examples of tacit annotation as we need extra information about the annotator, or the history of the annotation process in order to interpret them. An explicit annotation will carry sufficient information for its interpretation. As Marshall says, the dimension of explicit vs. tacit is crucially related to intelligibility – in the context of the provision of markup intended for software agents or processes the requirement of explicitness is particularly strong as such agents will not possess the real world knowledge, reading history, cultural background and so on, of human readers.

5 The COHSE System

COHSE [7] brought together an open hypermedia architecture (the Distributed Links Service [9] or DLS) with ontological services in order to provide an architecture for the Semantic Web [21].

The system consists of a *COHSE agent* (along with supporting services such as an *On-*

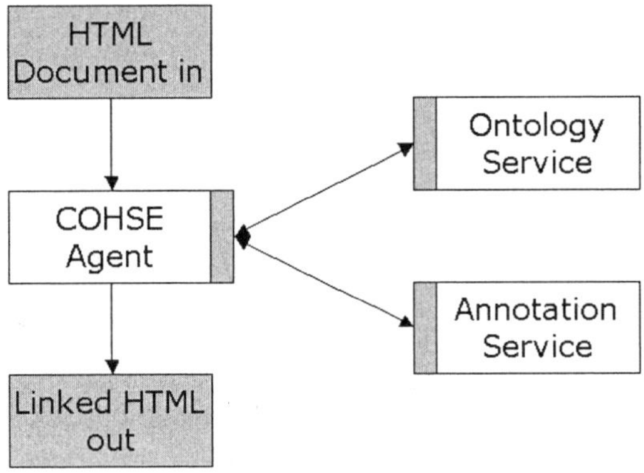

Figure 2: COHSE Architecture

tology Service and *Annotation Service*) that augments documents with links based on the semantic content of those documents. The Ontology Service supplies operations relating to the content of a conceptual model. The Annotation Service associates concepts with resources and provides mechanisms for querying those associations.

The system employs either a specialist browser (based on Mozilla[2]) or a proxy through which all HTTP requests are routed. The words and terms that appeared in a document are used as entry points to an ontology while annotation data provides further information to guide the linker. The relevant concepts in the ontology can then be used to determine appropriate targets for links out of the given resource. Central to the COHSE agent is the provision of an *editorial component* within the agent. This component uses information within the ontology (such as hierarchical classification) in order to determine whether the links are suitable or to perhaps expand or cull the set of possible targets. Figure 2 shows a simplified view of the basic architecture of the system.

Figures 3 shows a page taken from Sun's Java Tutorial web site. In Figure 4 we see the same page augmented by the COHSE agent. A number of link anchors (signified by the small "L" icon) have been added to the page. One of these has been opened up, and we see a collection of possible targets which have been annotated as being "about" the particular concept selected – in this case the concept of byte.

In addition to using the words and phrases that appear in the documents, rather than relying solely on mappings from words and terms, the COHSE agent can also use explicit metadata applied to the resources, e.g. annotations. These explicit annotations can then help guide the editorial component in its linking strategy. For example, if a passage in a web page has been annotated as being about a particular subject, say programming datatypes, the editorial component may know that there are certain terms that should be focused on within the context of that annotation (say the terms `int` or `float`) – an example of an agent using semantic information to make decisions as to its *behaviour*.

[2]`http://www.mozilla.org`

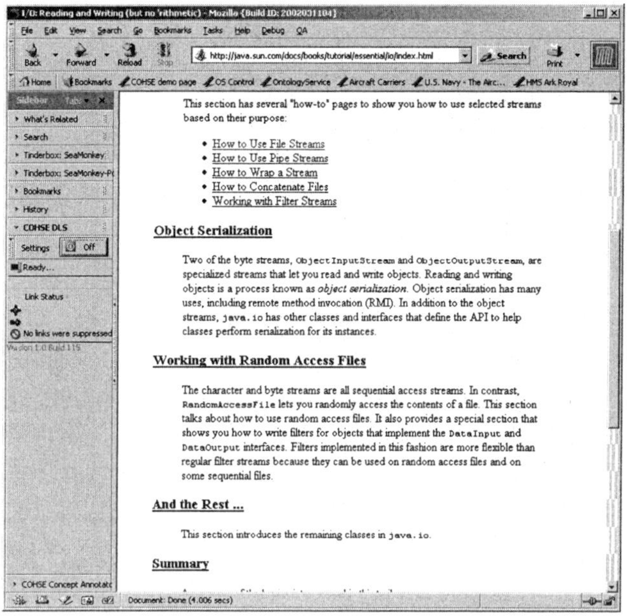

Figure 3: Before COHSE Linking

5.1 Editorial Knowledge & Behaviours

COHSE makes use of editorial knowledge in order to improve the linking performance of the system (see Section 7.5 for a discussion of how we might evaluate or characterise improved performance). The relationships between the classes that are found through lexical mapping and those due to annotation can be used to control the COHSE agent and alter linking strategies, through the use of *behaviours*. This can help to avoid problems of over-linking (see Section 3).

Two alternative behaviours are provided in the current implementation:

- Link Suppression: In this case, the annotation classes are used to suppress links found through lexical analysis. Within a section of annotated resource (annotations use XPointer [18] expressions to denote the resource being annotated and thus may refer to document fragments), any links which are due to classes which are a specialisation of the annotation class will *not* be shown.

- Link Promotion: When promotion is being used, *only* those links due to classes which are specialisations of the annotation class will be shown.

Although relatively simple, these behaviours provide a powerful mechanism to control interaction between generic and annotation linking and help avoid problems such as over-linking (see Section 3).

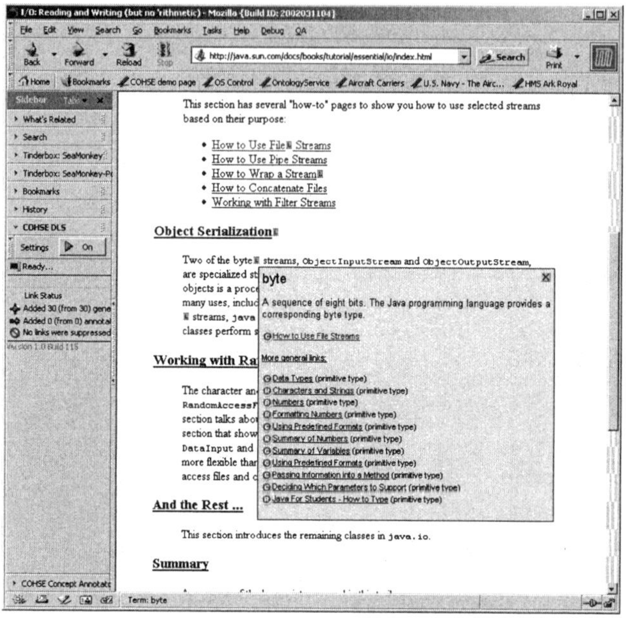

Figure 4: After COHSE Linking

This use of annotation to influence behaviour and provide source anchors is a key aspect of COHSE's novelty. To paraphrase a recent marketing campaign, annotation links provide an answer to the question *"Where do you want to go **from** today?"*. At the same time, the annotations are also being used to provide link targets (as is the case in other, resource-discovery based, systems). Thus within COHSE, the purpose of annotation is twofold: i) to populate a knowledge base for retrieval; and ii) to provide anchors for links as the annotations are used to derive outward links from resources.

5.2 *Annotation as Linking, Linking as Annotation*

Annotation within COHSE can be seen as a mechanism that allows the user to specify possible link anchors within a document, with the anchor being associated with a conceptual description. This description will then be used to determine appropriate links at read-time.

Alternatively, the provision of dynamic linking based on generic links (the words and terms that appear in the documents) as used by the COHSE project can itself be seen as a kind of annotation. In this case hypertext links are being provided rather than some textual/semantic annotation. Documents are annotated at read-time by the agent, producing a "just-in-time" hypertext.

Koivunen et al. [31] discuss approaches to Web annotations and categorise systems as, in the main, either **proxy-based** or **browser-based**. In a proxy-based approach, the annotations and document are merged by the proxy, with the browser seeing only the merged documents. In a browser-based approach, a specialist browser application will merge the annotations with the original documents while browsing. Annotations can be stored separately and provided via some annotation service (or kept within the proxy itself).

Similarly, COHSE has two implementations. In the **proxy**, all requests from a browser are redirected through the proxy. The proxy will rewrite the resulting pages, adding links where appropriate. The proxy implementation has the advantage that no specialist browsing software is required, and delivery can be targeted at a number of platforms (e.g. mobile devices). One drawback of a proxy, however, is that all processing (i.e. identification of links, reasoning about concepts, and retrieval of annotations) must be performed before the resulting page can be returned to the browser. This may impact on browsing performance. In addition, the proxy needs to be able to cope with malformed HTML (a common occurrence in the Web).

In the **browser** version[3], the COHSE agent is implemented as a browser plug in. The agent can thus directly manipulate the DOM object held by the browser. Once the document has been loaded, the agent can look for appropriate content (e.g. words/phrases) or query an annotation service for appropriate annotations. If suitable link sources are found, the DOM object is altered, and the rendering of the document in the browser will change accordingly. This has a number of advantages: the browser will take care of any bad HTML; and processing can occur after the document has finished loading which can improve browsing speed. A drawback is that a specialist browser is required.

6 The COHSE Annotation Tool

The COHSE browser implementation includes a plug-in that allows the user to create annotations. These can either be simple annotations that involve a class name (e.g. a URL) or can be composite class expressions (for example conjunctions) in DAML+OIL. Complex expressions are formed using a small browser built using components from the OilEd [3] tool.

A central Annotation Server holds the annotations and provides a basic interface for addition and retrieval of the annotations. For each annotation, the server holds:

- The URL of the document;
- An XPointer [18] expression denoting the specific portion or fragment of the resource being annotated;
- A simple textual description of the annotation;
- The DAML+OIL class that forms the body of the annotation;
- The ontology from which the class was taken.

The ontology is stored so that we can be sure that when the COHSE agent retrieves the annotations, the context within which the annotation has been made is explicit. For example, for single classes, the URL of the class is not enough for the agent to determine other information about that class (such as super- or sub-classes) – the context of the ontology (e.g. the assertions and class definitions in force) is required. If the presentation of annotation information is to be consistent with the original intention of the annotator, this reference to the original ontology is needed.

[3]Based on Mozilla: `http://www.mozilla.org`

The annotations are stored as a single table in a mySQL database. A simple HTTP/CGI interface is provided that allows clients to query for all annotations placed on a particular URL, or all annotations which use a particular class.

Constructing an annotation involves:

- Selecting a passage of the current resource. If no selection is made, the annotator will create an annotation that refers to the URL of the current document.
- Selecting a DAML+OIL class which forms the "body" of the annotation. If the class is a single class name, then this can be done using a list of classes displayed in the plugin. If a complex expression, then the mini-browser should be used.
- Optionally, providing a simple textual description of the annotation – this will then appear when annotations are displayed by the COHSE agent.

Upon creation, the appropriate information is sent to the Annotation Service. In the current implementation, no attempt is made to disambiguate the semantics of the relationship between the resource being annotated and the class: the resource is simply "about" the class in a loose way. A desirable extension to this would be to explicitly represent the relationship using, for example, an RDF Schema [2]. The COHSE agent would then be able to alter its linking behaviour based on this information – for example if the resource was annotated as being a direct instance of a class (e.g. the resource `R` has `rdf:type C`, where `C` is some DAML+OIL class), then the agent may choose to show links about other instances of the class – alternatively, the agent may show links about resources which have the looser "about" association. The point here is that the annotation would contain explicit information about the type of the relationship, allowing the agent to make a choice.

7 Case Study

As a case study we chose to investigate a commercially functional Web site to identify the hypertext linking issues that our approach could address. Through the project's connection with Sun UK, we chose the Java Tutorial site[4]. Its educational purpose provides many possibilities to increase the breadth and accuracy of the linking in order to help students learn about the Java language.

7.1 Background

The Java Tutorial is a high-traffic, promotional Web site established in 1995 which contains some 250,000 pages. The editorial team consists of approximately 10 members, in addition to the original authors of the material. The site consists of a wide range of individual Java tutorials ranging from introductory language material to advanced, specialised API concepts. The tutorial sources are stored in both HTML and Framemaker formats and the content is published both on the Web and in printed form. There are several trails available under the Tutorial. A trail represents a substantial aspect of Java programming, such as user interface design, and contains several lessons, each of which include numerous examples. This simple model forms a design constraint aimed at improving the navigational ease of the site.

[4]`http://java.sun.com/docs/books/tutorial/`

The Web site began as a Java tutorial document that was released in 1995. Using a custom preprocessor that handled simple structural links (links that help the user orientate and navigate within a site, such as Previous and Next), the editorial team produced the first version of the website. Initially, the website contained few non-structural links, for example, links to further information, glossary definitions and example Java source files were largely missing.

Several changes have been made over the years. The structural links have been modified to include trail information.

Search and feedback links were also added and an icon scheme was devised to help users quickly identify the target type of particular links in the tutorial. Link behaviour also varies depending on the destination material type. Intra-tutorial destinations replace the content of the current browser window, whereas extra-tutorial destinations bring up a new browser window. The trailmap is seen as an important navigation and structural tool for users. It provides a way of modularising the different themes in the Java tutorial, and provides users with a finer level of granularity for selecting material. Each trail itself is further split into sub-themes, easily accessible through the linked table of contents provided in each trail.

7.2 *Current State of Linking on the Java Tutorial Site*

The majority of the linking on the Java Tutorial site is produced using automation. All header and footer links are added automatically by a preprocessor which uses a configuration file to link the tutorial pages in the correct order and add the structural links. Links to glossary terms are also inserted by the preprocessor. Other types of links are rarely evident, but are occasionally added by the original authors. The editorial team frequently run link checkers (and receive feedback from their readers) to ensure the integrity of all links. Nevertheless, users still complain of getting lost while using the tutorial.

A number of different link types are used, including structural, extra-tutorial, intra-tutorial and narrative links.

Structural links generally tie sections of a lesson together, and help orientate the user when they become lost. This includes all the links in the headers and footers, as well as links within the body that refer to other sections of a lesson. Extra-tutorial links point to ancillary information that the users may be interested in while reading. These include glossary links, links to example Java source files and links into the Java API. Intra-tutorial links point to lessons outside the current trail. Narrative links aim to assist the user while they read a particular page, perhaps by providing a jump to a section further down the page.

Table 1 outlines the type of linking evident on the major sections of the I/O lesson in the trail "Essential Java Classes". The links have been classified according to their destination anchor.

Section	Pages	Structural Links	Extra-Tutorial Links	Intra-Tutorial Links	Narrative Links	Other Links	Total Links
Overview of I/O Streams	1	7	6	0	0	0	13
Using the Streams	8	61	35	1	0	1	98
Object Serialization	3	20	0	1	0	3	24
Working with Random Access Files	3	21	11	0	0	3	35

Table 1: Existing linking on Java Tutorial site

The link classification indicates inconsistencies within the site. The section *Using the Streams* is heavily linked, while the other sections, in particular *Object Serialization* have a distinct lack of links. The quantity of extra-tutorial links fluctuates greatly. Some pages include links when references to Java class names, section names and examples files are used, while other pages fail to link these phrases. The number of intra-tutorial links is also surprisingly low, given that the lessons frequently make references to concepts outside the current trail. Narrative links are not evident, although this might be due to the short length of the pages.

There are also inconsistencies in the identification of links. For example, a page on the *Object Serialization* lesson contains a link to another tutorial (*Putting It All Together*) which has not been indicated with the appropriate icon. In the *Filter Streams* lesson, an unindicated link has been constructed to an external resource, resulting in users blindly leaving the site.

Linking on educational sites is vital to ensure the student has access to the most suitable material at the right stage of their learning [28], material which can vary from background notes to specialist support information. It is also important to retain the focus of the student, ensuring they do not get lost due to a lack or an excess of links.

7.3 Developing the Case Study

To use a Web site effectively with the COHSE tools requires three stages of preparation: developing an ontology, choosing sets of useful destinations for concepts in the ontology and annotating Web pages with concepts from the ontology.

A basic DAML+OIL ontology of concepts relating to programming and the Java language in particular was produced using OILEd. [3].

With the significant concepts modelled, it is necessary to decide what the destination of any links should be. For example, if encountering a person's or company's name, it would be reasonable to link to their home page. However, we are largely dealing with programming concepts: Java class names and programming concepts. We took the decision that for this application, class names (e.g. `java.io.BufferedInputStream`) refer to a concrete implementation in the Java language, and so the most logical place to link to is the relevant API documentation. Programming concepts (e.g. buffered I/O) are less easily defined. Linking outside the Java tutorial is probably inappropriate as link integrity, document quality, and appropriateness of material cannot be guaranteed. This leaves information within the Java site, in particular, the Java Tutorial. Of special interest is the possibility of improving the intra-tutorial linking.

A feature of the annotation services is the ability to annotate entire Web pages or spans of text within a Web page with conceptual information. For example, the Web page on the tutorial site, *Filter Streams*, can be annotated as being about the concept Filter Stream. Alternatively, if we are annotating a page on Java streams and come across the phrase *Java also enables filters to be attached to streams* we may wish to indicate that some part of that phrase is about the concept Filter Stream.

7.4 Examples of Ontological Linking

At the very least, an ontology represents a community-agreed vocabulary that describes a collection of concepts significant to that community [39]. The first stage in applying the ontological hypertext techniques (described earlier) is to use the lexical representations of the ontology's concepts as search terms within the document. Any matches in the text indicate a site where a link to the matching concept could be attached (i.e. a potential ontological link anchor).

The aim of ontological linking is to improve the understanding of what is being linked (and why) so our system can exert greater control over the linking process. A frequent problem with naive link-matching techniques is the tendency for over-linking, when too many words are recognised as key terms. This is particularly true in tutorial material, where many concepts are being explained. Previous attempts to control this problem in the DLS have been indiscriminate thresholding systems, which simply delete links without reference to their utility [8].

The ontology provides a better way to manage this situation: we can examine each potential link and reject it if it is "uninteresting", for example, any link to the same kind of material as the current page.

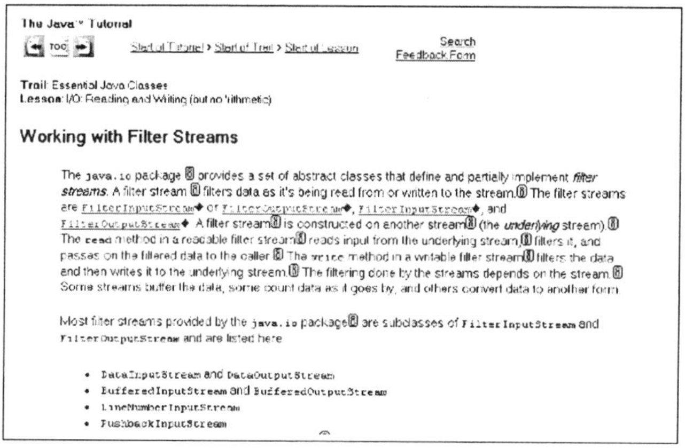

Figure 5: Overlinking

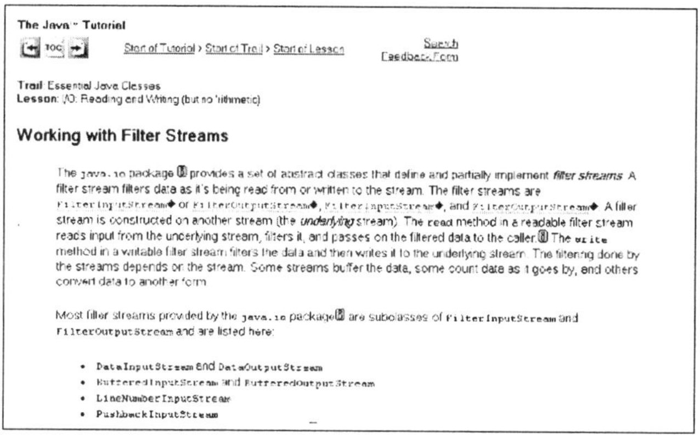

Figure 6: Pruning

Figure 5 shows a tutorial page about "Working with Filter Streams", including links that explain the terms stream and filter streams. Since these types are explained on the current page, the links are redundant. In this case the author may decide to annotate the page to declare that it is about the concept Stream. Our conceptual model has represented this term as a concept. It has subconcepts, such as Filter Stream, File Stream and Object Stream. The linker can now determine, through a query to the Ontology Service, that terms such as Filter Stream are subconcepts of the page's main topic. It can then decide on those unhelpful links that appear in the text (see Figure 6) and cull these while retaining links on unrelated terms such as package and caller.

7.5 Evaluation

We have undertaken a quantitative evaluation, counting and classifying the links available on the Java Tutorial site with and without COHSE linking. Specifically, the number of links between lessons within the same trail, and links between different trails were counted. Inter-trail links are particularly important as they connect trails in different parts of the tutorial. It was noted earlier that on the tutorial site these types of links are largely missing.

However, counting links is a difficult task for two reasons:

- The ontological linking is intensional and requires the user to select from a number of provided links.
- Due to the annotation mechanism, the number and quantity of linking can be customised and therefore coming up with concrete numbers to prove or disprove the usefulness of the environment is difficult.

A proxy version of the COHSE Agent was used in combination with an automated Web crawler to download Java Tutorial pages and count and classify (by comparing the current page location to the destination location) the linking on them. This was completed on the basic trails section of the tutorial. The results are given in Table 2. The link counting was applied without COHSE linking, with COHSE linking but without annotations, and with full COHSE linking. A moderate amount of annotation (i.e. 2 or 3 per page) was done on the tutorial pages. The table shows an increasing number of inter-lesson and inter-trail linking as more COHSE linking is applied. For example, on the trail Learning the Java Language the number of inter-lesson links jumped from 26 to 547 and the inter-trail linking from 9 to 82. These numbers may appear large; they do not represent the number of link anchors on a page however, as COHSE links offer several destinations per linked concept.

7.6 Hypertext Distance Metrics

The metrics discussed in [6] are used as the basis for the navigational analysis. *Compactness* and *Stratum* measure the connectedness and linearity of the site respectively. Both return a normalised magic number.

At the root of these metrics is the distance matrix – is a matrix that lists the shortest paths between each node of the hypertext (if one exists). The shortest path is calculated using the hypertext links between the documents.

			Without COHSE		Generic		Generic and Annotations	
Trail	No. of Lessons	Pages	Inter-Lesson	Inter-Trail	Inter-Lesson	Inter-Trail	Inter-Lesson	Inter-Trail
Getting Started	4	20	19	16	202	85	351	132
Learning the Java Language	5	106	26	9	361	58	547	82
Essential Java Classes	5	70	23	15	414	79	610	108
Writing Applets	4	34	40	26	271	114	430	143

Table 2: Comparing Linking

When calculating metrics, index pages and headers/footers are frequently removed as they distort the results. While these links are useful, they do not provide the same level of intuitiveness as links embedded in the actual content of Web pages. Having to continuously refer to index pages or header/footer links does not produce a coherent browsing experience. For this reason, the metrics were calculated with and without counting these links. As will become evident, metrics after these links have been removed prove more useful in determining the benefits of COHSE linking, than with them included.

A distance matrix was calculated for six versions of the site, with varying levels of COHSE linking and with/without the index links. Scripts were used to automatically download and analyse the Java Tutorial and to calculate the distance matrixes and metrics. Figure 7 illustrates the compactness formula which is used to measure the connectedness of hypertext pages. N represents the number of nodes, D the distance matrix, $Max = N^3 - N$, and $Min = N^2 - N$. The formula returns a number in the range of 0 and 1. A result of 1 means a complete graph, while a hyperdocument without links has a compactness of 0.

$\frac{Max-\sum_{i=1}^{N}\sum_{j=1}^{N} D[i,j]}{Max-Min}$	$\frac{4\sum_{i=1}^{N}(\lvert\sum_{j=1}^{N} D'[j,i]-\sum N_{j=1} D'[i,j]\rvert)}{N^3-N}$
Compactness	Stratum

Figure 7: Metrics

Figure 7 also shows the stratum formula which measures how linear a site is. N represents the number of nodes, D' the distance matrix with all 'no routes' replaced by 0, $Max = N^3 - N$, and $Min = N^2 - N$. Again the result is in the range of 0 and 1. A result of 1 means the site has a linear structure. A result of 0 means a circular link structure which gives users a great degree of navigational freedom.

The results of applying the metrics to the six distance matrixes are shown in Table 3.

Strategy	**With headers/footer**		**Without headers/footer**	
	Compactness	**Stratum**	**Compactness**	**Stratum**
Without COHSE	0.982	0.019	0.122	0.710
Generic COHSE	0.994	0.010	0.934	0.383
Generic & Annotation COHSE	0.996	0.006	0.945	0.323

Table 3: Hypertext metrics on the Java Tutorial site

The figures with index links included show that while the COHSE linking "improves" the metric, the change is minor as the original values are close to the limit. With the index links removed, however, it is clear the change that COHSE linking has made to the site. The generic linking has changed the compactness value by 0.8 and the stratum value by over 0.3.

With annotations enabled, these numbers changed further by approximately 0.01 and 0.06 respectively. Given that the generic linking has greatly changed the connectedness of the site, annotation linking is only ever going to marginally increase this factor. However, annotation linking is more useful for connecting parts of the site that are typically far apart (e.g. intra-tutorial linking). This is reflected by the greater change in the stratum number.

These results show us that COHSE linking dramatically alters the hypertext of the Java Tutorial Site. Both the connectedness and navigational freedom of the site have increased. While these numbers indicate a more interlinked site, further qualitative user trials would determine to what extent the navigation experience has improved.

8 Related Work

COHSE's main focus of interest is in the way in which semantic annotation data is *used* and presented.

Webscripter[5] produces reports based on annotated resources, for example the marked-up abstracts[6] of the ISWC conference [27]. SemTalk[7] [20] also provides diagrammatic renderings of annotation data. However, these systems adopt a different approach from COHSE, providing a direct view of the relationships between the annotated instance along with links *into* the resources.

SHOE and Ontobroker were two early projects concerned with semantic annotation. In the SHOE approach [25], ontologies are marked up in an extension to HTML and are stored and referred to using a URL. Ontobroker [15] also used in-document markup (relying on an extension of the `<A>` tag). An agent then crawls pages and uses the metadata to provide retrieval. These could be considered in some way "closed" or "centralised" approaches. With COHSE, pages are annotated, and at browsing or reading time, the annotations are then used to augment the documents. Of course within COHSE we will still require a number of known documents (or access to a service) in order to provide the linking targets.

W3C's Annotea system [30, 40, 31] allows the annotation of web resources with commentaries. The body of a resource is effectively a chunk of HTML, which simply provides the (textual) content of the annotation. Annotea relies on an RDF schema. Extensions to the basic schema allow the use of richer annotation types [11] (for example commentaries can be marked as replies or gathered into threaded discussions), but a principle characteristic of this approach is that it is primarily aimed at human readers (and authors).

CREAM [24] (and its implementation OntoMat) provides a framework for relational annotation metadata. However, the framework concentrates on the construction of such metadata rather than mechanisms for its presentation. An interesting experiment would be to integrate annotation data provided by OntoMat with the COHSE agent – a true test of interoperability in the Semantic Web.

9 Concluding Remarks

Semantic annotation is set to play a major part in the implementation of the Semantic Web. COHSE shows that i) ontologies and an open hypermedia architecture can work together

[5]`http://www.isi.edu/webscripter/`
[6]`http://annotation.semanticweb.org/iswc/documents.html`
[7]`http://www.semtalk.com/`

to support linking and the construction of hypertexts; and ii) annotation information can be used within this context to further enhance the link structure obtained. In particular, COHSE demonstrates that annotation not only provides a mechanism where resources can be decorated and then subsequently retrieved, but that this annotation information can also be used to influence the behaviour of a linking agent and the presentation of information.

10 Acknowledgements

This work was supported by EPSRC Grant GR/M75426. The authors would also like to thank Sun Microsystems for their assistance in providing access to the Java Tutorial materials and information about the editorial process. We are also grateful to Bernard Horan of Sun Microsystems for his support and comments.

References

[1] K. Andrews, F. Kappe, and H. Maurer. Hyper-G: Towards the Next Generation of Network Information Technology. *Journal of Universal Computer Science*, April 1995.

[2] S. Bechhofer, L. Carr, C. Goble, S. Kampa, and T. Miles-Board. The Semantics of Semantic Annotation. In *To appear in: ODBASE: First International Conference on Ontologies, Databases, and Applications of Semantics for Large Scale Information Systems*, Irvine, California, October 2002.

[3] S. Bechhofer, I. Horrocks, C. Goble, and R. Stevens. OilEd: a Reason-able Ontology Editor for the Semantic Web. In *Proceedings of KI2001, Joint German/Austrian conference on Artificial Intelligence*, Vienna, September 2001.

[4] T. Berners-Lee. *Weaving the Web*. Orion Business Books, 1999.

[5] T. Berners-Lee, R. Cailliau, and J.-F. Groff. The World-Wide Web. *Computer Networks and ISDN Systems*, 25(4-5):454–459, 1992.

[6] R. Botafogo, E. Rivlin, and B. Shneiderman. Structural Analysis of Hypertexts: Identifying Hierarchies and Useful Metrics. *ACM Transactions on Information Systems*, 10(2):142–180, 1992.

[7] L. Carr, S. Bechhofer, C. A. Goble, , and W. Hall. Conceptual Linking: Ontology-based Open Hypermedia. In *Proceedings of WWW10, Tenth World Wide Web Conference*, Hong Kong, May 2001.

[8] L. Carr, D. De Roure, H. Davis, and W. Hall. Implementing an Open Link Service for the World Wide Web. *World Wide Web Journal*, 1(2):61–71, 1998.

[9] L. Carr, D. De Roure, W. Hall, , and G. Hill. The Distributed Link Service: A Tool for Publishers, Authors and Readers. *World Wide Web Journal*, 1(1):647–656, 1995.

[10] World Wide Web Consortium. Web-Ontology (WebOnt) Working Group. `http://www.w3.org/2001/sw/WebOnt/`.

[11] P. Cross, L. Miller, and S. Palmer. Using RDF to Annotate the (Semantic) Web. In *K-Cap Workshop on Knowledge Markup and Semantic Annotation*, Victoria,B.C., Canada, October 2001.

[12] DAML+OIL. `http://www.daml.org/language`.

[13] H. Davis. Referential integrity of links in open hypermedia systems. In *Proceedings of the Ninth ACM Conference on Hypertext and Hypermedia, Hypertext '98*, pages 207–216, Pittsburgh, Pennsylvania, 1998.

[14] H. Davis, I. Heath W. Hall, G. Hill, and R. Wilkins. Towards an Integrated Information Environment with Open Hypermedia Systems. In *ECHT '92, Proceedings of the Fourth ACM Conference on Hypertext*, pages 181–190, Milan, Italy, 1992. ACM Press.

[15] S. Decker, M. Erdmann, D. Fensel, , and R. Studer. Ontobroker: Ontology Based Access to Distributed and Semi-Structured Information. In R. Meersman, Z. Tari, , and S. Stevens, editors, *Semantic Issues in Multimedia Systems. Proceedings of DS-8*, pages 351–369. Kluwer Academic Publishers, 1999.

[16] S. Decker, F. van Harmelen, J. Broekstra, M. Erdmann, D. Fensel, M. Klein I. Horrocks, , and S. Melnik. The Semantic Web — on the Respective Roles of XML and RDF. *IEEE Internet Computing*, 2000.

[17] S. DeRose. Expanding the Notion of Links. In *Proceedings of the Second Annual ACM Conference on Hypertext*, pages 249–257, 1989.

[18] S. DeRose, E. Maler, and R. Daniel Jr. XML Pointer Language (XPointer) Version 1.0. W3C Candidate Recommendation. `http://www.w3.org/TR/xptr/`, September 2001.

[19] S. DeRose, E. Maler, and D. Orchard. Xml linking language (xlink) version 1.0. W3C Recommendation, 27 June 2001.

[20] C. Fillies, G. Wood-Albrecht, and F. Weichardt. A Pragmatic Application of the Semantic Web Using SemTalk. In *Proceedings of WWW2002, Eleventh World Wide Web Conference*, Honolulu, Hawaii, May 2002.

[21] C. A. Goble, S. Bechhofer, L. Carr, D. De Roure, , and W. Hall. Conceptual Open Hypermedia = The Semantic Web? In *SemWeb2001 The Second International Workshop on the Semantic Web*, Hong Kong, May 2001.

[22] K. Grønbæk, J. A. Hem, O. L. Madsen, and L. Sloth. Designing Dexter-based cooperative hypermedia systems. In *Proceedings of ACM Hypertext 93*, pages 25–38, 1993.

[23] F. Halasz and M. Schwartz. The Dexter Hypertext Reference Model. In *Proceedings of the Hypertext Standardization Workshop by National Institute of Science and Technology (NIST)*, 1990. Reprinted in Communications of ACM, Vol. 37, No. 2, 30-39, February 1994.

[24] S. Handschuh, S. Staab, and A. Maedche. CREAM - Creating relational metadata with a component-based, ontology-driven annotation framework. In *Proceedings of K-CAP 2001, First International Conference on Knowledge Capture*, Victoria, B.C. Canada, October 2001.

[25] J. Heflin, J. Hendler, , and S. Luke. SHOE: A Knowledge Representation Language for Internet Applications. Technical Report CS-TR-4078 (UMIACS TR-99-71), Department of Computer Science, University of Maryland, 1999.

[26] S. Hitchcock, L. Carr, Z. Jiao, D. Bergmark, W. Hall, C. Lagoze, and Harnad S. Developing services for open eprint archives: globalisation, integration and the impact of links. In *Proceedings of 5th ACM Conference on Digital Libraries*, pages 143–151, 2001.

[27] I. Horrocks and J. Hendler, editors. *The Semantic Web - ISWC 2002, Proceedings of the First International Semantic Web Conference*, volume 2342 of *Lecture Notes in Computer Science*, Sardinia, Italy, June 2002. Springer-Verlag.

[28] F.M. Shipman III, C. C. Marshall, R. Furuta, D. A. Brenner, H. Hsieh, and V. Kumar. Using Networked Information to Create Educational Guided Paths. *International Journal of Education Telecommunications*, 3(4):383–400, 1997.

[29] International Standards Organisation. Hypermedia/time-based structuring language (hytime). ISO/IEC Standard 10744, 1992.

[30] J. Kahan, M.-R. Koivunen, E. Prud'Hommeaux, and R. Swick. Annotea: An Open RDF Infrastructure for Shared Web Annotations. In *Proceedings of the Tenth International World Wide Web Conference*, Hong Kong, May 2001.

[31] M.-R. Koivunen, D. Brickley, J. Kahan, E. Prud'Hommeaux, , and R. R. Swick. The W3C Collaborative Web Annotation Project ... or how to have fun while building an RDF infrastructure. `http://www.w3.org/2000/02/collaboration/annotation/papers/annotationinf%rastructure`, May 2000.

[32] S. Lawrence, M. David, G. Pennock, R. Flake, F. Krovetz, E. Coetzee, Å. Finn, A. Kruger, and C. Giles. Persistence of Web References in Scientific Research. *IEE Computer*, 34(2):26–31, 2001.

[33] M. Margolis and D. Resnick. Third Voice: Vox Populi Vox Dei? *First Monday*, 4(10), 1999. `http://www.firstmonday.dk/issues/issue4_10/margolis/`.

[34] C.C. Marshall. Towards an ecology of hypertext annotation. In *Proceedings of HT98, ACM Conference on Hypertext*, pages 40–49, Pittsburgh PA, USA, 1998.

[35] D. Ragget, A. Le Hors, and I. Jacobs. Html 4.01 specification. W3C Recommendation, 24 December 1999.

[36] J.L. Schnase, J.J. Leggett, D.L. Hicks, P.J. Nürnberg, and J. Alfredo Sánchez. Design and Implementation of the HB1 Hyperbase Management System. *Electronic Publishing: Origination, Dissemination and Design*, 6(2):35–63, 1993.

[37] SWISS-PROT Annotated Protein Sequence Database. `http://www.expasy.org`.

[38] The Gene Ontology Consortium. Gene Ontology: a tool for the unification of biology. *Nature Genetics*, 25:25–29, 2000.

[39] M. Uschold and M. Grüninger. Ontologies: Principles, methods and applications. *Knowledge Engineering Review*, 11(2):93–136, 1996.

[40] World Wide Web Consortium. Annotea Project. `http://www.w3.org/2001/Annotea`.

Annotation for the Semantic Web
S. Handschuh and S. Staab (Eds.)
IOS Press, 2003

Annotation for an Open Learning Repository for Computer Science

J. Brase and W. Nejdl
Information System Institute
and LearningLab Lower Saxony
University of Hannover

1 Introduction

In this case study we give you a brief overview how we annotate our computer science course and how we storage them in our learning repository. In section 2 we give you a brief introduction to the field of metadata and their binding and discuss which subset of the metadata schema LOM (Learning objects metadata) by the IEEE we find most useful to use for annotating our resources. We also present you the taxonomy we use to classify our learning resources by their content.

During the project PROMISE (Project oriented multimedia study of electric engineering and computer science), a joint project of three north german universities, founded by the government of Lower Saxony from 1999 to 2001, the department for knowledge based systems in the Information System Institute in the university of Hannover developed an open learning repository (the OLR) for the course of software engineering.

In the years 2001 to 2002 new repositories have been implemented based on the first OLR. We give you an overview of the standard OLR architecture in section 3. Taking a closer look at the content classification of the resources, we look at the metadata based queries inside our repositories in more detail.

In section 4 we finally present you the latest generation of the OLR3, that we use for our artificial intelligence course and present its new metadata schema editor.

2 Case study - Annotating courses

2.1 Finding relevant metadata standards

Metadata is data about data that helps us to receive better search results. Instead of hoping that a full text search through a learning resource will somewhere inside find the author's name nejdl for example, we can annotate the resource with a metadata attribute "author is nejdl". At once we see the two major difficulties this method holds: the technical realisation of "attaching metadata to a resource", and the standardization to avoid misunderstanding by using different attributes for the same purpose like "author is nejdl", "creator is nejdl" or "written by nejdl", etc.

Let us first discuss the idea of using a generalized vocabulary or schema for metadata.

One of the most common metadata schemes in the web today is "Dublin Core" (DC) by the DCMI. The Dublin Core Metadata Initiative (DCMI) is an organization dedicated to promoting the widespread adoption of interoperable metadata standards and developing specialized metadata vocabularies for describing resources, that enable more intelligent information discovery systems.

Each Dublin Core element is defined using a set of 15 attributes from the ISO/IEC 11179 standard for the description of data elements, including for example: title, identifier, language, comment. To annotate the author of a learning resource we would use the element creator, and write dc:creator = nejdl

Where "Simple Dublin Core" uses only the elements from the Dublin Core metadata set as simple attribute-value-pairs, "Qualified Dublin Core" employs additional qualifiers to further refine the meaning of a resource. The DCMI recommends a set of qualifiers simply called "Dublin Core Qualifiers" (DCQ), these include for example name, label, definition or comment as alternative qualifiers, that refine the element title. For a complete description, we refer to [4]. Since Dublin Core is designed as metadata for describing any kind of resource, it pays no heed to the specific needs we encounter in describing learning resources. The "Learning Objects Metadata Standard" (LOM) [8] by the Learning Technology Standards Committee (LTSC) of the IEEE was established as an extension of Dublin Core. Each learning object can now be described using a set of more than 70 attributes divided into nine categories responsible for general, technical, or even educational aspects of the resource.

Work on the LOM schema has started in 1998, the latest draft version was 6.4. Once the standard has been accepted, which hopefully will happen this year, it will be LOM 1.0. Since LOM defines metadata attributes for any kind of learning resource, it is obvious that one does not need to use all of the 70 attributes, but can use his own subset for annotation. On the other hand, regardless the very useful work that has been done in developing the LOM standard, the standard still fails to specify important educational aspects of learning resources. Therefore colleagues from the Learning Lab Lower Saxony (L3S) work on interesting ideas to even extend LOM in the field of educational metadata. I refer to [2] for more details. For our courses we mostly use a set of roundabout 12 attributes per resource, but having the wide variety of LOM to choose from gives us the opportunity to match the set perfectly to different types of resources.

2.2 Appropriate bindings

Mainly two possible ways to realize the "binding" of metadata to a resource have been developed in the last years, XML-binding and RDF-binding. XML stands for Extensible Markup language and is derived from the document description language SGML (The international standard for structured information). RDF stands for Resource Description Framework. A great amount of work in the field of binding is done by the IMS Global Learning Consortium, who have developed a XML binding and a RDF binding of LOM, the latter with cooperation from our institute under guidance of Michael Nilsson from the SweLL (Swedish Learning Lab) [10]. We will not discuss the details of these types of binding, but shortly describe, why we use the RDF-binding for our resources.

The XML Binding defines an exchange format for metadata. The metadata might be contained in a database and a XML representation is usually generated on demand, for export to other tools and environments. Thus, a XML metadata record is a self-contained entity with a well-defined hierarchical structure, so there is seldom a natural way to reuse other metadata standards.

A RDF statement is a triple consisting of a subject, a predicate and an object, where the subject is referenced by an URL. The most common way to represent RDF is in XML. Using the syntax proposed by the W3C the statement that a resource has a certain author could be written as:

```
<rdf:RDF
xmlns:rdfs="http://www.w3.org/2000/01/rdf-schema#"
xmlns:dc="http://purl.org/dc/elements/1.1#">
<rdf:Description about=http://www.xyz.com/resource.html>
<dc:creator>nejdl</dc :creator>
</rdf:Description>
</rdf:RDF>
```

We still can identify the triple-structure of RDF: the resource, referenced by the URL "http://www.xyz.com/resource.html" is the *subject*, "dc:creator" is the *predicate* and the literal value "nejdl" is the *object*. The namespace "dc:" refers to an URL containing a RDF file that describes the structure of the metadata attributes of Dublin Core, dc:creator in this case. That file is called the RDF-binding for DC. If we want to describe a resource with RDF and use LOM, we write triples like the one above in a rdf-file and refer to the RDF binding of the LOM attributes we use. A final metadata description is just a set of these triples. The use of namespaces makes it a part of a global network of information, where anyone has the capability of adding metadata to any resource, using standardized or specialized schemas describing these metadata. This modularity of the architecture leads to naturally reusable constructs. The LOM RDF binding is directly compatible with Dublin Core RDF binding, and therefore Dublin Core elements are used directly instead of defining new LOM elements for these DC properties. This of course helps a lot to enhance the interoperability between resources that are annotated with DC and others that are annotated with LOM. In the latest draft for the RDF binding of LOM ([10]) for example, about 80 percent of the LOM elements are defined using DC and DCQ.

2.3 An example course for software engineering

In our system a whole course is represented by a single rdf-file. In the following you see a simple example of a course consisting of one lecture-unit with the slides and the streaming video of the lecture as learning resources, containing description, title, rights, language and a classification entry

```
01 <?xml version='1.0' encoding='ISO-8859-1'?>
02<rdf:RDF
03 xmlns:rdf="http://www.w3.org/1999/02/22-rdf-syntax-ns#"
04 xmlns:rdfs="http://www.w3.org/2000/01/rdf-schema#"
05 xmlns:dc="http://purl.org/dc/elements/1.1/"
```

```
xmlns:dcq='http://dublincore.org/2001/08/14/dcq#"
xmlns:lom_cls='http://www.imsproject.org/rdf/imsmd_classificationv1p2#"
xmlns:lom='http://ltsc.ieee.org/2002/09/lom-base#"
xmlns:vCard='http://www.w3.org/2001/vcard-rdf/3.0#'>

<rdf:Description rdf:ID='SELecture'>
<rdf:type rdf:resource='http://telemann.kbs.uni-hannover.de:3333/
                                    olr/olr_v9#Course'/>
        <dc:title>SE Lecture in winter 2001</dc:title>
        <dc:creator>
            <lom:entity>
                <vCard:FN>Friedrich Steimann</vCard:FN>
            </lom:entity>
        </dc:creator>
        <dcq:created>
            <dcq:W3CDTF>
                <rdf:value>2001-09-15</rdf:value>
            </dcq:W3CDTF>
        </dcq:created>
        <dcq:hasPart>
            <rdf:Seq>
            <rdf:li rdf:resource='#Unit1'/>
            </rdf:Seq>
        </dcq:hasPart>
</rdf:Description>

<rdf:Description rdf:ID='Unit1'>
<rdf:type rdf:resource='http://telemann.kbs.uni-hannover.de:3333/
                                    olr/olr_v9#Unit'/>
    <dc:title>1. Lecture unit 22.10.2001</dc:title>
    <dc:description>Introduction to the course</dc:description>
    <dcq:isPartOf rdf:resource='#SELecture'/>
        <dcq:hasPart>
            <rdf:Seq>
            <rdf:li rdf:resource='http://www.kbs.uni-hannover.de/Lehre/SWT1/
                                    /S1T1.pdf'/>
            <rdf:li rdf:resource='http://www.mml.uni-hannover.de/
                                    meta/kbs.cgi?SWT1WS01S01T1.rm'/>
            </rdf:Seq>
        </dcq:hasPart>
</rdf:Description>

<rdf:Description rdf:about='http://www.kbs.uni-hannover.de/Lehre/
                                    SWT1/OLR/S1T1.pdf'>
<rdf:type rdf:resource='http://telemann.kbs.uni-hannover.de:3333/
                                    olr/olr_v9#PDF'/>
    <dc:title>Slides for the first lecture</dc:title>
```

```
53     <dc:description>Overview of the discipline. And a brief intodruction
54                        to the Function-Point-Method</dc:description>
55     <dc:rights>balzert</dc:rights>
56     <dc:language rdf:resource='http://www.kbs.uni-hannover.de/~brase/
57                        lang.rdf#en'/>
58     <dc:subject rdf:resource='http://www.kbs.uni-hannover.de/~brase/
59                        SWT_Ontologie.rdf#MeasSWDevelopment'/>
60     <dc:subject rdf:resource='http://www.kbs.uni-hannover.de/~brase/
61                        SWT_Ontologie.rdf#FuncDesMeasures'/>
62     <dcq:hasFormat rdf:resource='http://www.mml.uni-hannover.de/meta/
63                        kbs.cgi?SWT1WS01S01T1.rm'/>
64     <dcq:requires rdf:resource='http://www.kbs.uni-hannover.de/Lehre/
65                        SWT1/OLR/S3T2.pdf'/>
66     <dcq:isPartOf rdf:resource='#Vorlesungseinheit4'/>
67 </rdf:Description>
68
69</rdf:RDF>
```

Line 11-30 define the structure of the complete course, Line 32-46 of the unit, using rdf:Sequence. Also between these description tags stands all metadata concerning the whole course respectively the unit. Between line 48 and 67 is the metadata concerning the pdf-slides as one of the learning resources.

For a complete description of the attributes used, we refer to [10] and [4]. In the following we give you a brief overview of the subset of LOM, we use to annotate our courses in software engineering.

rdf:type (line 12, 33, 50): The type *course* or *unit* stands for a self-created structure in contrast with a learning resource, which is physically present somewhere in the internet. Also rdf:type is used to ensure that the resources are displayed in the best possible way. For type *pdf* or *video*, a new window will open, including a small navigation bar for "Play", "Pause" and "rewind" in case of type *video*.

rdf:ID (line 11, 32): Each structure element like the course or a unit, that can not be physically located via its URI, needs a unique ID to be referenced by inside the database.

dc:title (line 13, 35, 52): The title of the resource will be displayed in the navigation tree. Often the title is displayed as the result of a query. Therefore it is very useful to choose a title that is short, but rich and understandable.

dc:creator, dcq:created (line 15, 20): These attributes to describe author and time are usually only used once in the course metadata description and then inherited to every unit and sub-unit inside the system.

dc:description (line 36, 53): Contains a short description that can be displayed, when opening the resource.

dcq:isPartOf, dcq:hasPart (line 25, 37, 38, 66): This attributes are used to define the structure of a course.

dc:rights (line 55): Some parts of the lecture "Software Engineering I" are based on a lecture by Prof. Balzert from the university of Bochum. We use this attribute to cope with any problems of copyright by identifying resources from other authors.

dc:language (line 56): A useful attribute for querying resources to make sure that you will be able to understand the language of the learning resources you get as a result.

dcq:hasFormat (line 62): As the lectures are represented by a pdf-file with the slides and a streaming video we use dcq:hasFormat and dcq:isFormatOf to receive better search results by eliminating resources that are only a different version of an already known search-result.

dcq:requires (line 64): This metadata instance from the Relation category binding (see [10] for the details) is needed for an adaptive version of the script. It shall prevent readers from starting with chapters that build up on other chapters the reader has not yet looked at. This adaptive version of the script is developed as a diploma and will be presented in a later paper.

dc:subject (line 58, 60): This attribute is used to classify the content of the learning resource. We will discuss it in detail in the next chapter.

The list above represents our best practice list. It turned out that these 12 attributes are enough to richly annotate our resources and gain a high quality in querying the system, but they are far less than the over 70 attributes that form the LOM schema.

2.4 *The SWEBOK taxonomy*

As mentioned before we are interested in classifying the content of our resources as well. It is obvious that using self-defined keywords can only be a first solution to this problem. To receive the best search results the used keywords should be part of an international accepted and used classification system, such as the ACM CSS [1] for example. For the discipline of software engineering, we decided to use the SWEBOK as a taxonomy.

The SWEBOK has been developed as a Guide to the Software Engineering Body of Knowledge in a context of an IEEE/ACM working group. On their webpage [14] we find the definition "The purpose of this guide is to provide a consensually-validated characterization of the bounds of the software engineering discipline and to provide a topical access to the Body of Knowledge supporting that discipline." Almost 500 software engineering professionals from 41 countries have hierarchically structured the field of software engineering in 10 Knowledge Areas and almost 300 topics, based on their number of publications. The Knowledge areas are:

- Software requirements
- Software design
- Software construction
- Software testing
- Software maintenance

- Software configuration management
- Software engineering management
- Software engineering process
- Software engineering tools and methods
- Software quality

Compared to the already established ACM classification, that tries to catalogue the whole discipline of computer science, the SWEBOK classification is more detailed and covers more theoretical aspects of software engineering.

Therefore we decided to use the SWEBOK Classification to receive a larger amount of annotation entries. Since using more than one classification system to annotate learning resources is very useful, we consider an automated mapping from SWEBOK to ACM.

2.5 A machine readable version of the taxonomy based on LOM

To classify a resource the IEEE learning object RDF binding guide (Draft version) [10] suggests the use of dc:subject with elements of a taxonomy that must be found on the Internet. Such a taxonomy hierarchy is an instance of lom-cls:Taxonomy and must be formated in a RDF file where the topics and subtopics are separated following the example below.

Based on the SWEBOK we created a RDF-file with a taxonomy for the area of software engineering called mySWEBOK. The complete ontology can be found at [3], The main structure is as follows:

```
<dcq:SubjectScheme rdf:ID='mySWEBOK'>
<rdfs:label>Software Engineering Book of Knowledge Field Classifi cation</rdfs:label>
</dcq:SubjectScheme>

<lom_cls:Taxonomy>
    <lom_cls:rootTtaxon>
    <swtOnt:mySWEBOKrdf:about='http://www.kbs.uni-hannover.de/~brase/
    SWT_Ontologie.rdf#SWEnginManagement'>
    <rdf:value>Software engineering management</rdf:value>
        <lom_cls:taxon>
        <swtOnt:mySWEBOK rdf:about='http://www.kbs.uni-hannover.de/
        ~brase/SWT_Ontologie.rdf#SWEnginMeasurement'>
        <rdf:value>Software engineering measurement</rdf:value>
            <lom_cls:taxon>
            <swtOnt:mySWEBOK rdf:about='http://www.kbs.uni-
            hannover.de/~brase/SWT_Ontologie.rdf#MeasSWDevelopment'>
            <rdf:value>Measuring software and its development</rdf:value>
            </lom_cls:taxon>
        </lom_cls:taxon>
    </lom_cls:rootTaxon>
</lom_cls:Taxonomy>
```

This extract from the ontology shows the definition of one knowledge area (Software engineering management) divided in this example in one subtopic (Software engineering measurement), which is itself divided in one subtopic (Measuring software and its development).

All the RDF Triples building the ontology are stored in the database of the OLR as well. Since the SEWBOK is more a classification than an ontology we find almost no dependencies between the different topics, as we would aspect of an ideal ontology.

Nevertheless mySWEBOK is exactly what we need for our purposes, an universal structure of the discipline of software engineering that is widely accepted.

3 OLR

Our Open Learning Repositories, Versions 1 to 3, are connected to an Oracle Database. In the database we store the metadata of a course, never the content itself. Therefore, it is easy to include material from different sources throughout the internet to a course, if the copyright is granted (Otherwise we recommend the use of dc:rights). As shown above, a course is represented by one single rdf-file containing the structure and all metadata of a course. The rdf-Triples are stored as triples in the database and are used by the system to display the system.

For further information about the OLR we refer to [16].

3.1 Architecture

The basic architecture of the different OLR versions is the same. The first two versions were php-based. Our newest Open Learning Repository, the OLR3 system however, that we use for our artificial intelligence course, is implemented in Java and works as a JavaServlet, running on an Enhydra [5] Application Server (open source software). It is connected to an Oracle Database via JDBC, which is used to store the metadata entered by course authors and students. RDF schemes, needed for either the annotation of metadata or the import of externally prepared metadata, can come from anywhere in the internet.

The database does only hold the metadata annotated by the user or imported from RDF files, that are prepared to act as a data source for the courses metadata. The resulting RDF statements are defined on basis of arbitrary RDF schemes, which are used as a guideline to the user whenever he wants to add new metadata.

The central part of the system is a storage called "StatementPool". It holds all metadata that is known to the system at runtime. When an author starts working on a course, the pool is filled with the already existing data about that course from the database, and all statements from the used RDF schemes.

Any referenced RDF schema will be parsed using the SiRPAC RDF parser [12], whereas imported RDF files are parsed by a VRP RDF parser [15] , which provides semantical checks against given RDF schema rules.

OLR3 offers a web-browser based metadata editor/viewer and provides two major user interfaces: One for readers with a more graphically oriented view and only minor functions for manipulation of the underlying metadata. The other one designed for authors to provide a schema-driven and browser-based metadata editor with flexible binding to different RDF schemes.

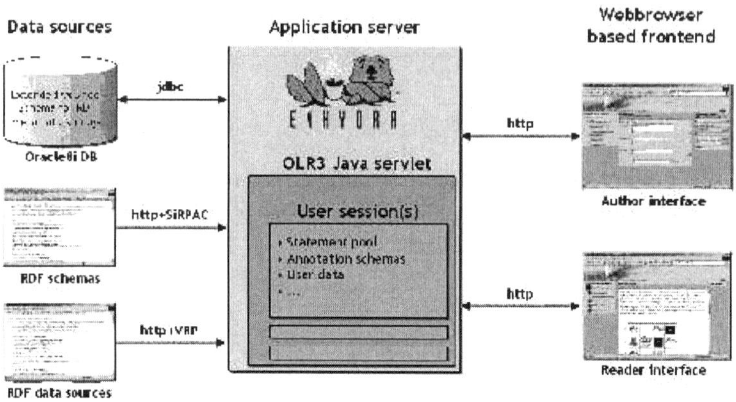

Figure 1: The architecture of the OLR3 system

3.2 Reader Interface Layout

Readers of courses using this interface can navigate through an existing course structure, displayed as a tree and extended by additional, metadata-defined images for better understanding. Within that tree they may select single course elements, whose content will be shown in the center of the screen. A specific engine prepares and filters the elements metadata ("content"), and displays it in a certain manner - e.g. show inline links to linked web pages, or display the course elements title at the top of the content screen.

The reader interface also offers the reader the possibility of making minor additions to the metadata of a selected course element by providing functions like "add comment", "add bookmark", etc. All those additions can be made private or public to other course readers.

3.3 Querying the course meatdata

We assume that we can access the triples with a view STATEMENT(Subject,Predicate,Object). Let us also consider that every resource has an ID that was automatically generated, when the RDF file was stored in the database. We will now have look at how the metadata is queried in more detail. Therefore we return to our software engineering course, and the way it is represented in the OLR2.

Parts of our little software engineering course and of the mySWEBOK Taxonomy can be found in the database as:

...
STATEMENT(http://www.kbs.uni-hannover.de/Lehre/SWT1/OLR/
S1T1.pdf, ID, 577)
STATEMENT(577, dc:title, "Slides for the fi rst lecture")
STATEMENT(577, dc:language, http://www.kbs.uni-hannover.de/
~ brase/lang.rdf#en)
STATEMENT(577, dc:subject, http://www.kbs.uni-hannover.de/~ brase/

```
                              SWT_Ontologie.rdf#FuncDesMeasures)
...
STATEMENT(http://www.kbs.uni-hannover.de/~ brase/
                              SWT_Ontologie.rdf#FuncDesMeasures, ID, 1004)
STATEMENT(1004, rdf:value, 'Measuring software and its development')
STATEMENT(1017, lom_cls:taxon, 1004)
STATEMENT(http://www.kbs.uni-hannover.de/~ brase/
                              SWT_Ontologie.rdf#SWEnginMeasurement, ID, 1017)
...
```

When we display a learning resource, one can decide between looking at the content, by choosing a layer labelled "content" or looking at the classification-entry, by choosing the layer labelled "taxon".

If you choose "taxon" the system will first retrieve the ID of the current learning resource, which is 577 in this example and then look if there are any dc:subject entries in the Oracle-Database via:

SELECT **Object** FROM STATEMENTS WHERE **Subject**='[577]' AND
Predicate='dc:subject'

The taxon entry is displayed not with its original entry but the system will retrieve the rdf:value entry of it from the taxonomy as the title. The system will also retrieve the taxon-structure identified by the taxon-attribute. Remember that the complete SWEBOK taxonomy is also stored in triples in the database. In our example the entry *MeasSWDevelopment* will be displayed as:

Software engineering management / Software engineering measurement / Measuring software and its development

We decided to display the entry as a hyperlink to the user leading to a brief description of the subject, that this resource was described as belonging to by the entry (see Fig 2).

3.3.1 Related Resources

Furthermore, the related resources (Resources with the same classification entry *MeasSWDevelopment* from the same taxonomy mySWEBOK) are retrieved from the database via:

SELECT **Subject** FROM STATEMENTS WHERE **Predicate**='dc:subject'
AND **Object**='[http://www.kbs.uni-hannover.de/~ brase/SWT_Ontologie.rdf
#MeasSWDevelopment]')

and displayed as a hyperlink to the resource (see Fig 2).

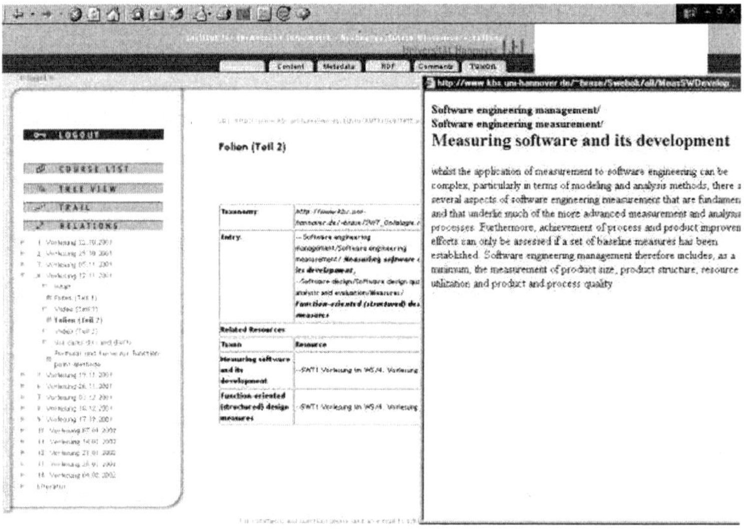

Figure 2: Taxon entries and related resources for a specifi c resource in the OLR2

3.3.2 Annotating chapters

Since a course is only represented by a RDF-Schema, a single learning resource can be annotated via its RDF description. A whole course, or a single lecture exists only inside the schema. Of course it has a description that we could annotate, but since we want to be as flexible as possible in creating different views of different lectures from the same learning resources, lectures and courses inherit their taxon-entries from their child-units. If the user chooses the layer "taxon" while he is not in a learning resource, but looking at the structure of a unit, the sub-units of this unit are retrieved via:

SELECT [The sub-units names] FROM STATEMENTS WHERE **Subject** IN
(SELECT **Object** FROM STATEMENTS WHERE **Prediacte** ='dcq:hasPart'
AND **Subject**=[The ID of the current unit])

Then their taxon entries are displayed together with the learning resource they come from. Displaying the taxon entries of a whole course works in the same way, it only takes one iteration more to receive the taxon entries from the "grandchildren"

4 OLR3 Schema Editor

The major difference between the OLR3 and its ancestors is the schema editor. Mainly two considerations led to the development of the OLR3 metadata editor: Firstly, the need for an editor which allows to edit content online from anywhere in the world without additional client software, plug-ins or configuration. And secondly, the demand for an extensible and flexible authoring interface, which should not be limited to a certain metadata standard or schema, but be open for arbitrary future developments, ideas and resulting schemes.

The OLR3 editor can handle any given RDF scheme and - once it is registered to the editor - use it for metadata input. Thus, the set of available RDF properties will only be limited by the number of available schemes that define the properties. An author can choose any desired property from existing standards (e.g. LOM, DC) and compose his own set of metadata attributes to annotate learning resources.

4.1 Author Interface Layout

The OLR3 offers a second interface, the actual metadata editor, which is intended for course authors, who can navigate through the structure tree of a course and select any sub-element. All existing editable metadata for this element is shown in the center of the screen, and the user can choose from a set of existing RDF properties to add to the metadata or to modify the existing data. The author can also bind RDF schemes (e.g. DC, DCQ, LOM) from anywhere in the Internet to extend the set of available properties for annotation, or unbind RDF schemes, that are not needed anymore. A "toolbar" holds those bound RDF schemes and offers the possibility of navigating through their structure by displaying an expandable tree view of any available property.

4.2 Structural Schema Viewer

The "Toolbar" within the author interface does not only hold all system-bound RDF schemes, but also provides the possibility of investigating the structure of any included schema. One can bind or unbind RDF schemes given by their URI. Then each bound schema may be expanded to show all included properties. A mouse-click on a property or subitem exposes all its attributes with their corresponding values. Thus, one can navigate through all elements defined by the RDF schema. The underlying technique used here is very similar to the one used for the Course Viewer.

4.3 Interface - Input Types

Whenever the user selects an item from the course viewer in the author mode, all its editable attributes will be displayed in the content area of the editor. In this context, editable means: The property is contained in one of the RDF schemes of the toolbar. This way, its possible to reduce the shown properties to a subset of significant ones by simply removing some bound RDF schemes from the toolbar.

A property can be displayed in several different manners, depending on the properties range settings and the state of the object.

4.4 Properties with Literals

If the value of a property is a literal value, the user interface will show a plain entryfield, containing the literal. If the property does not have a value yet (object is empty) and there is

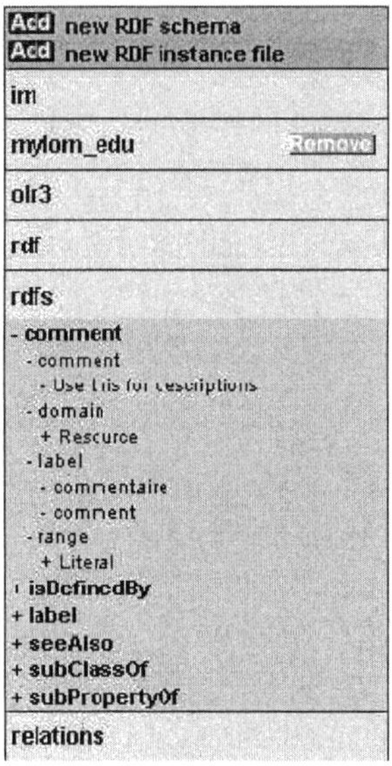

Figure 3: The Toolbar here contains several schemes, with "rdfs" expanded and showing the subitems for the property "comment"

Figure 4: A property with a literal value

no range definition given for the property, the interface will show an empty entryfield, where the user may enter any valid URI.

4.5 Properties with Range

If a property has no value yet (the object is empty) but has a range definition, the user will see - depending on the existing resources in the system - a select list with all instantiable classes for that range and/or a select list with all existing resources, that fit into the range. If rdfs:Literal is part of the instantiable classes, one will see an additional empty entry field for any literal. In any case, the system respects rdfs:subClassOf and rdfs:subPropertyOf definitions to find all valid classes and resources.

One can either choose to create a new instance from one of the offered classes, select an existing resource or enter a literal as the new value for the given property.

Figure 5: A property with range and an empty value

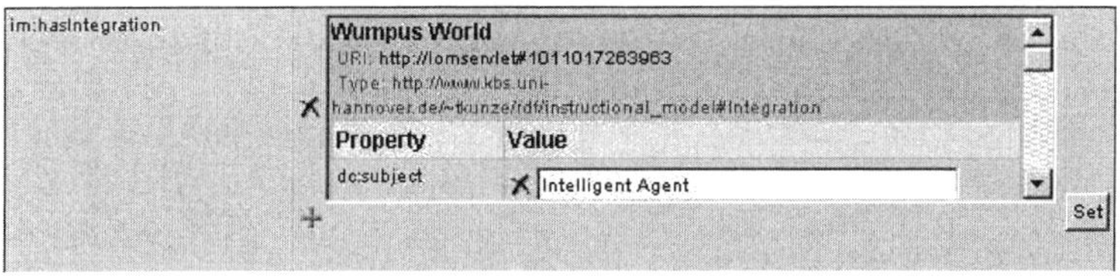

Figure 6: A property with a resource

4.6 Properties with Resources

Properties with an existing object resource that is known to the system, will show an internal frame that contains the attributes of that resource

4.7 Adding Properties

For any subject, the user can extend the existing annotation by adding properties from the toolbar that fit to the type of the resource. "Fit" means all properties with either no domain definition, or a domain definition that somehow (by respecting super-classes) refers to the origin class of the given subject. This way, OLR3 ensures the construction of valid statements.

One relevant element of the editor is the list containing all properties available for annotation. For a selected resource (course element), the editor will filter and provide only those properties from the toolbar schemes with either no domain attribute or a domain attribute that somehow (by respecting subClassOf and subPropertyOf definitions) includes the type of the selected resource. Thus, a user automatically gets a list with "valid" properties for annotation,

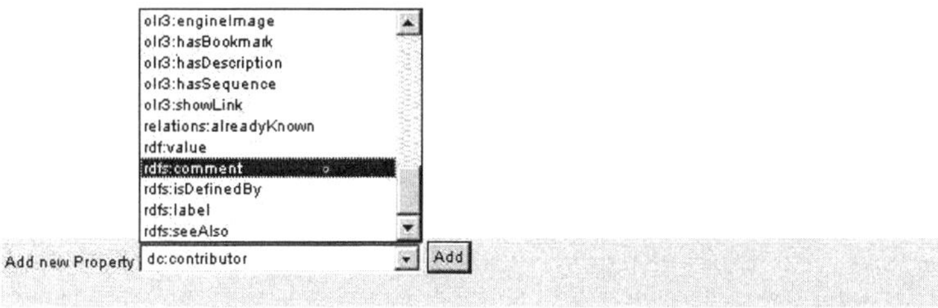

Figure 7: The list with valid properties for annotation

from which he can choose to add attributes to the given resource.

5 Related work

Even though the number of digital libraries and Learning repositories have started to increase rapidly, we haven't yet encountered a similar approach to classify the resources than our use of the LOM Standard together with a machine readable rdf-file as a classification scheme. Whereas the use of metadat to annotate resource is widely accepted and common, the traditionalway of annotating the content of a resource is by using keywords, and query these keywords later via a full text search.

Even Portal the Digital library of the ACM [11] itself uses the ACM CSS Classification for a simple keyword annotation of the resources, the same as for example the SMETE Digital Library [13].

We decided to develop OLR3 on the basis of regular web-browsers, to give every student the opportunity to access our courses without further software installation. This is a different approach from document viewers like CREAM from the University of Karlsruhe [6], although the schema-driven metadata approach is very similar.

A similar approach was developed in the K-Med project by the university of Darmstadt [7]. The courses presented in their editor are also only represented by metadata-schemes, using LOM metadata. The system however is focused only on LOM and therefore lacks our possibility to include new, self-created metadata elements in the course schema.

Conzilla the Concept-Browser, developed by the CID [9], is a very interesting metadata-focused tool, with an editor using the LOM standard, which is very similar to our approach. It is however no course editor. Its main goal is to present complete fields of science and their concepts.

6 Conclusion

In this chapter we have discussed the annotation of courses with metadata. We have presented an example RDF file for a course description and introduced the metadata standard LOM from the IEEE we use to describe our learning resources. We identified a subset of 12 attributes that are enough to richly annotate our resources and gain a high quality in querying the system, but are far less than the over 70 attributes that form the LOM schema.

The content of a resource is classified using the attribute dc:subject. Instead of having self-defined keywords as a value, dc:subject points to a taxon in a taxonomy hierarchy. We have identified the Software Engineering Body of Knowledge (SWEBOK) developed in context of an IEEE/ACM working group as a content classification for this discipline and have implemented a machine readable version of it as a taxonomy. We have discussed how to use this content classification inside our open learning repository to easily identify related resources for example.

To add and edit metadata annotation in a comfortable way, we have included a metadata schema editor in the latest version of our open learning repositories, which supports us in linking different schemas and creating our own metadata sets. This editor is server based and accessible for authors via the internet by simply using a browser.

7 Acknowledgements

The basic versions of the OLR were created and implemented by Boris Wolf. The OLR3 and the Schema-editor were implemented by Tobias Kunze. We also gratefully acknowledge important input and discussion on the design and use of the OLR3 editor from Hadhami Dhraief

References

[1] *The ACM Computing Classification System–1998 Version* valid in 2002 http://www.acm.org/class/1998/

[2] H. Allert, H. Dhraief, W. Nejdl. *How are Learning Objects Used in earning Process?* ED-MEDIA 2002, World Conference on Educational Multimedia, Hypermedia & Telecommunications, Denver Colorado, United States, June 24-29, 2002

[3] J. Brase *mySWEBOK – A classification for Software enginering, based on the SWEBOK* http://www.kbs.uni-hannover.de/~brase/SWT_Ontologie.rdf

[4] The Dublin Core Metadata Initiative http://dublincore.org/

[5] *Enhydra Open Source Java/XML Application Server* http://enhydra.enhydra.org

[6] S.Handschuh, S. Staab, A.Maedche. *CREAM- Creating relational metadata with a component-based, ontology-driven annotation framework ACM K-CAP*, First International Conference on Knowledge Capture, October 2001 , Vancouver.

[7] S. Hoermann, A. Faatz, et.al *Ein Kurseditor fr modularisierte Lernresourcen auf der Basis von LOM zur Erstellung von adaptierbaren Kursen*.LLWA 01 - GI-Workshopwoche 'Lernen-Lehren-Wissen-Adaptivit", 2002

[8] Learning Technology Standards Comittee of the IEEE: *Draft Standard for Learning Objects Metadata IEEE P1484.12.1/D6.4*12. June 2002). http://ltsc.ieee.org/doc/wg12/LOM_1484_12_1_v1_Final_Draft.pdf/

[9] Nilsson, M. & Palm M., *Conzilla - Towards a Concept Browser*, (CID-53), KTH, 1999.

[10] M. Nilsson.*IMS Metadata RDF binding guide*May 2001 http://kmr.nada.kth.se/el/ims/metadata.html

[11] *PORTAL to computing literature* http://portal.acm.org/portal.cfm

[12] *SiRPAC RDF Parser, Stanford* http://www-db.stanford.edu/ melnik/rdf/api.html

[13] *SMETE Digital Library* http://www.smete.org/

[14] *The guide to the Software engeneering body of Knowledge* http://www.swebok.org

[15] K.Tolle*VRP RDF Parser, ICS Forth, Greece* http://www.ics.forth.gr/proj/isst/RDF

[16] B. Wolf, H. Dhraief, M. Wolpers, W. Nejdl. *Open Learning Repositories and Metadata Modeling* International Semantic Web Working Symposium (SWWS) Stanford University, California, USA,July 30 - August 1, 2001

Author Index